Checking for
FRAGMENTS
(Dependent Clauses)

1. Every real sentence must have a subject and a verb.
2. The subject and verb cannot be cancelled out by converter words (also called **subordinating conjunctions**).

REMEMBER
- "ing" words by themselves are never verbs
- "to" + verb is never a verb
- "be" by itself is never a verb
- the YOU UNDERSTOOD rule (page 223)
- the THIS or THAT rule (page 228)
- hidden THAT (page 226)

ALWAYS VERBS

am	will	must
is	shall	do
are	would	does
was	should	did
were	can	seem
has	could	seems
have	may	seemed
had	might	

CONVERTER WORDS (Subordinating Conjunctions)

after	unless	although
until	as	as if
what	whatever	before
how	where	wherever
even if	if	which
since	in order that	while
whichever	who, whom	whose
why	so that	that (can be hidden)
til	for (used as because)	

Checking for
SEN

1. Count
2. Look f conjur.
3. See how many SENTENCES you have.

WRONG

SENT	SENT	(Sentence NOTHING Sentence): Run-on Sentence
SENT ,	SENT	(Sentence COMMA Sentence): Comma Splice

RIGHT

SENT .	SENT	(Sentence PERIOD Sentence)
SENT ,	and SENT	(Sentence COMMA CONJUNCTION Sentence)
	but	
	so	
	yet	
SENT ;	SENT	(Sentence SEMICOLON Sentence)

Checking for
SUBJECT / VERB AGREEMENT

1. Find the SUBJECT and VERB.
   (Remember, the subject will not be in a prepositional phrase.)
2. Put the SUBJECT in one of these groups.

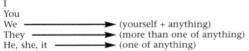

I
You
We ⟶ (yourself + anything)
They ⟶ (more than one of anything)
He, she, it ⟶ (one of anything)

3. Read the following chart.

BASIC CHART

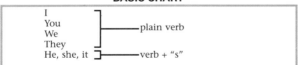

I
You
We ⟶ plain verb
They
He, she, it ⟶ verb + "s"

CHART for TO BE

	PRESENT	PAST
I	am	was
You		
We	are	were
They		
He, she, it	is	was

PREPOSITIONS

on	in	with	over	beside	upon
within	at	of	below	above	inside
by	below	above	under	among	behind
from	without	beneath	to	except	around
into	during	before	across	until	against
past	toward	through	like		

Checking for
PAST TENSE

1. Add "ed" *or* change the spelling to show past tense. Don't do both.

   walk adds "ed"   Yesterday Cedric *walked* three miles.

   take changes spelling   Last week Juanita *took* the bus to work.

2. Use your SUBJECT / VERB Agreement rules for "was" and "were."

3. Words that end in the "n" sound must be used with helpers: *has, have, had.* (past perfect tense)

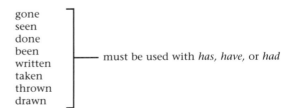

gone
seen
done
been
written
taken
thrown
drawn

⟶ must be used with *has, have,* or *had*

The Visual Guide to

COLLEGE

COMPOSITION

with Readings

The Visual Guide to

COLLEGE

COMPOSITION

with Readings

Joanna Leake
James Knudsen
University of New Orleans

New York • San Francisco • Boston
London • Toronto • Sydney • Tokyo • Singapore • Madrid
Mexico City • Munich • Paris • Cape Town • Hong Kong • Montreal

Vice President and Editor in Chief: Joseph Terry
Senior Acquisitions Editor: Steven Rigolosi
Development Manager: Janet Lanphier
Development Editor: Art Pomponio
Marketing Manager: Melanie Craig
Supplements Editor: Donna Campion
Media Supplements Editor: Nancy Garcia
Production Manager: Joseph Vella
Project Coordination, Text Design, and Electronic Page Makeup:
        Thompson Steele Production Services, Inc.
Photo Research: Photosearch, Inc.
Cover Designer/Manager: Wendy A. Fredericks
Cover Photos: © Photo Disc, © Corbis, © Stockbyte, and © Digital Vision
Manufacturing Buyer: Lucy Hebard
Printer and Binder: R.R. Donnelley & Sons, Inc.
Cover Printer: Phoenix Color Corp.

For permission to use copyrighted material, grateful acknowledgment is made to the copyright holders on pp. 457–459, which are hereby made part of this copyright page.

Library of Congress Cataloging-in-Publication Data

Leake, Joanna
    The visual guide to college composition with readings / Joanna Leake, James Knudsen.
        p. cm.
    Includes bibliographical references and index.
    ISBN 0-321-06099-7 (student ed.) -- ISBN 0-321-06100-4 (instructor ed.)
    1. English language--Rhetoric. 2. College readers. 3. Report writing. I. Knudsen,
James. II. Title.

PE1408 .L36 2002
808'.0427--dc21

                                                                    2001038604

Please visit our website at http://www.ablongman.com/leake

ISBN 0-321-06099-7 (Student Edition)
ISBN 0-321-06100-4 (Annotated Instructor's Edition)

1 2 3 4 5 6 7 8 9 10—DOC—04 03 02 01

For David and Madeleine (and Waylon)

J.L.

For Jeanne, Seth, and Celeste

J.K.

BRIEF CONTENTS

DETAILED CONTENTS

PART 9 FOR SECOND LANGUAGE LEARNERS   **371**

PART 10 SEVENTEEN READINGS   **399**

PREFACE

We've designed *The Visual Guide to College Composition* to give students a strong foundation in all the basic skills they'll need to succeed in their college writing classes. Since reading and writing skills are so strongly linked, we've also included a large selection of readings and solid suggestions for improving reading skills. Because we know that today's students are frequently visual learners, our book is full of the kind of photos, illustrations, and charts that can make learning easier. We've presented the kind of basic information college writers need in a way that keeps ideas clear and inviting. Students who have had difficulty reading texts in the past will be engaged in a whole new way.

The Visual Guide to College Composition focuses on the writing process: from finding topics and generating ideas to polishing a final draft with careful evaluation of content and the elimination of both serious and minor grammatical problems. Instructors will find sections on the modes of development—from examples and comparison/contrast to description and cause and effect. We've also included a section on argumentation and the kinds of fallacies that can ruin an effective argument. Reading selections that illustrate the various modes are found in Part 10.

We've set this book up with a modular format so that instructors can easily adapt it for use in their own classrooms. Whatever an instructor's approach to teaching composition may be, this book will do the job.

We are convinced that your students will enjoy learning from this text. We'd love to hear your thoughts. Please send them to us care of Developmental English Editor, Longman Publishers, 1185 Avenue of the Americas, 25th Floor, New York, NY 10036.

Features

The Visual Guide to College Composition offers a number of unique features to help students succeed in college writing at the paragraph and essay level. Throughout the book we put our emphasis on writing as a process. We begin with an overview of the entire process and then break it down into easy-to-follow sections. This book covers everything from exploring ways to start a successful essay to solving grammar problems so necessary to successful proofreading.

VISUAL APPROACH

Today's students are used to the easy access to information provided by the visuals of television and computers. Students who are less prepared for college-level writing are frequently the ones who will benefit most from a more visual approach. We have used color and graphics and clear design to help students learn what they need to learn.

PROOFREADING CARDS

You've probably already noticed perforated cards at the front of this book. These cards have been designed to assist students in reviewing and mastering proofreading skills. These cards clearly condense the most important parts of the proofreading section of this book.

MODULAR DESIGN

Because we know that instructors organize their courses and use textbooks in different ways, we have presented the material in this book in ten parts and 46 sections. This modular design makes the book easily accessible and flexible. You can precisely identify the material you want to cover and make assignments that will work best for you and your class. Each concept presented here is followed by at least one activity, and each section ends with additional activities.

READABILITY

One of our goals has been to create a book that college students will actually read. We pose questions to make them think, and we use a friendly, encouraging tone to keep them engaged. Students with writing problems frequently have reading difficulties, so we have tried to keep our explanations brief and clear. Each section ends with "We're Glad You Asked," a casual question-and-answer session where we anticipate student questions and problems.

HUMOR

When it makes good sense, we use humor to sell our points. Cartoons and other visual humor help students stay involved as they absorb the important lessons of this text.

THINKING ABOUT THE WRITING PROCESS

We believe that students can profit from learning more about their own individual writing process. Once they understand the stages involved in successful writing, they can begin to look at their own process and locate the areas where they have problems. Locating these problems can be a major step toward eliminating them. To this end, we have included an entire section devoted to "thinking about your writing."

RHETORICAL MODES/STRATEGIES OF DEVELOPMENT

Since many instructors use modes of development as an important component in developing their students' writing skills, we have included sections on Example, Comparison and Contrast, Cause and Effect, Division and Classification, Process, Narration, Definition, and Description. We explore ways to use each mode to write successful paragraphs and essays. Working from a basic blueprint, we show students how they can adapt it to a variety of purposes.

LOGICAL FALLACIES

Since argumentation skills are crucial to any college-level writer, we have included a section that examines how they work and explains the various fallacies that can undercut a writer's success: faulty analogy; argument in a circle; post hoc, ergo propter hoc; non sequitur; begging the question; ad hominen; slippery slope; and either/or. Students will receive practice in recognizing these fallacies and what to focus on in order to avoid them. Clear thinking goes hand in hand with clear writing.

WRITING FOR DIFFERENT PURPOSES

Students are often called upon to put their writing skills to use in their other classes. In order to help them adapt to these somewhat specialized writing situations, we've devoted a special section to two essential skills that any college writer must have: taking essay exams and writing summaries.

ACTIVITIES AND MASTERY TESTS

Most students need plenty of practice in all of the areas covered by this book. For this reason, we've included many activities in each section as well as a section of additional exercises and mastery tests. These added exercises and tests may be used for in-class practice, homework assignments, or quizzes. In addition, we've prepared a separate test bank for use with the text. (For more information on the test bank, please see the description below.)

READINGS

Since improving reading skills is one of the most important goals of this book, we've included information on how to read better and a large selection of readings (including some that illustrate the modes of development).

We've included articles on a variety of subjects including "Life Lessons for Students" and "Success Takes Time, Sacrifice, and Hard Work" as well as more traditional argumentative essays on topics such as women in athletics, air-conditioning, small town life, and prisons.

The Teaching and Learning Package

Several supplements are available to help make *The Visual Guide to College Composition* easy to teach and learn from.

The **Annotated Instructor's Edition** (0-321-06100-4) is a replica of the student edition, with all answers provided within the text.

The **Instructor's Manual** (0-321-06103-9) includes teaching tips, sample syllabi, and overhead transparency masters. Also available is a separate **Test Bank** (0-321-06104-7), with reproducible quizzes for each chapter in the text.

For additional activities and quizzes, be sure to visit the text's book-specific Website at **http://www.ablongman.com/leake**.

Also available free upon adoption of this text is **The Longman Electronic Test Bank for Writing** (0-321-08117-X). This electronic test bank features more than 5,000 questions in all areas of writing, from grammar to paragraphing, through essay writing, research, and documentation. With this easy-to-use CD-ROM, instructors simply choose questions from the electronic test bank, then print out the completed test for distribution.

The Longman Developmental English Support Package

In addition to the book-specific supplements described above, many other innovative supplements are available for both instructors and students. All of these supplements may be obtained without charge or at greatly reduced prices.

FOR ADDITIONAL READING AND REFERENCE

The Dictionary Deal. Two dictionaries can be shrinkwrapped with this text for a nominal fee. *The New American Webster Handy College Dictionary* is a paperback reference with more than 100,000 entries. *Merriam Webster's Collegiate Dictionary*, tenth edition, is a hardback reference with a citation file of more than 14.5 million examples of English words drawn from actual use. For more information on how to shrinkwrap a dictionary with this text, contact your Longman sales representative.

Penguin Quality Paperback Titles.   A series of Penguin paperbacks is available at a significant discount when shrinkwrapped with *The User's Guide.* Some titles available are Toni Morrison's *Beloved,* Julia Alvarez's *How the Garcia Girls Lost Their Accents,* Mark Twain's *Huckleberry Finn, Narrative of the Life of Frederick Douglass,* Harriet Beecher Stowe's *Uncle Tom's Cabin,* Dr. Martin Luther King Jr.'s *Why We Can't Wait,* and plays by Shakespeare, Arthur Miller, and Edward Albee. For a complete list of titles or more information, contact your Longman sales representative.

The Pocket Reader, **First Edition** (0-321-07668-0).   This inexpensive volume contains 80 brief reaings (1 to 3 pages each) on a variety of themes: writers on writing, nature, women and men, customs and habits, politics, rights and obligations, and coming of age. Also included is an alternate rhetorical table of contents.

100 Things to Write About (0-673-98239-4).   This 100-page book contains 100 individual assignments for writing on a variety of topics and in a wide range of formats, from expressive to analytical. Ask your Longman sales representative for a sample copy.

Newsweek **Alliance.**   Instructors may choose to shrinkwrap a 12-week subscription to *Newsweek* with any Longman text. The price of the subscription is 57 cents per issue (a total of $6.84 for the subscription). Available with the subscription is a free "Interactive Guide to *Newsweek*"—a workbook for students who are using the text. In addition, *Newsweek* provides a wide variety of instructor supplements free to teachers, including maps, skills builders, and weekly quizzes. For more information on the *Newsweek* program, contact your Longman sales representative.

ELECTRONIC AND ONLINE OFFERINGS

The Longman Writer's Warehouse.   The innovative and exciting online supplement is the perfect accompaniment to any developmental writing course. Developed by developmental English instructors specially for developing writers, The Writer's Warehouse covers every part of the writing process. Also included are journaling capabilities, multimedia activities, diagnostic tests, an interactive handbook, and a complete instructor's manual. The Writer's Warehouse requires no space on your school's server; rather, students complete and store their work on the Longman server, and are able to access it, revise it, and continue working at any time. For more details about how to shrinkwrap a free subscription to The Writer's Warehouse with this text, please consult your Longman sales representative. For a free guided tour of the site, visit **http://longmanwriterswarehouse.com**.

The Writer's Toolkit Plus CD-ROM. This CD-ROM offers a wealth of tutorial, exercise, and reference material for writers, including almost 2,000 grammar questions. It is compatible with either a PC or Macintosh platform, and is flexible enough to be used either occasionally for practice or regularly in class lab sessions. For information on how to bundle this CD-ROM free with your text, contact your Longman sales representative.

The Longman English Pages Website. Both students and instructors can visit our free content-rich Website for additional reading selections and writing exercises. From the Longman English pages, visitors can conduct a simulated Web search, learn how to write a resumé and cover letter, or try their hand at poetry writing. Stop by and visit us at **http://www.ablongman.com/englishpages**.

The Longman Electronic Newsletter. Twice a month during the spring and fall, instructors who have subscribed receive a free copy of the Longman Developmental English Newsletter in their e-mailbox. Written by experienced classroom instructors, the newsletter offers teaching tips, classroom activities, book reviews, and more. To subscribe, visit the Longman Basic Skills Website at **http://www.ablongman.com/basicskills**, or send an e-mail to **Basic Skills@ablongman.com**.

Teaching Online: Internet Research, Conversation, and Composition, **Second Edition** (0-321-01957-1). Ideal for instructors who have never surfed the Net, this easy-to-follow guide offers basic definitions, numerous examples, and step-by-step information about finding and using Internet sources. FREE to adopters.

FOR INSTRUCTORS

Competency Profile Test Bank, Second Edition. This series of 60 objective tests covers ten general areas of English competency, including fragments; comma splices and run-ons; pronouns; commas; and capitalization. Each test is available in remedial, standard, and advanced versions. Available as reproducible sheets or in computerized versions. (Free to instructors. Paper version: 0-321-02224-6. Computerized IBM: 0-321-02633-0. Computerized Mac: 0-321-02632-2).

Diagnostic and Editing Tests and Exercises, Fourth Edition. This collection of diagnostic tests and exercises helps instructors assess student's competence in Standard Written English for the purpose of placement or to gauge progress. Available as reproducible sheets or in computerized versions, and free to instructors. (Paper: 0-321-10022-0. CD-ROM: 0-321-10459-5).

ESL Worksheets, Third Edition (0-321-07765-2). These reproducible worksheets provide ESL students with extra practice in areas they find the most troublesome. A diagnostic test and posttest are provided, along with answer keys and suggested topics for writing. FREE to adopters.

80 Practices (0-673-53422-7). A collection of reproducible, ten-item exercises that provide additional practices for specific grammatical usage problems, such as comma splices, capitalization, and pronouns. Includes an answer key. FREE to adopters.

CLAST Test Package, Fourth Edition. These two 40-item objective tests evaluate students' readiness for the CLAST exams. Strategies for teaching CLAST preparedness are included. FREE with any Longman English title. (Reproducible sheets: 0-321-01950-4. Computerized IBM version: 0-321-01982-2. Computerized Mac version: 0-321-01983-0).

TASP Test Package, Third Edition. These 12 practice pretests and posttests assess the same reading and writing skills covered in the TASP examination. FREE with any Longman English title. (Reproducible sheets: 0-321-01959-8. Computerized IBM version: 0-321-01985-7. Computerized Mac version: 0-321-01984-9).

Teaching Writing to the Non-Native Speaker (0-673-97452-9). This booklet examines the issues that arise when non-native speakers enter the developmental classroom. It includes profiles of international and permanent ESL students, factors influencing second-language acquisition, and tips on managing a multicultural classroom. FREE to instructors.

FOR STUDENTS

The Longman Writer's Journal (0-321-08639-2). This journal for writers offers students a place to think, write, and react. FREE with any Longman English text. For an examination copy, contact your Longman sales consultant.

The Longman Researcher's Journal (0-321-09530-8). This free journal is a resource designed to help first-time researchers brainstorm, research, write, revise, and document a research paper.

Researching Online, **Fifth Edition.** A perfect companion for a new age, this indispensable new supplement helps students navigate the Internet. Adapted from *Teaching Online*, the instructor's Internet guide, *Researching Online* speaks directly to students, giving them detailed, step-by-step instructions for performing electronic searches. Available FREE when shrinkwrapped with any Longman text. Ask your Longman sales representative for more information.

Learning Together: An Introduction to Collaborative Theory. This brief guide to the fundamentals of collaborative learning teaches students how to work effectively in groups, how to revise with peer response, and how to co-author a paper or report. Shrinkwrapped FREE with any Longman Basic Skills text.

A Guide for Peer Response, **Second Edition.** This guide offers students forms for peer critiques, including general guidelines and specific forms for different stages in the writing process. Also appropriate for freshmen-level course. FREE to adopters.

Thinking Through the Test **by D. J. Henry [For Students in Florida].** This special workbook offers ample skill and practice exercises to help student prepare for the Florida State Exit Exam. To shrinkwrap this workbook free with your textbook, please contact your Longman sales representative. Also available: Two laminated grids (one for reading, one for writing) that can serve as handy references for students preparing for the Florida State Exit Exam.

Acknowledgments

We'd like to acknowledge several individuals: John Cooke, who continues as the ideal chair; Gabi Gautreaux, our guru; Tara Jill Ciccarone, ace xeroxer and staunch assistant; and Mike Kabel, our man in the copy room and researcher.

At Longman, we'd like to thank Art Pomponio for his good sense and good humor in putting this book together (and for introducing us to Time Trolls and Newton). Thanks also to Steven Rigolosi, our acquisitions editor and unending source of support, great stories, and top-drawer dinner conversation. Thanks also to master marketer Melanie Craig, and for keeping things running smoothly, Meegan Thompson and Donna Campion.

Special thanks to Jennifer Bradner for setting up our Website and to Nancy Freihofer and Sally Steele at Thompson Steele for their enthusiasm about our project and for being a pleasure to work with.

We'd also like to thank the following instructors for their insightful reviews of the book:

Ruth Callahan, Glendale Community College

Donneva Crowell, South Plains College

Lisa Dague, Santa Monica College

Patrick Haas, Glendale Community College

Marian Helms, College of Southern Idaho

Janene Lewis, Huston-Tillotson College

Candace Mesa, Dixie State College

Linda Robinett, Oklahoma City Community College

Joanna Leake
James Knudsen

New Orleans, LA

Authors James Knudsen and Joanna Leake
Photo Credit: David Leake

PART
1
THE WHY AND HOW
OF EFFECTIVE WRITING

1

THE WRITING PROCESS

Suppose you've decided to go on a trip, maybe to see the Grand Canyon or to attend a family reunion at Grandpa Wally's ranch. You want your trip to be a success.

Before you leave, you get a map and plan your route. You decide what sights you want to see on the way (Moe's Alligator Ranch, Water World), what roads you want to travel (I-10, Route 66), where you want to stop for the night (Motel-O-Rama, Betty Jean's Guest House). You drive to your destination, following the route you planned. When you arrive, you take a burro ride to the bottom of the Grand Canyon or spend a weekend partying with your relatives.

After you return home, you can enjoy thinking about your trip: You can look at the photos you took and play back camcorder tapes showing you atop a burro or Grandpa Wally doing the limbo. You might decide that on your next trip you're not going to stay at Motel-O-Rama again and you're definitely going to stick to the newer interstate highways.

Your trip wasn't just a single event. It was a process—a process that began with the planning of the trip, continued during the actual trip, and concluded with your evaluation after the trip was over.

Writing an essay, like going on a trip, is a process. Usually an instructor will start the process rolling by giving you an assignment—a key part of the plan that will help you end up with an essay. Let's take a look at the process that will get you from the assignment to the finished product—a successful essay. In this process you will move from **planning to drafting to revising and proofreading.**

Planning

Your first step will be to make a plan. The basic plan for every essay divides material into three parts:

1. Introduction (the beginning)

2. Body (the middle)

3. Conclusion (the end)

Each of these three parts has a role to play.

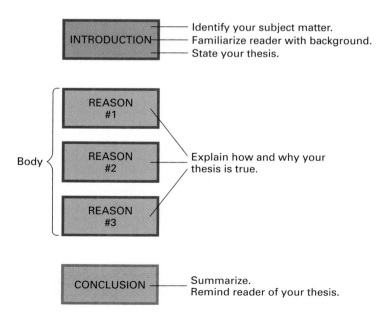

INTRODUCTION

The beginning of your essay should provide your reader with the following information:

◆ **The subject matter**

Are you writing about pollution?

The upcoming election?

The newspaper's editorials?

◆ **Enough background to become familiar with the subject matter**

Pollution is increasing in your city.

The upcoming election is between two newcomers to politics.

The editorials in the newspaper are all written by the same journalist.

◆ **Your opinion about the subject matter**

Industrial waste is the cause of air pollution.

Rupert Tibbs is the best choice for mayor.

The newspaper's editorials are too predictable.

Your opinion leads to a very important part of your essay—your thesis. The *thesis* is the statement that reveals your opinion on a limited subject. It is a debatable statement that reveals your side of an argument. The thesis will lead to the next step in the process: convincing readers that your thesis is true.

BODY

In the middle of your essay—the main part, or body—you'll offer your readers reasons that will convince them that your thesis is true. You'll also provide some specific details to explain how these reasons work. Each paragraph in the *body* needs to show how and why your thesis is true. The body is where you build your case.

Industrial waste is the cause of air pollution in our city. Why?

A new factory dumps waste in the river.

The paper mill's exhaust stacks discharge clouds of black smoke.

The toxic waste from the pharmaceutical plant ends up in the air and water.

Rupert Tibbs is the best choice for mayor. Why?

He has long-standing ties to the community.

He is in favor of improving the school system.

He has been endorsed by respected leaders.

The newspaper's editorials are too predictable. Why?

They express no interest in political reform.

All decisions by politicians in office are praised.

Controversial issues are consistently ignored.

CONCLUSION

In this part you briefly summarize the thesis of your essay. You remind your readers of your opinion. It's your last shot to make your case.

PUTTING IT ALL TOGETHER

Later on we'll show you how special kinds of essays will take this basic Introduction/Body/Conclusion plan and vary it to meet their requirements. But the basics won't change. Plan your beginning, middle, and end, and you're on your way to a successful essay. Let's look at the Tibbs for mayor essay as an example. A short outline for it might look like this:

Introduction: Tibbs best candidate for mayor

Body: Longstanding ties; favors school improvements; endorsed by leaders

Conclusion: No better candidate

ACTIVITY 1-1

Directions: Your instructor has assigned the topic "Why I Decided to Attend College" to your class. Make a brief outline (like the one on page 5) of how you might develop it as an essay.

Introduction:

Body:

Conclusion:

Drafting

This is the second step in the writing process, the point when you turn your engine on and go. Go fast. You have your plan to follow. You know what your main points will be. Now let your fingers fly. Either with pen or pencil in hand or at the computer keyboard, let your fingers try to keep up with the flow of your ideas. Don't worry about spelling words incorrectly or making grammatical errors. This is the part of your essay where you can find your voice and develop your own style, your own way of expressing yourself. If your mind is moving faster than your hands, just try to keep up. Just get your ideas down. If you think you've written yourself into a trouble spot, jot a question mark in the margin and write on!

ACTIVITY 1-2

Directions: Return to the topic "Why I Decided to Attend College" that you just outlined in Activity 1-1. Now try writing a draft. Remember that your goal is just to get your ideas out at this point.

Revising and Proofreading

Now you've come to the part of the process where you need to sit back and slow down. Read over what you've written and think about how you can improve it. You'll want to think about three basic areas:

❶ *Mechanics:* Look for mistakes in capitalization, punctuation, and grammar: the hard and fast rules.

❷ *Sense:* Are you being clear? Have you left out a word?

❸ *Style:* Think about ways to get and keep your reader's interest. Are you being too wordy? Can you liven up your language?

We'll give you tips later on what will help you find and correct mistakes related to mechanics, sense, and style.

Things to Remember in Order to Write a Successful Essay

❶ Writing is a process.

❷ You need to plan, draft, and edit to create a successful essay.

❸ You want to end up with an essay that will convince a reader that your thesis is true.

Important: Keep the three stages separate. Don't draft while you plan. Don't edit while you draft.

2

AUDIENCE: WHO WILL BE READING THIS?

Suppose someone has asked you to describe what you did at a party last Saturday night. Imagine what you would say. How would your reply change if the questioner was a ten-year-old child? Your best friend? A nun? Obviously the version of your Saturday night adventures will vary depending on who will be hearing it. The details you include and the vocabulary and tone of voice you use will all depend on whether you are talking to a ten year old, your best friend, or a nun. The same kind of thing should happen when you write. You make changes to fit the **audience**—the reader or readers who will be reading what you write. The details, vocabulary, and tone of an essay should be appropriate to your audience. Most of the time your audience for college writing will be your instructor and your classmates.

ACTIVITY 2-1

Directions: This writing activity has two parts.

Example:

a. The atmosphere in Ms. Morse's classroom is unpleasant. The students behave poorly. The air conditioner is broken. It is hard to hear what people are saying. The writing on the chalk board is impossible to read.

b. The atmosphere in Ms. Morse's classroom is unpleasant. The students pay no attention to what she is saying. Instead they talk loudly among themselves, slouch in their desks, and throw crumpled up wads of paper onto the floor and at each other. The air conditioner is broken, and the hot, muggy air settles oppressively over the room. There is a disturbing level of background noise. As Ms. Morse drones on at the head of the class, her voice mixes with the unruly clatter of student conversation, making it impossible to hear what anyone is saying. On the chalk board, a maze of indecipherable scribbling added to the feeling of general chaos.

a. Write a letter to your grandmother describing your first day of college.

b. Write a letter to your best friend describing your first day of college.

Here are some general rules to keep in mind when considering *audience*.

What's a level 2 incandescent semiconductor?

❶ **Define technical or specialized terms:** If you're a car nut, you'll know what a manifold exhaust is, but many of your readers will not.

That's the bomb, man!

❷ **Watch the slang:** The terms and expressions you use with your friends may not be a good choice for an essay. Some instructors don't even want you to use contractions (*that's, I'm, isn't, etc.*) or first person voice (*I*) in essays. Know the limits and respect them.

What's in it for me?

❸ **Make your readers care:** Even though your instructor has to read your essay, she doesn't have to like reading it. Think how much better you'll do if she does enjoy it. Remember that an actual human being will be reading your essay. Try to make it a pleasant, even a rewarding experience. Your reader should be entertained, informed or, ideally, both.

Huh?

❹ **Make your meaning clear:** You know what's in your mind, what you mean to say, what you're talking about when you refer to "the thing on the wall of the office." Your reader isn't a mind reader. Try to imagine the confusion or problems a reader might have trying to figure out what you're talking about. It's your job to communicate, not simply to fill up the pages with words.

ACTIVITY 2-2

Directions: One of the best ways to make your meaning clear is to be specific. Rewrite the following paragraphs adding specific details.

My room is a disaster. There is junk all over the floor and under the bed. The closet is packed with all my stuff. My desk is just about buried. Even the ceiling of my room is gross.

_____

_____

I'm in favor of putting a streetlight at the corner of Main and Hawthorne. It's a good idea. Everyone will benefit. We have needed a streetlight at that corner for a long time.

_____

_____

ACTIVITY 2-3

Directions: Match the appropriate audiences to the following passages.

Passages:

_____ 1. Wash the cut with warm water. Make sure to use lots of soap so that the bubbles will wash away the germs. Use clean toweling to dry off the cut. Then put on a Band-Aid to keep it clean.

_____ 2. Irrigate the wound with warm water and clean the area thoroughly. Dry the affected area with clean toweling. Apply a sterile dressing.

_____ 3. Wash the cut thoroughly with warm, soapy water. Use a clean towel to dry the area. Place a Band-Aid over the cut to prevent infection.

Audiences:

a. physicians   b. parents   c. children

Passages:

_____ 1. Dress as your favorite super hero and save up to 50%! Win prizes! We have the biggest collection of comics in the city. Come to the Grand Opening of our new location in Parkland Mall. Arrive early for the best bargains and the widest selection.

_____ 2. The opening of Clyde's Comix in Parkland Mall is another indication of the current upswing in retail sales outlets. Six new commercial sites have opened this year, representing a 4% increase over last year's rate. This trend has spurred the projected expansion of the mall, expected to be complete within two years.

_____ 3. Parkland Mall will welcome a new retailer, Clyde's Comix, this weekend. The Grand Opening will begin at 10:00 A.M. on Saturday with a costume party. Shoppers who most resemble comic book characters will be eligible to win prizes and store discounts.

Audiences:

a. Newspaper readers   b. comic book buyers   c. Chamber of Commerce

3

PURPOSE: WHY AM I WRITING THIS?

There are many reasons to write. Going to the grocery store? You might make a list so you don't forget Aunt Thelma's raisin bran. Feeling down? You might want to write about what you're feeling in a diary. Having trouble in biology class? You might start taking notes. Feeling inspired? You might write a poem. Most of the writing you'll do in college will be assigned: a term paper, the answer to a question on an exam, an essay for a composition class. You can save yourself trouble and do a lot to ensure your success if you pay attention to the following guidelines.

❶ *Time:* When is it due? Will you have to turn in your essay at the end of the class period? In a week? In assigning some research papers, the instructor may allow you several weeks to complete your writing. On tests, instructors often indicate how much time should be allotted to each question.

   If your time is limited, you need to spend less of it on each step, but the important thing is to leave time for all of the steps. Jot down a few notes to collect your thoughts, draft quickly, then be sure to proofread for grammatical and "sense" problems. Obviously, the more time you have, the more you can spend on each step. Don't put yourself in the position of doing an assignment at the last minute. Some writers claim they are inspired at the last minute, but it's a very risky choice and often results in little if any time for the important editing stage.

❷ *Length:* How much should I write? Knowing even a ballpark figure for the expected length of your assignment will help. The important thing to remember is that the length of the assignment means more than just the number of words or pages that are required. It gives you an idea of the amount of space you have in which to convince

13

your reader that your thesis is true. In a short essay, you'll need to hit the high points, to make your points quickly. In a longer essay, you'll have time to go into more detail, to offer more complete discussions of examples. Don't be one of those misguided students who just quit writing when they get to five pages or 800 words; they think they've finished just because their writing contains the right number of words.

❸ *What's the point?* Know your assignment. Make sure you're staying on target when you respond to the instructions your instructor gives you. Answer the exact question that has been put to you. Suppose this essay question appeared on a history test:

Near the end of World War II, the United States dropped a nuclear bomb on Japan. This resulted in massive death and injury to civilians. But the overwhelming display of force is thought to have shortened the war, thereby saving lives. Do you agree or disagree with the decision to drop the bomb?

Which of these responses would lead you to the best essay?

A. Bombing civilians is inhumane.

B. The military must do what it takes to protect its troops, even if such actions result in civilian deaths.

C. The Japanese also committed wartime atrocities.

D. There were other ways to shorten the war preferable to dropping the bomb.

Both B and D are possible responses to the question that would lead to interesting essays. Answer A almost goes without saying. Answer C limits what you can talk about in your essay.

The Three Purposes of Writing

When writers put words down they are addressing three main purposes:

◆ to inform

◆ to entertain

◆ to persuade

Writing that is intended to **inform** is sometimes called expository writing. Here the writers explain something to their readers: the life cycle of the meal worm, the reasons for economic inflation, or the history of underwear. Textbooks and encyclopedia entries are written to inform. Writing that informs is ideal for answering essay questions on exams or for doing research papers.

Writing that is intended to **entertain** is designed to keep readers interested and involved, and to make them want to keep turning the pages. Entertaining writing makes readers laugh or cry. It can shock, surprise, horrify, or delight. It amuses and intrigues. Readers keep reading because the writer's words make them curious, suspenseful, or amazed. Writing that entertains is well suited for storytelling or personal narratives (see Part 4, Section 23).

Writing that is intended to **persuade** is sometimes called argumentation. Persuasive writing is designed to convince the reader of something. To do this, it is important that writers have strong reasons to make the case. If writers are writing to persuade, there must be another side of the argument. This means that the arguments presented must be logical and the support for them must be solid. Writing that persuades is often used for editorials or personal opinion essays. Anytime a writer has a thesis, there is an obligation to persuade the reader that the thesis is true.

THE SECRET FORMULA

Now that you know about the three main purposes of writing, we'll let you in on a secret: the best writing combines all three.

It doesn't matter if you are answering an essay question, doing a term paper, or writing a composition in an English class. If you ignore one of these purposes, you run the risk of having readers who are confused, bored, or unconvinced. Anything you write will be better if you can inform your readers, while keeping them entertained and persuading them that your take on the subject matter is convincing.

ACTIVITY 3-1

Directions: Come up with thesis statements for the following essay exam questions.

a. In a short essay, discuss how television changed for better or worse during the 1990s.

_____

_____

_____

b. Write an essay in which you discuss how the current president won the election.

_____

_____

_____

c. Discuss the significance of the space program to the average person.

_____

_____

_____

d. Identify the most important quality a doctor needs to be effective.

_____

_____

_____

e. Discuss the circumstances that contribute to the rising rate of juvenile crime.

_____

_____

_____

f. In a short essay, explain the best plan to combat blighted housing.

_____

_____

_____

g. Identify the election reforms that would result in a more democratic voting process.

_____

_____

_____

h. Industrial pollution effects our quality of life. Discuss some of the consequences of industrial pollution.

_____

_____

_____

THE WHY AND HOW OF EFFECTIVE WRITING **Q&A**

Q How can I write about a topic that doesn't interest me?

A Your best bet is to take some time and see if you can find an angle on the topic that does interest you. The topic "cars" might not sound all that interesting, but describing your "dream car" might be fun. If all else fails, think of it as a challenge. A good writer can write reasonably well about anything.

Q Did great writers like William Shakespeare and Willa Cather and Richard Wright actually have to learn how to write?

A Of course they did.

Q What is luck?

A Luck, we are told, is where preparation meets opportunity.

PART

2

STARTING UP

WHERE EARL GETS HIS IDEAS

4

GENERATING IDEAS: WHAT WILL I WRITE ABOUT?

Sometimes getting started seems like the hardest part of writing. A writing assignment can be specific (the positive/negative effects of television, why real estate is/is not a good investment) or more general (a childhood memory, the prison system in the United States). Some assignments may simply call for you to write an essay on a subject of your choice. Have you ever received an assignment and just stared at it, unable to begin? You're not alone. Very few writers can receive an assignment and immediately begin to write. For most of us, a successful piece of writing requires thought and planning. We need to take time to find an approach to the topic that will really work for us. Occasionally we will need time to find the topic itself. There is an old Chinese saying that goes, "The journey of a thousand miles begins with a single step." What it says is that every task can be handled if we take it in steps and that what we must do is get started.

In this part of the book, we are going to discuss various ways of getting started. We'll begin by looking at a couple of methods of finding material you already know about which may lead you to topics for future essays, the writer's inventory and keeping a journal. These methods will help you when you are given an open ended assignment, one where you can choose your topic or shape it in some significant way to your liking.

In Section 5, we are going to ask you to take a look at how you feel about writing and what your experiences as a writer have been. By examining your attitudes about writing and thinking about where they came from, we hope you will be able to find ways to make the process easier.

Section 6 will introduce you to a way of generating and storing ideas that may come in handy whenever you have a new writing assignment.

In Section 7, we'll talk about some methods you can use when the assignment you've been given involves a specific topic. You can use these methods for any kind of writing—whether it's in or out of class, a short essay, an essay question response, or a research paper. The important thing is not to stall before you start. Once you've mastered the strategies we discuss in Part 2, you'll always be ready to take that first step on your writing journey.

5

WRITER'S INVENTORY

If you want to run a profitable business, you need to keep good records of the goods you have on hand. The manager of an auto parts store needs to know how many mufflers she has in stock and what sizes they come in. The owner of an ice cream shop needs to know what flavors to reorder and whether he has enough cherry-bomb chocolate chip swirl ice cream for the Sunday afternoon crowd.

A writer also has "goods on hand." A writer's goods are ideas, thoughts, opinions, and feelings. Before you start writing essays, you need to take stock of the things you might write about. You need to do an inventory. Having a list of things that interest you and issues that matter to you will make your job as a writer easier. When writers care about their subjects, it makes writing easier and the results more successful. Readers can sense when writers are really enjoying what they're doing.

Writers can also benefit from exploring their attitudes toward writing and analyzing their own process. Let's take some time right now to see what you've got in your inventory. The inventory is made up of four sections: (1) you, the writer; (2) questions; (3) thoughts; and (4) big ideas. We will cover each of these throughout this section. Later you might come back and turn your answers to some of these questions into essays.

Write your answers to the following questions in the spaces provided, so you'll have them handy.

Section 1: You, The Writer

If you're like most people, you learned to write your name and short words like "cat" and "dog" back in nursery school or kindergarten. What do you remember about learning to write? Did it excite you and the people around you? Take a moment to write down your thoughts in the space below.

What kinds of writing did you do in grade school? Did you write poems and stories? Book reports? Did you enjoy writing them? Why or why not?

What kinds of writing did you do in middle school or junior high school? Did your teachers expect more of you than they did in grade school? Did you enjoy writing back then? Why or why not?

What kinds of writing did you do in high school? Use the following questions to help formulate your answer: Did you write essays? Did you write a term (research) paper? If yes, how long was it? Did you have essay exams in any of your classes?

Did you enjoy the writing you did in high school? Why or why not? How do you feel about writing now? Is it something you enjoy, something you find difficult, something you don't have feelings about one way or another?

Have you ever kept a diary or journal? When? For how long? Did you enjoy it? Why or why not?

Section 2: Your Thoughts and Opinions

At some level, your best writing always involves your thoughts and opinions. Whenever you're assigned a topic to write about, you need to find an angle that engages your thoughts and strongest feelings. Here are some questions that will help you identify subjects you really care about. Jot down your responses in the space provided.

What is a recent news event that affected your life?

What did you think of the principal at your high school?

What do you think of the job the president of the United States is doing?

Should the mayor of your town or city be reelected? Why or why not?

What is something you know now that you wish you had known a long time ago?

What is one thing you like that none of your friends seem to like (could be a movie, magazine, or restaurant, or something else of your choice)? If you think of more than one thing, make a list.

What is one thing that seems to be popular with your friends that you don't like? Once again, it might be a movie, magazine, or restaurant, or something else of your choice. Explain why you don't like it.

Did your parents do a good job raising you? Explain your answer.

Do you think you were a good child? Explain why.

What career have you chosen? Why? If you haven't chosen a career, write about the problems you have faced in making this decision.

If you were going to run for a political office in your city or state, which one would you choose? Why?

Describe your favorite hour of the day. Provide details that explain your answer.

What has living in your neighborhood taught you about life?

Should music contain parental advisory labels? Why or why not?

Should parents allow children to have TV sets in their bedrooms? Why or why not?

Should parents install computer programs that prevent their children from visiting certain Websites? Why or why not?

Should new parents be required to take training classes? Why or why not?

Should couples who want to get married be required to go to couples counseling before being issued a license? Why or why not?

Should people who want to buy guns be required to have a license? Why or why not?

Have you ever felt you were cheated by a business? What happened?

What was the most important thing—positive or negative—that happened to you while you were in high school? Describe why it was important.

How do you expect college will change your life? In what way or ways?

Name the person you most admire in each of the following categories. Briefly explain your answers.

athlete _____   actor _____

politician _____   writer _____

teacher _____   relative _____

musician _____   comedian _____

Choose a sport or hobby. What are the benefits of being involved in that activity?

How have computers changed your life?

If you could own only a TV or a computer, which would you choose? Why?

KEEPING A JOURNAL

Dear Diary: Repeat yesterday's entry.
Delete "ham." Enter "pastrami."

Writing is like just about every other skill: the more you do it, the better you get at it. Keeping a journal gives you a place to practice your writing. Even when you don't have a specific writing assignment to work on, you can always write in your journal. A journal is a place to express your thoughts and blow off steam; it's a place to jot down ideas for upcoming writing assignments; it's a place to record interesting things you hear or read. Anything you want to write about can go into a journal. That's the great thing about it. You can write anything you want in your journal at just about any time.

Tools of the Trade

Although you can keep a journal on a disk and write at your computer, unless you have a laptop, you're probably going to be limited in the places and times you can write in it. As a practical alternative, we suggest that you get a notebook that you devote especially to journal keeping. This may be a fancy blank book you buy at a bookstore or an inexpensive spiral notebook you buy just about anywhere. The main thing is that you want something you'll feel comfortable writing in that won't be too bulky to keep with you wherever you go. Keep in mind that your journal should be used for journal entries only. Don't use it for taking notes in class or writing down assignments.

If you prefer writing on your computer and don't have a laptop, you might want to keep a journal disk and have a notebook only for times when you're away from your computer. It really doesn't matter how and where you keep your journal—just that you do it.

You might want to find a specific time in every day to spend writing in your journal. You don't need a lot of time—you can get a lot down in ten or fifteen minutes—but once you make it a habit, you may find yourself full of things to say. Before an athlete takes part in a major sporting event, he or she will do stretching exercises. Think of keeping your journal as the stretching exercises you should do before a major writing assignment.

Though "anything goes" in your journal (from recording what happens to you every day to writing short stories and poems), sometimes it helps to have a little push to get you started. You can use your journal as a continuation of your Writer's Inventory, coming up with your own questions or using some of ours. Here are some possible ideas to write about in your journal:

1. What's your favorite class this semester? Why?

2. Think about something at home or at work that recently made you mad. What did you do about it?

3. What is the last thing you bought that wasn't worth what you paid for it? Why?

4. What are the three best things about the town or city you live in? What are the three worst things?

5. What are three things your parents did right in raising you? What are three things they did wrong? Explain.

6. If you could change one thing about this country, what would it be? Explain.

7. What does "integrity" mean to you?

8. What does "tragedy" mean to you?

9. What does "freedom" mean to you?

10. Describe your first best friend and what the two of you liked to do together.

11. Describe your bedroom five or ten years ago and compare it with how it looks today.

12. Describe your dream car. Compare it with the car you are currently driving.

13. Describe a stressful day at work or school.

14. Describe your perfect night on the town.

15. Compare the career plans you had as a kid with your career plans today.

16. Describe the steps you follow when you get ready for school or work every morning.

17. Explain the steps you follow when you do a particular job—like making perfect popcorn or washing the car.

18. Explain what a great teacher or a bad teacher does and give specific examples from your own experience.

A journal is a great place to try out essay ideas. As you read on through this book, you may find topics for essays developing out of some of the suggestions above. You may also find that some of your own entries can be developed into full length essays. Your journal can become an important part of your growth as a writer.

ACTIVITY 6-1

Directions: During the next week, choose a notebook you can keep as a journal and fill at least two pages (on one side) with entries. The entries can be on the subject of your choice. If you find it difficult to come up with subjects on your own, feel free to use some of the ones listed in this section.

7

STRATEGIES FOR DISCOVERING SUPPORTING MATERIAL

In the writer's inventory in Section 5, you were often asked to explain your feelings and opinions. Without even thinking about it, you were providing your reader with "supporting material." There may be times, though, when you won't be completely sure how to proceed, when you need to set aside time to collect enough material to write an essay that will adequately support a thesis.

In order to discover your supporting material, you must first have a topic—a topic that is assigned or one you have come up with on your own. Once you have it, there are three particularly useful strategies for discovering supporting material: (1) brainstorming, (2) freewriting, and (3) mind-mapping. The method you use will depend on various factors. We encourage you to experiment with each method—you may find that one works better than another for a particular topic. Keep in mind that there is no one way of doing things—all writers make their own paths by choosing the methods that work best for them.

Brainstorming

Sometimes writers have trouble getting started because they're sorting through a lot of ideas and nothing seems good enough. They get an idea and before their pens hit the paper or their fingers hit the keyboard of their computers, they've already discarded it. Sometimes writers have trouble getting started because too many irrelevant ideas get in the way. They're hungry or tired and keep thinking about being hungry or tired. Or they can't get some song lyric out of their mind.

The perfect method for getting past this obstacle and for clearing the path to your best ideas is brainstorming—the process of making a list of everything you think of when you think of a given topic. Your goal here is not to judge or censor anything. Write down everything—single words as well as parts of sentences. You must think of brainstorming as the process of emptying your mind of the "storm" of ideas that a topic sets in motion.

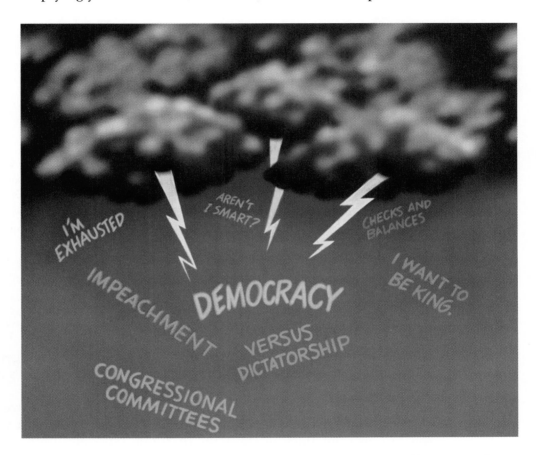

One way to brainstorm is to set up a timer. Tell yourself to write down everything that comes to mind as you think about your topic over the next five minutes. (The first time, you might try it for three minutes.) The trick is to write down everything that comes to mind. Don't question whether it relates to the topic. Don't worry if it is obviously off the subject. You want to clear your mind of everything that is distracting you as well as everything you can use.

Here is an example of a brainstorm a writer came up with on the benefits of owning a car:

transportation when you want it

go where you want

starving

Lexus

steering wheel

bored

impress other people

cruising fun

Another writer came up with this on the space program:

moon

Mars

expensive

experiments

astronauts

tired

clothes to cleaners

Notice how both brainstorms include items that obviously would never turn up in an essay on the topic listed ("starving," "tired," "clothes to cleaners"). Sometimes writing such things down allows you to get them off your mind, so you can get to what really matters. That's why it's important when you brainstorm to write everything down.

When you have finished brainstorming, you can go back over your list and cross out anything that obviously has nothing to do with your topic. You can also put stars beside items that look especially promising as supporting points for your thesis. One of the great things about brainstorming is that you sometimes find things on your list that surprise you. Some of your best ideas come when you let loose and think creatively.

ACTIVITY 7-1

Directions: Pick one of the following topics and brainstorm for three minutes.

The advantages of living on your own

A high school diploma is not enough

Freewriting

In freewriting—which is in a way like brainstorming—you write without censoring your thoughts, allowing everything to come out. The difference between freewriting and brainstorming is that you write in complete sentences and may end up with a piece of writing that resembles a draft rather than a list.

Remember the topic we just brainstormed on the benefits of owning a car? Here is what freewriting on that topic might look like:

> There are many benefits of owning your own car. You've got it when you want it. You can drive it anywhere. You don't have to wait for a bus. Having a car means freedom. You can go wherever you want whenever you want. It's great. Feeling that breeze as you roll down the streets, everybody watching your every move.

The writing here is not polished, but the writer has come up with a couple of ideas that are worth developing in an essay: having a car means you can go where you want; having a car means you can go whenever you want. The purpose of freewriting is to help you get your ideas out. When you've finished writing, go back and take a look—circle or underline those ideas which seem promising. It's difficult to write when you have a critic looking over your shoulder and many times that critic is you. Freewriting allows you the freedom to write without anyone looking over your shoulder.

ACTIVITY 7-2

Directions: Freewrite on one of the following topics.

How having a computer has changed the way I do homework

My first week at college

Mindmapping

For some writers, the best way to plan what they're going to say is through mindmapping—the process of "mapping out" thoughts on paper. When you mindmap, you get your ideas down and make quick connections. You begin with your topic and move outward, drawing lines to connect whatever ideas come to mind. Imagine that you have been assigned to write an essay about your first day at college. Here's how a mindmap of that topic might look.

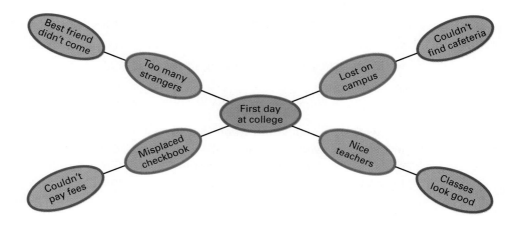

ACTIVITY 7-3

Directions: Try mindmapping the topic "Why I want a college diploma" for yourself.

Let's take a single topic and look at how brainstorming, freewriting, and mindmapping would look.

A brainstorm on the topic of the minimum wage might look like this:

$5.25

too low

not enough to live on

late paying rent

hard work

McDonald's

two cheeseburgers for the price of one this week

stay poor

write to representative in Congress

Freewriting about the minimum wage might look like this:

I've worked for minimum wage for the past three years at Bob's CD Barn. I put in 20 hours a week and only make about $100. My rent is $500 a month and my other bills are another $500. I can't make it on the minimum wage. It's driving me crazy. They've got to raise it. Even an extra dollar an hour would really help. When they invented the minimum wage it was a lot cheaper to live.

A mindmap on the topic of the minimum wage might look like this:

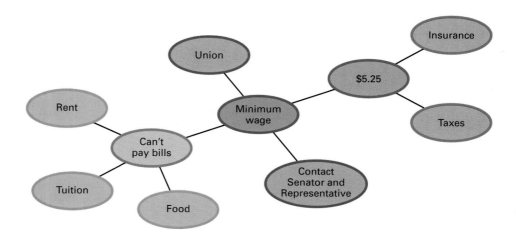

Notice how some items in the mindmap directly relate to each other (*can't pay bills* links bill items *rent*, *tuition*, and *food*); while these items remain indirectly related to others (*tuition* and *taxes*). Mindmapping can help you to see different relationships among ideas.

Whatever method you choose, the important thing to remember is that many times you will find out what you think by writing. You get your ideas out on paper any way you can, and that sets you on the path that will make what you want to say clear to yourself and your readers. You need a method to get your ideas out just so you'll have something to examine and polish. Brainstorming, freewriting, and mindmapping are all great ways to get what you have to say out on paper. Once you've got a few ideas going, you'll have the confidence you need to develop and refine them.

WE'RE GLAD YOU ASKED
GENERATING IDEAS **Q&A**

Q Is there one method of generating ideas that is better than all the others?

A The best method of generating ideas is the one that works for you. It may change depending on the topic. That's why it's good to know more than one way. If you're having trouble generating ideas using one method, try another.

Q If I don't take the time to write down or type out my ideas before I begin, will my essay be a disaster?

A It might not be a disaster, but it probably won't be as good as it could be. Why settle for less? To build a good essay you need to use the best materials you can find.

Q Who put the ram in the rama-lama-ding-dong?

A It's a closely guarded government secret.

3

WRITING EFFECTIVE PARAGRAPHS AND ESSAYS

8

WHAT ARE THE COMPONENTS OF AN EFFECTIVE PARAGRAPH?

Suppose you went into a grocery store with a list of items to buy: a loaf of bread, a gallon of milk, some apples, a pound of hamburger, a bunch of bananas, some Swiss cheese and a rump roast. Would you have to wander all over the store, looking down each aisle for your items? Of course not. You'd find the milk and cheese in the dairy section, the hamburger and roast with the meat, the apples and bananas in the produce department. All grocery stores are so organized that similar items are grouped together. So are good essays.

At their most basic, paragraphs are simply a way of grouping sentences together to make things a little easier for your reader. Imagine what reading would be like if there were no such things as paragraphs:

Over the years I've considered many careers. As a kid I wanted to be a fireman and then when I was in sixth grade I wanted to be a sixth grade teacher because I liked my teacher so much. When I got to high school, I took biology for the first time and began to reconsider my career goals. There are many reasons I have decided to become a doctor. First of all, I love the science of medicine. I love learning about various medicines and how they interact. I'm fascinated by the idea that someone can be sick and after taking a pill can feel so much better. Another reason I would like to be a doctor is that I want to help people in need. Doctors have the opportunity to change peoples lives. Imagine that—you can make a good living while helping others . . .

What would it be like to read page after page of endless, unbroken lines of words? It wouldn't be easy.

When you indent the first line of a paragraph, you give your readers an opportunity to rest for a second. You signal them that you may be changing course, moving on to talk about other things. By grouping sentences together, you make reading easier and help your readers to understand what you're trying to say. It's not just a matter of breaking your writing into pieces to make the writing easier on the eye visually; it's a matter of breaking the content up into sections that will be easier for the writer to absorb.

Let's take a look at the selection above, but this time we'll break it down into paragraphs, indenting five spaces to show where each new paragraph begins.

Over the years I've considered my careers. As a kid I wanted to be a fireman and then when I was in sixth grade I wanted to be a sixth grade teacher because I liked my teacher so much. When I got to high school, I took biology for the first time and began to reconsider my career goals. There are many reasons I have decided to become a doctor.

First of all, I love the science of medicine. I love learning about the various medicines and how they interact. I'm fascinated by the idea that someone can be sick and after taking a pill can feel so much better.

Another reason I would like to be a doctor is that I want to help people in need. Doctors have the opportunity to change people's lives. Imagine that—you can make a good living while helping others . . .

The first thing you notice is how different the writing looks when you indent for new paragraphs. Suddenly it seems more manageable to the eye. Notice how each paragraph contains ideas that belong together, so it's easier for the reader to follow the points being made.

Good paragraphs are the basic building blocks of successful essays. If you can write good paragraphs, you can write successful essays. In many ways, a paragraph is built on the same model as an essay. A successful essay has a thesis and includes supporting points that prove it. A successful paragraph has a topic sentence and supporting points that develop it.

9

WHAT IS THE MAIN IDEA?

Every successful paragraph has a main idea—an idea that is called the **topic sentence.** The topic sentence is frequently the first sentence in a paragraph, but in some cases it may come later. (The situation is similar in a full-length essay, where the thesis is commonly stated in the first paragraph but in some cases may appear elsewhere.) Look at the following paragraph:

> Today's cars are safer than ever. Many models feature specially reinforced bumpers. The air bag is now required in all new vehicles, and some even contain side air bags. Even that early safety device, the seat belt, has been improved so that it does an even better job.

Which sentence is the topic sentence? In this case the first sentence, as expected, is the topic sentence. It tells the reader what the paragraph is about and then the next three sentences give examples to support the claim made by the topic sentence:

◆ **Topic sentence:** Today's cars are safer than ever.

◆ **Support sentence 1:** Many models feature specially reinforced bumpers.

◆ **Support sentence 2:** The air bag is now required in all new vehicles, and some even contain side air bags.

◆ **Support sentence 3:** Even that early safety device, the seat belt, has been improved so that it does an even better job.

The topic sentence determines the limits of a paragraph. Your paragraph should contain only those ideas that support the topic sentence. If you can't relate a point back to your topic sentence, it needs to be cut. The topic sentence is an organizing principle that makes writing easier for you. Use it to help map out the development of your essay.

ACTIVITY 9-1

Directions: Come up with a good topic sentence for the following paragraphs.

1. _____

   Restaurants are sometimes full of people who smoke. At home you can eat smoke free. At restaurants they charge huge prices for a small amount of food. Home cooking is cheap by comparison and you can fix as much as you want to eat. Some restaurants can be really dirty. At home you can be sure that everything is as clean as it should be.

2. _____

   Computers are found in most homes. Some households even have more than one computer, one used by the kids to play games on and another used by parents to manage budgets and pay bills. In schools, computers are now as common as chalkboards. They are found in almost every classroom, and some schools have special computer labs for students. It's hard to imagine a business, from the corner hardware store to the global corporation—that doesn't rely on computers to get through their daily transactions.

10

HOW DO I CONVINCE MY READER?

Coming up with a good topic sentence is just the beginning of writing a paragraph. It's an important first step, but then you must follow it up by writing sentences that will support and clarify it.

Which of the following paragraphs do you think is the more convincing:

> Our campus is not very student-friendly. Many students are not comfortable here. They just get in their cars and leave. No one around here even tries to be nice.

> Our campus is not very student-friendly. There are no comfortable places for students to gather and talk inside or outside of the buildings. The only food service available is too expensive and offers only full meals like stewed chicken and rice or roast beef with mashed potatoes. The financial aid and other administrative offices make you feel like you should just go home and stop bothering them.

Is there any doubt which paragraph is better? The second example is better not just because it's longer. Some writers can go on and on without ever saying anything specific. What makes this paragraph work is that it provides the reader with several specific examples of ways in which the campus is not student-friendly. Choice A is just too general to convince the reader that the topic sentence is reasonable.

This raises an important question. Where do you find the kind of specific material you need to develop an effective paragraph? If you're lucky, it will pour out of you. You're so mad at your home football team for sinking into a five-game losing streak that the reasons just keep coming. You've seen so many great movies recently that you can hardly wait to list all of the examples for your essay on how the present is Hollywood's Golden Age.

49

Many times, though (and believe us, this is true for all writers), development ideas trickle out. They're just aren't enough. Possibly you have no ideas at all. This is when those strategies for discovering supporting material we talked about in Part 2 will come in handy. You can do a quick brainstorm or mindmap or try freewriting.

ACTIVITY 10-1

Directions: Brainstorm, mindmap, or freewrite on the following topic sentences.

I'm looking forward to owning my own car/renting my first apartment/retirement. Our school really needs a new . . .

It might be useful to think about the modes of development we'll be discussing in more detail in Part 4: can you think of examples to support your topic? Would division and classification or comparison and contrast help? Might you discuss causes and effects or describe a process or tell a story (narration) to develop your topic sentence?

Look at your topic sentence and consider the ways it might be developed.

ACTIVITY 10-2

Directions: Look at the following topics and list which of the modes might be used to develop them successfully. The modes to choose from are (1) examples, (2) division and classification, (3) comparison and contrast, (4) causes and effects, and (5) process.

1. Children today watch too much TV. _____

2. The driving age should be raised to 18. _____

3. My first date was a disaster. _____

4. Drugs are a major problem in this town. _____

5. Politicians are not public servants. _____

ACTIVITY 10-3

Directions: Write a well-developed paragraph on one of the topic sentences on the previous page.

An effective paragraph is one that has a single clear topic that tells what the paragraph is about. An effective paragraph contains specific examples, reasons, and details that further explain and/or support the topic sentence. An effective paragraph is as long as it needs to be to get its point across.

WE'RE GLAD YOU ASKED
WRITING EFFECTIVE PARAGRAPHS Q&A

Q Exactly how long is an effective paragraph?

A There is no magic number of sentences in an effective paragraph. Three sentences would seem like a good minimum number (though you could probably find an essay with a dramatic one- or two-sentence paragraph that works). The important thing is to be honest with yourself and take the time to make sure you've said enough about your topic sentence.

Q Is it possible to combine different modes of development into a single paragraph?

A Sure—an effective paragraph might compare and contrast examples or reasons. It might tell a story that contains examples. Your goal should be to write clearly and make sure your development clearly relates to your thesis.

Q Are the best things in life free?

A Without a doubt.

11

WHAT ARE THE COMPONENTS OF AN EFFECTIVE ESSAY?

"I bark. I get fed. That works for me."

If we asked you to describe a "good" essay, you would probably answer by using words like "interesting" and "well written." You might even say it "doesn't have many mistakes." Well, certainly, good essays are interesting and well written and don't have many mistakes, but this doesn't give the writer who hopes to write a good essay much to go on. In this chapter we will introduce you to the basic qualities of a good essay and give you some ideas of what to keep in mind as you write. As you read through the rest of the book you will find these ideas explored in more detail. Good writing is much more than not making mistakes with grammar and spelling. Many students come to college with memories of papers being returned to them full or red marks. Or maybe they come with the memory of no comments and a mysterious grade scrawled across the top or bottom of the essay. It's easy to get the wrong idea about how to write good papers. It's not simply about avoiding red marks and it's not about trying to guess what your grade means and making another wild stab at successful writing in your next essay.

Good writing is about generating a lot of ideas about what you want to say and then thinking about them before you begin a first draft. It's about making a plan before you start. It's about writing a draft of your essay already knowing that it won't be your last, that you don't have to get everything right the first time. It's about getting your ideas down on paper in a way that a reader other than yourself can understand. It's about being specific and detailed. It's about not worrying about grammar and spelling until you're working on the final, polishing draft and proofreading as if your life depended on it.

A good essay contains three parts:

❶ Introduction

❷ Body

❸ Conclusion

None of these parts can exist without the others. You can't have an essay that is all introduction or all conclusion. Similarly, it can't be all body. Each part of the essay depends on the other two parts. Each part must be working well in order for the total essay to shine. Let's take a look at the three basic elements of the essay in more detail.

Introduction: How Can I Make a Good First Impression?

Your first paragraph, what we'll be calling the introduction, is the beginning of your paper, and in writing, just as in life, first impressions count. Your introduction should serve three main functions:

❶ *I.D. the general topic*: The introduction should let the reader know what the overall topic of the paper is. Will you be writing about wildlife in Africa? Air pollution in Los Angeles? Your long lost Uncle Louie? The title of the essay can help here, but titles can be vague or even misleading. The introduction should leave no doubt as to what the subject matter at hand will be.

❷ *Set the hook*: The introduction should catch your readers' interest and make them want to read more. This is called setting a "hook"— something that will grab readers and pull them into the rest of your essay.

❸ *State the thesis*: The introduction should state your thesis. There may be exceptions to this rule, but for the most part, unless you deliberately want to mislead your reader to set up a surprise, it's best to come out and state your thesis somewhere in your introduction.

12
THESIS: WHAT IS IT AND DOES MINE WORK?

The introduction of almost every essay asserts a **thesis.** It is very important that you understand what a thesis is and how it works in the essays that you read and the essays that you write.

A thesis is the main point you want to communicate to your reader.

> Starting your own small business isn't easy.

A thesis is the stand you take, an opinion you must support.

> Bob Wilson is the best candidate for governor.

A thesis is not a statement of fact.

> Every June thousands of Americans graduate from college.

A thesis is not a title.

> How to Buy a Car

A thesis is not an announcement of a subject.

> My essay is about the importance of vitamins.

ACTIVITY 12-1

Directions: Look at the following statements. Put a "T" beside the thesis statements you find. Put "NT" beside any statement that is not a thesis and be sure you can explain why it's not.

_____ 1. Olympic figure skating in the 1990s.

_____ 2. Kevin Spacey won the Academy Award in 2000.

_____ 3. The policemen in this city are underpaid.

_____ 4. Nursing is an excellent career for men.

_____ 5. *The Great Gatsby* and *The Sun Also Rises*

HOW DO I SET UP AN INTRODUCTION?

There are several strategies you can use when you are planning your introduction:

◆ **Tell a story:** Everyone likes to hear stories. A good story will grab the reader's attention:

> Last Sunday I was driving home after having breakfast at Shoney's. When I got to the corner of Milne and Harrison, a car ran a stop sign and nearly crashed into me. As the car sped away, I noticed that the driver was talking on a cell phone. He was so busy yakking I don't think he even saw me. It was this experience along with some others I've heard about that have convinced me that drivers should not be allowed to use cell phones.

◆ **Ask a question:** An interesting question will get your readers thinking. Because they want to know the answer, they'll read on:

> We are currently reaping the benefits of modern technology particularly in the field of communications. We can reach people via computer or telephone at virtually any time. I wonder sometimes, though, whether this is a good thing. Should we be talking on phones while we're driving? Is it worth the risks?

◆ **This means you (nail the reader):** This strategy draws readers into your essay in a way they simply can't ignore:

> If you own a cell phone, listen up. I enjoy talking on my cell phone just as much as you do. You'll see me walking across campus talking to my dad or reserving tickets for a concert. I love the convenience. One thing I don't do, however, is mix my cell phone and driving. I don't think you should either.

◆ **Big-to-little (general to specific):** Following this method you get the reader's attention and gradually focus it down to a narrow statement (thesis):

> There have been many technological innovations over the past twenty years that have really improved our lives. Where would we be without the benefits of cable television and the personal computer? Telephones, too,

have been greatly improved. We now have the capacity to be connected by phone virtually wherever we are. This mobility however, has begun to cause problems. People are using their cell phones at inappropriate times like when they're driving and they shouldn't be.

◆ **Little-to-Big (specific to general):** Here you begin with a small statement and slowly expand outward until you reveal the central point you want to make:

It takes a driver three seconds to get his eyes back on the road after dialing a number on his cell phone. In those three seconds, anything can happen. A car can begin braking in front of him or a car in the next lane can make a sudden swerve. Drivers don't have time to take their eyes off the road. Therefore, drivers should not be allowed to use cell phones.

◆ **Try Bartlett's:** A quotation can grab your reader's attention. Quoting a respected person can add credibility to your argument. Sometimes, though, a quotation will simply add a bit of interest to your opening:

Police Chief Jack Jones was recently quoted as saying, "If I could launch all the cell phones into outer space, I would." He was speaking in reference to a recent spate of accidents in our area involving drivers who were talking on cell phones. It's easy to understand his frustration; these accidents didn't need to happen. Talking on cell phones while driving should be outlawed.

How long should the introduction be? It's probably going to be short in relation to the whole essay.

ACTIVITY 12-2

Directions: Read the following introductory paragraphs and identify the method (from the list above) that the writer is using.

1. Going to college is an expensive proposition. In addition to tuition and fees, students have to buy expensive textbooks and other supplies. They often have to pay for transportation costs and housing. In order to afford college, many students have to work while attending school. Balancing the world of work and the world of school isn't easy.

    Method: _____

2.　　　When Cedric started college in September, he quickly ran into financial problems. Though he'd taken out a loan, he still found it difficult to pay for his books and supplies and still have some left over for his social life. He decided to get a part-time job and was happy when he found one almost immediately. Getting a job, however, provided Cedric with a whole new set of problems. Balancing the world of work and the world of school isn't easy.

Method: _____

3.　　　More than 60 percent of the students at this university are currently working while going to school. Counselor Mary Scroggins says, "We have many jugglers who try to keep their jobs and rarely find a free moment as they move from one activity to the next." Balancing the world of work and the world of school isn't easy.

Method: _____

4.　　　While driving to his job on an ordinary Monday morning, Bill Wharton was killed by a drunk driver, a man with two prior DWI convictions. Could this tragedy have been prevented?

Method: _____

5.　　　If you own oceanfront property, you can't afford to ignore the problem of coastal erosion. Not only can it have disastrous economic effects, such as reducing your property value, but it can also have negative repercussions on your quality of life, forever altering the view that enriches the beauty of your land.

Method: _____

13

BODY: WHAT IS IT, AND DOES IT SUPPORT MY THESIS?

The body of your essay is where you convince your reader that your thesis is true. There are many ways to do this, ways that we will be exploring in detail later in this book. Here are the main methods. They are sometimes called *rhetorical modes*.

◆ **Examples:** Gives examples, often exploring a few of the best ones in detail (see p. 75).

◆ **Comparison and contrast:** Shows the similarities and differences between two subjects (see p. 92).

◆ **Cause and effect:** Examines the causes and/or effects of something (see p. 105).

◆ **Division and classification:** Examines a subject by breaking it down into parts (see p. 120).

◆ **Process:** Explains how to do something or how something happened (see p. 131).

◆ **Narration:** Tells a story to prove a point (see p. 144).

◆ **Definition:** Defines a term that means different things to different people (see p. 151).

◆ **Description:** Uses a detailed description to make a point (see p. 157).

Each of these methods has special requirements. We'll show you how to design a blueprint for each type of essay so that you can build an essay that will work effectively.

The body of your essay may be one or two paragraphs (though this is rare) or it may be three to five or more. It all depends on your thesis and how much you need to say in order to convince your reader. There's no magic formula or recipe or rule here. You simply have to determine what you need to do to convince your reader and then do it.

14

CONCLUSION: HOW DO I WRAP THINGS UP?

Have you ever listened to a bad singer try to perform? All too often the final notes just kind of fade away, as if the singer ran out of breath or got too embarrassed to carry on. You don't want that to happen when you're writing.

The conclusion needs to serve three functions:

❶ *Summary:* The conclusion should summarize your main points; it should never bring up a brand new point.

❷ *Rerun the thesis:* The conclusion should restate your thesis.

❸ *Leave an impression:* The conclusion should leave your readers thinking about what you had to say.

Here are some strategies for you to use in setting up your conclusion:

❶ *Call to action:* Suggest something that readers can do, now that they have read your essay. It might be a physical action. ("Remember to get out and vote on election day. Your future depends on it.") It might be a mental action. ("The next time you feel too lazy to go to the polls, think about what others have sacrificed for your right to vote.") This kind of language in a conclusion urges the reader to make use of the ideas you've expressed in writing.

❷ *Ask a question:* One easy way to get readers to think about the ideas you've discussed is to throw a question directly in at them. ("If election day was tomorrow would you be standing in line ready to cast your vote? Or would you be at home, watching TV and leaving your future in the hands of someone else?")

❸ *Look into the crystal ball:* This strategy requires you to predict the future. You offer your reader a glimpse into what might happen "if." ("If voter turn-out continues to decline, political decisions will be made by a small percentage of the citizens, while the majority leaves the important decisions in the hands of a few motivated voters.")

❹ *Back to Bartlett's:* Again, if you can find a quote that fits, it could be a nice way to wrap things up. Don't force it; this is a good strategy only if you find the right quote for the occasion. "Vote early and vote often."

ACTIVITY 14-1

Directions: Remember the introductions for the essay on cell phones we looked at in Section 12? Read the following concluding paragraphs and determine which method from the list above that the writer is using.

1.   Given the fact that there have been numerous accidents attributed to cell phones, the time has come to do something. All citizens should contact their congressmen and senators about this issue. Starting on the local level might even be more effective. Citizens should make sure their lawmakers come up with a law that prohibits the use of cell phones by drivers of moving vehicles.

Method: _____

2.   Next time you're in your car, ask yourself if talking on your cell phone to your Aunt Margaret about what she is fixing for dinner is important enough to take the chance of impairing your driving. Do you really want to be responsible for injuring someone else not to mention damaging your own car in such an accident? Worse still, how would it feel to be hit by another driver who lost control while talking on the phone? It is time for our nation's phone obsession to end.

Method: _____

3.   While we've all heard about cell phone related accidents, no one knows the extent of this tragedy as well as our police officers and ER doctors and nurses. Almost every day they see victims of this avoidable problem. As Police Chief Jack Jones said recently, "If I could launch all the cell phones into outer space, I would." Since we can't do that, outlawing their use by drivers is the next best thing.

Method: _____

4.   The growing reliance on computers has certainly made life easier. However, if this trend continues, it has a dark side. A single computer glitch could cause the wheels of society to grind to a total standstill.

Method: _____

5.   Greta Garbo, film star of the 1930s, said, "I want to be alone." Little did Garbo know the terrible burden celebrity would become in the years that followed. Celebrities today are all too familiar with the curse of being constantly in the public eye.

Method: _____

6.   The fate of many endangered species rests not in the faraway jungles, oceans, or arctic seas, but in the cities and suburbs of our country. Sitting at your kitchen table, in your livingroom, or on your patio, you can make a difference. Get involved in conservation. Volunteer your time, energy, money—or all three. You can make a difference.

Method: _____

15
TITLE: HOW DO I CLAIM MY READER'S INTEREST?

"That's O.K., Dad. I think I'll go with the ambient waterfall sounds tonight."

The title of an essay is probably always going to be the first thing readers notice, yet it's not something writers need to worry about until the end of their writing process. After all, something that hasn't been written yet really doesn't need a title. You can jot down title ideas as you go along, but you really don't need to make a final decision (and really don't know what will fit best) until you've finished writing.

Have you ever read something just because the title caught your eye. What if you saw a headline in a newspaper that said "Giant Pink Reindeer Invades College Dormitory"? Would you want to read about it? Or how about "Money to Be Given Away on Thursday—Come and Get It!" Wouldn't you want to read on immediately, find out all the details?

The trick to writing good titles is to find a line or group of words that conveys the content of your essay while stimulating the reader's curiosity. You could call an essay about your brother, "My Brother" or you could call it, "My Brother—The Pint-Sized Hero." Which essay sounds more interesting to you? By revealing a few details and an attitude toward the subject, you come up with a much stronger title.

ACTIVITY 15-1

Directions: Circle the better title in each of the following pairs. Think about why one title is better than the other.

1. "Cars Today"/"My Late Great Dodge Dart"
2. "My Vacation"/"The Amtrak Seven-Day Disaster"
3. "Freedom at Risk"/"Voter Apathy"
4. "Healthy Eating"/"Add Years to Your Life in the Supermarket"
5. "Shopping"/"How to Spend Money and Save"

WE'RE GLAD YOU ASKED
WRITING EFFECTIVE ESSAYS Q&A

Q If I'm running out of time, should I just skip the conclusion?

A A one sentence conclusion that restates the thesis would be better than no conclusion. If you run into this problem, you probably need to reevaluate how you manage your writing time.

Q How do I know if I've come up with a good title?

A After reading your essay, look at the title. Does it clearly connect to your thesis in some way? Does it shed any light on your main point? Do you think it will make the reader want to read on? If so, you have a good title, maybe even a great one.

Q Do cats really have nine lives?

A We may never know, but look for full coverage on the Discovery Channel or Animal Planet if scientists ever figure this one out.

P A R T
4
EXPLORING WAYS
TO DEVELOP IDEAS

"Nevermore. And you can quote me."

16

CATEGORIES

No matter what plan you decide to use to build your essay, you'll need to be able to work with the concept of categories. A **category** is a group of terms each of which has something in common with the rest. See if you can figure out what makes the following list of items a category:

Big Bird
a lemon
the sun
a school bus
a coward
butter

Is there anything that all of the items have in common? Yes, all are yellow.

What about this list?

table
chair
twins
horse
dog

All have four legs.

ACTIVITY 16-1

Directions: What do the items in the following lists have in common? Write your answers in the blanks below.

List A

toothpaste
soap
sink
aftershave
towel

_____

List B

The White House
The Lincoln Memorial
The Smithsonian Institution
The National Gallery
The Capitol

_____

List C

keep
loop
liar
star
stew

_____

When you write an essay, you'll have a collection of information. Think of it as a list. Some items on the list may have something in common. The way you group the items into categories will help you decide how to build your essay, how to organize it.

Remember that there may be many ways to divide items into categories. You'll need to decide which way works best for you. Suppose you have a room full of dogs.

Collie
Poodle
Great Dane
Dachshund
Basset hound
Chihuahua

Pit bull
Doberman
Sheep dog
Irish setter
Cocker spaniel

You could divide your dogs into categories according to size: big dogs, medium dogs, and small dogs. Or you could have categories according to ears: long ears or short ears. You might decide to show the differences between groups: dogs that are good with children and dogs that aren't; dogs that are easy to care for and dogs that require lots of grooming. Some categories could highlight similarities: dogs used for guard work, dogs used for hunting, etc.

The decisions you make about the categories you find will lead you to your decisions about what kind of essay you'll write and how to build it.

After you brainstorm (brainstorming works particularly well here as a prewriting activity—see p. 34), take a minute to look over your ideas. Think about the categories you might find and what the different items on your brainstorming "list" could have in common.

17
CHOOSING A MODE: WHAT BLUEPRINT WILL I USE?

Look up the word **mode** in the dictionary. One definition is "a **manner** of doing something"; another is "a particular **form** of something." When it comes to writing essays, these definitions apply. There are many modes that we'll introduce you to shortly. Some examples are: Comparison and Contrast, Cause and Effect, Division and Classification, Process, Narration, Definition, and Description. The mode you pick will determine the **form** of your essay and determine the **manner** in which you will build it.

Think about houses. Although there are countless ways to design a house (ranch style, split level, and bungalow, to name a few), all houses (or at least all of the decent ones) have certain basic features: kitchens, bathrooms, bedrooms. There are countless ways to construct an essay. But all essays (or at least the decent ones) have certain basic features: a beginning (the Introduction), a middle (the Body), and an end (the Conclusion).

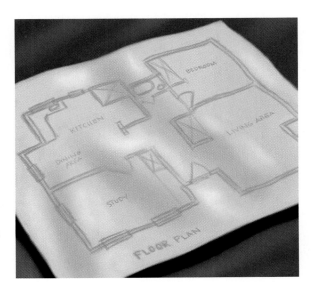

If you are a gourmet cook, you need a house with a big kitchen. You might also like a large dining room. If you have a lot of out-of-town visitors, you might want a guest room. And a guest bathroom might be nice too. If you are a serious athlete, your house should have a home gym for your workout equipment. If you have lots of children, your house should have a big playroom. And so on.

Planning your essay works much the same way. You want to build the kind of essay that will meet your particular needs. The modes are particular variations of the basic Introduction/Body/Conclusion essay plan. The way you design your essay, just the way you'd design your house, depends on what your needs are.

Think about your assignment (how long your essay should be, how much time you have to write it), your audience (who will be reading your essay), and your resources (what information you have access to).

Each mode has its own special design to tell you how to build it. We'll show you blueprints for each mode.

18

EXAMPLES: DON'T LEAVE HOME WITHOUT THEM!

Example Essay—When to Use It

Examples are among the most important modes in writing. They are a basic tool every writer needs. Examples will help you convince readers that your ideas are reasonable, that what you say makes sense, that your thesis is valid. You may want to use examples within a paragraph to back up

your topic sentence. In fact, it's hard to write a good essay without using examples. Sometimes you may want to build your whole essay around examples.

An example is one item that comes from a larger group or category that it's part of. Let's use cans as an example. Suppose you brought home a can from the grocery store only to find out that the label had fallen off. How can you go about convincing me about what the can holds? You might open the can, reach in, and pull out a green pea. Okay, you say, this is a can of peas. But I'm not convinced yet. You reach in again and pull out another green pea.

Pretty soon you have fifteen green peas sitting on the table. But I'm not convinced yet. You reach in one more time. Aha! This time you bring out a carrot. Okay, you say, this must be a can of peas and carrots. Not necessarily,

I say. You reach in again and bring out . . . a green bean! This is, in fact, a can of mixed vegetables. You convinced me by presenting several examples.

Let's think about laundry. Suppose you find a mystery laundry bag on the street and want to figure out who the laundry belongs to so that you can return it. Each time you reach into the laundry bag, you pull out an item of clothing. If you find a football jersey with the name Felix B. Jones on it, you might jump to the conclusion that the bag belongs to Felix. If the next item you pull out is a miniskirt, you might change your mind. Maybe the bag of laundry belongs to Felix's girlfriend.

You can see how examples can help you convince your reader. The trick here is to know what's in the can or in the laundry bag. The contents of the laundry bag make up the large group. The example is a single item that comes from the big group.

Example Essay—How to Build It

INTRODUCTION

The introduction to your example essay should include a thesis statement. Like all introductions, it should try to capture the reader's attention and give a general idea of the subject matter at hand. In an example essay, the introductory paragraph should clearly identify the big group from which the examples are drawn.

BODY

The body design of an example essay depends on the number of examples you are using. If you have a few examples, say three to five, that you can develop in detail, each example can get a paragraph for itself.

What happens if you have a lot of examples, say fifteen or twenty? Writing fifteen or twenty fully developed paragraphs could end up as an essay far too long for most class assignments. And writing fifteen or twenty short, sketchy paragraphs would lead to a very choppy essay. The answer is to find categories. This way you'll end up with four or five paragraphs. You could spend a few sentences on each specific example and your body will have well-developed paragraphs.

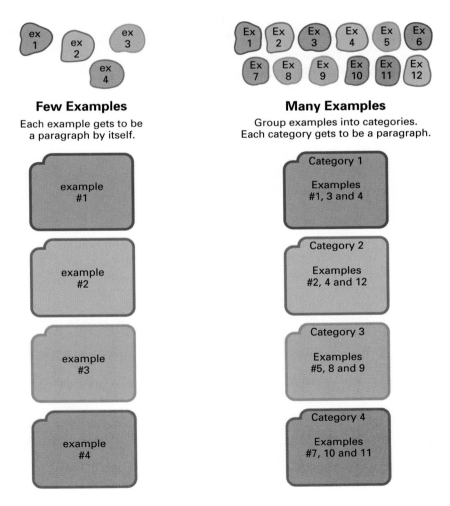

Few Examples

Each example gets to be a paragraph by itself.

| example #1 |
| example #2 |
| example #3 |
| example #4 |

Many Examples

Group examples into categories. Each category gets to be a paragraph.

| Category 1 — Examples #1, 3 and 4 |
| Category 2 — Examples #2, 4 and 12 |
| Category 3 — Examples #5, 8 and 9 |
| Category 4 — Examples #7, 10 and 11 |

CONCLUSION

There are no special requirements for the conclusion of an example essay.

ACTIVITY 18-1

Directions: Suppose the mayor of your town has made many improvements. Here is a list of examples to support that claim.

1. There are more meetings between police and community leaders.
2. He started an antilitter campaign.
3. The stoplights on Main Street are now synchronized.
4. The garbage pickups have been increased.
5. There are more police on the street.
6. The parks are maintained better.
7. Potholes on the streets are being repaired.
8. He appointed a new police chief.
9. Roadside crews now mow the grass on highways leading into town.
10. Two lanes have been added to Elm Street.

Rather than have ten short paragraphs, one for each of these examples, try to see if you can group these examples into the three categories below. We've started you off.

Police	**Traffic**	**Atmosphere**
example #_1_	example #_3_	example #_2_
example #_5_	example #_9_	example #_4_
example #_8_	example #_10_	example #_6_
		example #_7_

What Blueprint Should I Use?

There are two basic ways to set up an example essay. You can follow the few examples blueprint or the many examples blueprint. When you have a few examples, write a well developed paragraph for each example.

Introduction

◆ **Thesis:** Freshmen at State College have resources to help them adjust to college life.

Body

◆ **Paragraph 1:** The Counseling Center has 24-hour walk-in services.

◆ **Paragraph 2:** Dorm advisors talk monthly with freshmen.

◆ **Paragraph 3:** Peer support groups are available to advise freshmen.

Conclusion

◆ Sum up.

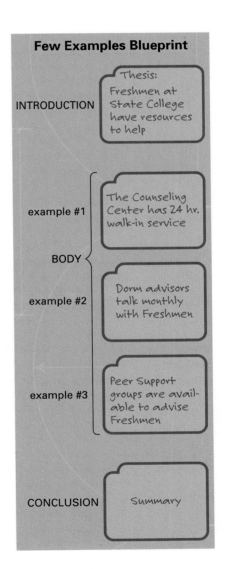

Few Examples Blueprint

INTRODUCTION — Thesis: Freshmen at State College have resources to help

BODY
example #1 — The Counseling Center has 24 hr. walk-in service

example #2 — Dorm advisors talk monthly with Freshmen

example #3 — Peer Support groups are available to advise Freshmen

CONCLUSION — Summary

By contrast, when you have many examples, group them into categories and write a paragraph for each category.

Introduction

◆ **Thesis:** The mayor has made many civic improvements during his term.

Body

◆ **Paragraph 1:** Police

Example: more police on the street

Example: more meetings with police and community leaders

Example: appointed new police chief

◆ **Paragraph 2:** Traffic

Example: synchronized stop lights on Main Street

Example: repaired potholes

Example: added two lanes to Elm St.

◆ **Paragraph 3:** Atmosphere

Example: increased garbage pickup

Example: work crews mow roadside grass

Example: parks maintained better

Example: anti-litter campaign

Conclusion

◆ Sum up.

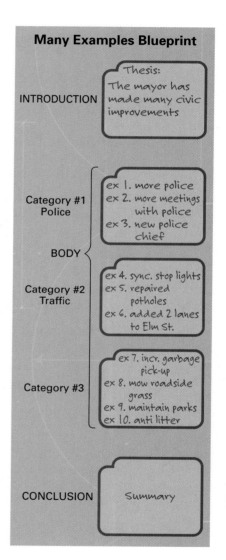

Many Examples Blueprint

INTRODUCTION — Thesis: The mayor has made many civic improvements

BODY

Category #1 Police
- ex 1. more police
- ex 2. more meetings with police
- ex 3. new police chief

Category #2 Traffic
- ex 4. sync. stop lights
- ex 5. repaired potholes
- ex 6. added 2 lanes to Elm St.

Category #3
- ex 7. incr. garbage pick-up
- ex 8. mow roadside grass
- ex 9. maintain parks
- ex 10. anti litter

CONCLUSION — Summary

ACTIVITY 18-2

Directions: Using the plan outlined above, set up an example essay on one of the following topics.

1. The cafeteria food is unacceptable.
2. Driving during rush hour is a horrible experience.
3. My last job was a satisfying experience.

Example Essay—Tips to Make It Work

❶ *Make your examples specific.* All good writing needs to be specific, and examples can't help but be specific. You can say the weather was horrible during your vacation, but when you begin to give examples, the notion of bad weather becomes much clearer and more vivid:

There were gale force winds.

More than three feet of rain fell in two weeks.

The lake overflowed and flooded our cabin.

Lightning struck our roof and destroyed the hotel's satellite dish.

ACTIVITY 18-3

Directions: Give three examples to make each of the following statements more vivid.

1. That car is in bad shape.

The appearance of that car is too old.

The color is too bad.

2. Owning a personal computer improves a person's life.

_____

_____

_____

❷ *Make your examples convincing.* If you suggest that spending August in Storm Beach, Florida, is not a good idea, you'll need to have something to back up your opinion. The most vivid examples of your bad experience will be strong enough to convince your reader.

ACTIVITY 18-4

Directions: Circle the set of examples that will convince readers that your trip to Storm Beach was a disaster.

A. The weather was unpleasant.

   My hotel room needed repairs.

   The hotel staff was discourteous.

   Prices for our stay were unreasonably high.

B. Gale force winds and driving rains left three feet of water flooding the ground.

The windows in our room did not close properly and the rainwater drenched the bed and carpet.

The bellhop refused to carry our bags to our room and the desk clerk read a comic book instead of listening to our complaints.

The cost of our room was $450 for the weekend.

❸ *Use examples in a lively way.* Using specific examples brings your writing to life, helps your reader understand what you mean. Those gale force winds, the three feet of rain, the overflowing lake, the lightning strike, all bring vivid images and feelings to mind.

ACTIVITY 18-5

Directions: Read the following paragraphs. Circle the one you think is the more lively.

A. The weather at Storm Beach was horrible. Jagged flashes of lightning and huge booms of thunder kept us up all night. Sheets of rain fell all weekend; it was storming so hard that the rain obscured even our view of the beach. When the storm began to let up, there was a flood. Water up to our ankles made walking to the parking lot like sloshing through the Amazon.

B. The weather at Storm Beach was horrible. It stormed all weekend with lots of thunder and lightning. After the storm, there was deep water all over the parking lot. We never got to the beach.

❹ *Make sure you have enough examples.* Easy for us to say, right? In fact, the truth is that the right number of examples depends on a number of things. Sometimes a few well-chosen examples will be enough to support your thesis. Other times fifty examples may not do the job. For instance, three examples of violent behavior (arson, an armed robbery, and an assault and battery) may be enough to convince the parole board to send a parolee back to jail. Fifty or even a hundred examples of mothers yelling at their toddlers won't be enough to convince someone that women with kids have bad dispositions.

If your examples don't seem to be working, no matter how many you pile up, you should at least consider that your thesis may be too weak. If you need a solid rule, try this one: It's hard to put together a convincing example essay with fewer than three examples.

ACTIVITY 18-6

Directions: Are the examples below sufficient to support the thesis statements?

A. Professor Smith is unfair.

Example 1: He didn't give me a good grade on my midterm.
Example 2: He took two points off my average for being late.
Example 3: He doesn't allow students to retake tests they fail.
Example 4: He told me to pay more attention in class.

_____ yes

_____ no

B. Oak Street is unsafe.

Example 1: There is a two-foot pothole in front of the bank.
Example 2: The stoplight at the corner of Oak and Main is broken.
Example 3: There is no school crossing in front of the elementary school.

_____ yes

_____ no

❺ *Play fair!* Examples need to be typical of the larger group. Suppose you consult 100 drivers, all of whom say the vehicle they drive at work is yellow. Is this enough to say that yellow is the most popular color for work vehicles? What if all 100 drivers you used as examples were school bus drivers? Since school bus drivers aren't typical of all workers, we can't conclude that the color of vehicles is the same as the color used by other kinds of workers and their vehicles.

You could offer examples showing that students in a local high school suffer from attention deficit disorder because you observed them fidgeting at their desks, talking in class, and ignoring their teacher's instructions. But suppose you observed them in the last class before school let out for spring break? You're not playing fair. It wasn't a typical day at school.

If you state that Americans have bad manners and you draw all of your examples from guests on the Jerry Springer show, you're not playing fair. We hope the Springer guests aren't typical of all Americans.

ACTIVITY 18-7

Directions: Do the examples shown below give a fair picture about the thesis statements?

A. Athletes at State College don't make good students.

Example 1: Bob Smith flunked his history test.
Example 2: Joe Lane has to have a tutor in English.
Example 3: Betty Johnson is enrolled in a remedial math class.

_____ yes

_____ no

B. Teenagers dress too skimpily.

Example 1: Britney Spears
Example 2: Lil' Kim
Example 3: Christina Aguilera

_____ yes

_____ no

C. Movie stars have good marriages.

Example 1: Paul Newman and Joanne Woodward
Example 2: Tom Hanks and Rita Wilson
Example 3: Arnold Schwarzenegger and Maria Shriver

_____ yes

_____ no

❻ *Pick a pattern.* When it comes time to arrange your examples, you could just toss them up in the air and let random selections take over. After all, they're all examples so what difference does it make?

In some cases, the order of your examples can make the difference between a "just OK" essay or a really effective one. Look for a pattern that can enhance the strength of your examples. Ask yourself, what are my best examples? The most striking example may be a good one to lead off with. It will help capture your reader's attention because it's very convincing or shocking or funny. You might want to put your second best example last, to end on a strong note. Or, if you'd like, you can build up to your strongest example.

❼ *Don't be afraid to call attention to an example.* It's o.k., even desirable, to straightforwardly label examples as such ("One example is . . ." "Another example is . . ." "For instance . . ." and so on). This helps your examples stand out. If they're strong examples (and we have great confidence they will be), there's no reason to avoid calling attention to them.

❽ *Let your examples lead you.* Examples give you a helpful push down the road to being specific. Don't resist. Remember the State College essay plan on page 79? Tell about a specific student who benefited from State College's counseling service. Or discuss a specific incident when the mayor's improved garbage pickup helped you.

❾ *Don't get sidetracked.* Remember that your examples should be used to prove that your thesis is true. Stay that course. For instance, if your thesis is "State College has resources to help freshmen adjust to college life," don't start discussing *why* freshmen have troubles adjusting to college life. Use your examples to show that there are indeed helpful resources for freshmen at State College.

Free Samples

Few Examples Essay

Introduction ⌐
Thesis ⌐

Example 1 ⌐
Body ⌐

Students beginning their college careers often find their first year on campus traumatic. Many are away from home for the first time, without anyone to help them cope with new pressures in and out of the classroom. Freshmen at State College, however, are fortunate to have resources to help them adjust to college life.

The Counseling Center, for example, is always available for students who want help. The center is open twenty-four hours a day, so that troubled students have a place to go even in the lonely hours late at night when they often feel most isolated and depressed. Although students may call ahead for appointments, this is not necessary. Trained counselors are there to talk with students who walk in without appointments.

Example 2 — Another way State College supports new students is through the Dorm Advisors Program. Each dormitory has live-in faculty advisors. In addition to having meals with students and maintaining informal contact during the semester, these resident faculty advisors have monthly meetings with freshmen to discuss how college life is going.These discussions range from open-ended gripe sessions, in which student air various complaints, to specific discussions of problems in a class or with a peer.

Body

Example 3 — The most innovative example of help available to State College freshmen is the peer support program. Freshmen can meet weekly with upperclassmen to talk about strategies to cope with life on campus. This student-eye perspective gives a particularly helpful view on how to adjust to demanding homework assignments, the party scene, difficult professors, or incompatible roommates.

Conclusion — Unlike some students who are left adrift in the often choppy waters of their first year at college, State College freshmen have resources to help them. Professional counselors, faculty advisors, and other students are available to help freshmen sail smoothly through their first year.

Many Examples Essay

Thesis ——

Introduction — After a closely fought, sometimes controversial election, some had their doubts, but the citizens of Somerville have seen Mayor Roland Brinkly make many improvements during his first term. His initiatives have made the city a better place to live and have earned him widespread support for his efforts.

Example Category #1 — Clear examples of improvement under Mayor Brinkly can be seen in Somerville's police department. With the hiring of ten new officers, there are now more police on the street. The increased police presence makes citizens feel safer. Under the mayor's direction, police representatives meet monthly with community leaders to discuss problems. Mayor Brinkly's hiring of Joe Marti as police chief also has helped make the department more effective. Chief Marti has made cleaning up police corruption a top priority.

Example Category #2 — Another area which has been strengthened under the mayor's leadership is traffic. For instance, the stop lights on Main Street are now synchronized, easing the congestion that commuters used to face. Another benefit comes from filling the pot holes that frustrated drivers, damaged cars, and slowed traffic on the city's streets. The mayor's decision to widen Elm Blvd. to four lanes also has helped the flow of traffic in town.

Example Category #3 — Perhaps the most striking improvement the mayor has brought about is in the atmosphere of Somerville. Increased garbage pickup, for example, has made the streets cleaner and more fragrant. Work crews now mow roadside grass regularly, giving the town a more manicured look. The parks are better maintained. Groundskeepers paint picnic tables, plant flowers, and keep play-ground equipment in good working order. Another important improvement is

Mayor Brinkly's energetic antilitter campaign. Now everyone from preschoolers to senior citizens are picking up trash and depositing it in the bright yellow litter bins the mayor has placed around town.

From a more effective police presence, to smoothly flowing traffic, to the cleaner, brighter look of the town, Somerville has benefitted from having Roland Brinkly as mayor.

Free Sample Example Questions

1. Do the Free Sample example essays indicate which examples are the strongest?

_____

_____

2. Which do you think is most persuasive, the few example or the many example format? Why?

_____

_____

3. Does your college have any resources to help students adapt to college life?

_____

_____

4. What steps would you like to see your college take to help students adapt more successfully to college life?

_____

_____

Shrink-Wrap

WRITING AN EXAMPLE PARAGRAPH

Since a paragraph is really just a mini essay (see p. 47), it's pretty easy to shrink an example essay down to an example paragraph. Let's take a look at our essay about the resources State College has for freshmen.

The thesis will become the topic sentence for your example essay. Each of the examples becomes a sentence in the paragraph. Details can be added as needed to develop the paragraph a bit more.

Few Examples Paragraph

Freshmen have many resources to help them adjust to college life at State College. There is a counseling center where psychologists are on staff 24 hours a day to see students who walk in or schedule appointments. The counseling center has a hot line to receive student calls. The freshmen dorms have live-in advisors who meet monthly with students to discuss problems and answer questions. Peer support groups are available to help students with any difficulties they encounter. There are peer panels to discuss problems such as alcohol abuse, test anxiety, and date rape.

Many Examples Paragraph

Somerville has become a better place to live during Mayor Brinkly's first term. The police department has improved in many ways. For example, there are now ten more police officers on the street patrolling. Police representatives now meet regularly with community leaders to discuss problems. Another improvement is the hiring of the new police chief who has vowed to clean up corruption. Traffic is one more area that has improved. The lights on Main Street, for instance, are now synchronized. Potholes are being repaired. And adding two lanes to Elm Blvd. also helps with traffic. The atmosphere of Somerville has changed for the better too. Increased garbage pickup is one example of how the mayor's leadership has made the town look better. Another is the work crews who now mow the roadside grass every week. Crews also keep the parks neat and clean, painting picnic tables and planting flowers. And the mayor's anti-litter campaign is a big success, motivating citizens to pick up trash.

WE'RE GLAD YOU ASKED
EXAMPLES Q&A

Q How do I know if I'm using a valid example?

A Think about the unmarked can. If you reach into the can, the item you draw out should be a fair example of what's in the can.

Q Can I use a personal experience as an example?

A Yes, if it's relevant, convincing, and representative. You can use your own experiences (or those of friends and relatives) as examples.

Q How many hours does a lion spend sleeping every day?

A Some lions sleep up to twenty-three hours a day! What a life!

Examples Topics Bank

Here are some topics you might use to practice writing example essays.

1. College students are under too much pressure.
2. Gossip is destructive.
3. Some Websites are too good to pass up.
4. Politicians are not trustworthy.
5. Weddings have become too elaborate.
6. Our healthcare system is sick.
7. Video games are too violent.
8. Exercise can improve your quality of life.
9. The holiday season has become too commercial.
10. Average citizens can make a difference.

19

COMPARISON AND CONTRAST

"No, I don't want to change you, Darryl. But sure,
it would be great if you were completely different."

Comparison/Contrast Essay—When to Use It

A comparison and contrast essay examines the similarities (compare) and/or differences (contrast) between two things in order to make a point. Here are a few examples of comparison and contrast ideas:

You might compare and contrast going to high school and going to college to show how going to college is more challenging.

You might compare and contrast the platforms of the Democratic and Republican parties to show which you believe offers better solutions to our nation's problems.

You might compare and contrast this year's Toyota Camry with this year's Ford Taurus to show which is the better family car.

Notice how in each case the similarities and differences lead to a conclusion. This is an important feature in a comparison and contrast essay. It is not simply a list of similarities and differences. Comparison and contrast is one of the most common types of writing because it is such a common thought process. We use it every day whenever we have decisions to make.

Which toothpaste should I buy? (How do toothpastes compare in terms of price, whitening power, flavor, packaging?)

Should I drive or take the bus to work? (Which will be faster? Which will be cheaper? Which will allow me to arrive at work more relaxed?)

Should I adopt a cat or a dog at the animal shelter? (Which pet is friendlier? Which pet requires less care? Which pet does better tricks?)

"Do you have this one in a cat?"

Since writing often requires you to consider various possibilities, you'll need to use comparison and contrast often. Whether you're writing an essay on a history exam comparing the causes of the Korean War with the causes of the Vietnam War or two different ways of treating depression for a psychology class, you're going to need to know how to write an effective comparison and contrast essay.

Comparison/Contrast Essay—How to Build It

INTRODUCTION

In your introductory paragraph, your thesis should identify the two items being compared or contrasted and state your opinion about them. You need to convince your reader. Here are some sample comparison and contrast statements:

McDonald's French fries are better than Burger King's.

Stephen King's earlier novels are scarier than his later ones.

Michael Jordan was a more dominant basketball player than Bill Russell.

Nurses are more respected now than they were twenty years ago.

Bikes offer many advantages to the commuter over cars.

Each of these statements takes a stand, makes a point. Avoid wishy-washy thesis statements like these:

There are many similarities between McDonald's and Burger King.

Stephen King's early novels are different in some ways than his later ones.

Michael Jordan and Bill Russell were alike in some ways, yet different in others.

Nurses today are somewhat different than in the past.

Bikes and cars provide different commuting experiences.

ACTIVITY 19-1

Directions: Turn the following comparison and contrast topics into workable thesis statements.

1. Compare and/or contrast two brands of athletic shoes.
2. Compare and/or contrast living in an apartment and owning your own house.
3. Compare and/or contrast eating in a restaurant and eating in a cafeteria.
4. Compare and/or contrast watching a movie in a theater and watching a video at home.
5. Compare and contrast high school and college English classes.

BODY

There are two patterns you can follow to set up the body of a compare and contrast essay:

◆ **Pattern 1–Chunk-by-Chunk:** Write about the first item, discussing each point of comparison or contrast in a separate chunk. You then write about the second item in another chunk, making the same points in the same order.

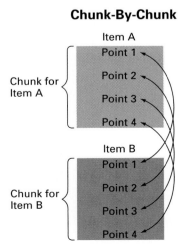

Chunk-By-Chunk

◆ **Pattern 2–Point-by-Point:** Write about each point of comparison or contrast, applying it to the first item, then the second.

Point-By-Point

Point 1
Item A
Item B

Point 2
Item A
Item B

Point 3
Item A
Item B

Point 4
Item A
Item B

Once you pick a pattern, it's important to stick with it. Be strict. Clear organization is especially important in comparison and contrast writing.

To set up the body of your comparison or contrast essay, you first need to identify the points of comparison or contrast. Let's suppose you decide to contrast cars and bikes as ways to commute to work. You come up with the following differences:

cost to operate

speed

health benefits

environmental impact

If you first discuss how these four points apply to a bike and then discuss how the same four points apply to a car, you're following Pattern 1 (Chunk-by-Chunk).

If you take the first point, and discuss how it applies to a bike and then to a car, then take the second point and apply it to a bike and then to a car (and so on) you're following Pattern 2 (Point-by-Point).

CONCLUSION

In a comparison and contrast essay, the conclusion must do the same job that it does in all essays: It sums up the main points and reinforces the thesis. If the essay presents a choice to the reader, the conclusion may suggest an action. (Try riding a bike to work instead of driving a car.) Here's how the blueprint for each type of comparison and contrast essay might look.

What Blueprint Should I Use?

BLUEPRINT 1: CHUNK-BY-CHUNK

Introduction

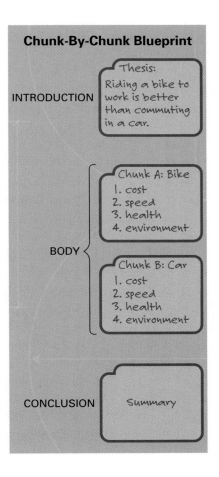

◆ **Thesis:** Riding a bike to work is superior to commuting in a car.

Body

◆ **Chunk A:** Bike

1. Operating costs (low)

2. Speed (competitive in traffic)

3. Health benefits (good)

4. Environmental impact (positive)

◆ **Chunk B:** Car

1. Operating costs (high)

2. Speed (slow in traffic)

3. Health benefits (none)

4. Environmental impact (negative)

Conclusion

◆ Sum up or suggest an action.

BLUEPRINT 2: POINT-BY-POINT

Introduction

◆ **Thesis:** Riding a bike to work is superior to commuting in a car.

Body

◆ **Point 1:** Cost

   a. Bike (low)

   b. Car (high)

◆ **Point 2:** Speed

   a. Bike (competitive)

   b. Car (slow)

◆ **Point 3:** Health benefits

   a. Bike (good)

   b. Car (none)

◆ **Point 4:** Environmental impact

   a. Bike (positive)

   b. Car (negative)

Conclusion

◆ Sum up and suggest an action.

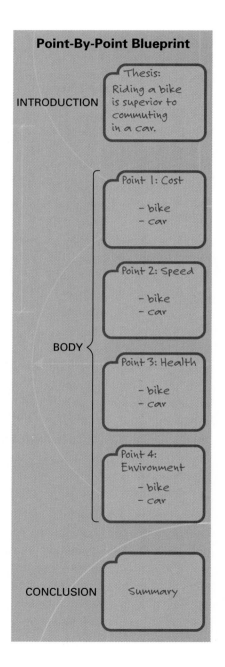

Point-By-Point Blueprint

INTRODUCTION — Thesis: Riding a bike is superior to commuting in a car.

BODY
- Point 1: Cost
  - bike
  - car
- Point 2: Speed
  - bike
  - car
- Point 3: Health
  - bike
  - car
- Point 4: Environment
  - bike
  - car

CONCLUSION — Summary

Comparison/Contrast Essay—Tips to Make It Work

❶ *Stick to two items only;* at first don't try to juggle three or more.

❷ *Make sure your thesis convinces readers of your opinion:* an opinion based on significant similarities or differences. Suppose you want to compare a bike and a car as ways to commute to work and have come up with the following list of similarities:

Cars and bikes are both used for transportation.

Cars and bikes both have wheels.

Cars and bikes both have brakes.

Cars and bikes both need drivers.

Do any of these factors seem significant? If you make a point of similarity or difference and the reader says "so what?" you've wasted your words.

❸ *If you mainly focus on differences (contrast), you can briefly mention similarities (compare).* Often the introduction is a good place to point them out. It's usually better to mainly focus on similarities or differences instead of trying to give equal attention to both.

❹ *Remember to use the same points in the same order if you are following the chunk-by-chunk pattern.* Establish the order in chunk A. In chunk B refer back briefly to chunk A to remind your reader what you had to say about the point.

❺ *Begin by identifying your main points of comparison or contrast.* These will serve as the points in both chunks or each point will be a paragraph in the point-by-point plan.

❻ *Don't forget about categories.* If you have a long, long list of points of comparison or contrast, you may want to divide the points into categories.

Free Samples

Here are two sample essays based on the chunk-by-chunk or point-by-point blueprint plans. Look at the plans on pages 97 and 98 to see how the bike versus car essays based on these plans might work.

Chunk-by-Chunk Essay

Introduction —
Thesis —

The commute to work is a daily event for us. Too often it's a ritual we dread as we sit in traffic jams while our tempers flare. Riding a bike is a better way to commute than driving a car.

1st Point of Contrast

Body
CHUNK A
(bike)

2nd Point of Contrast
3rd Point of Contrast
4th Point of Contrast

A bike provides many benefits to the commuter. First, the bike rider will save money. The bike itself costs a fraction of what a car costs. A bike uses no gasoline. It never needs an oil change or brake fluid. A flat tire on a bike costs almost nothing to fix if you do it yourself. Next, surprisingly, a bike can be competitive in speed to a car on short commutes. A bike can pass by cars stalled in snarled traffic. A bike can take off-road short cuts—through a park or a parking lot—unavailable to cars. Another benefit to commuting by bike is better health. Riding a bike increases the heart rate and builds cardiovascular conditioning and muscle tone. Bike riders burn calories, which helps them keep their weight down. Finally, the environment benefits when commuters ride bikes. There are no emissions, no smog-building pollutants, no noxious discharges from a bike.

1st Point of Contrast

Body
CHUNK B
(car)

2nd Point of Contrast

Unlike a bike, a car can cost the commuter thousands of dollars, starting with the purchase price. Car owners must pay for not only gas and oil but mandatory auto insurance, which may run over a thousand dollars a year. Although cars can travel 60 to 70 miles per hour on interstate highways, these speeds are rarely reached in a commute to work. Rush hour traffic moves

3rd Point of Contrast

Body CHUNK B (car)

slowly and, factoring in time spent stopped in traffic jams, the average auto commute speed is 20 miles per hour. When bike commuters are pedaling, working their muscles and building their strength and conditioning, no such advantages come to those driving cars to work. They are sitting passively, burning no extra calories. The tension of gridlock commuter traffic can even raise blood pressure and stress to unhealthy levels. Finally, unlike the emission-free bikes, cars continually spew unwanted elements into the air. Often the fumes during rush hour commutes are so thick that they hinder both breathing and visibility.

4th Point of Contrast

Conclusion

Clearly, the bike is a superior way to make short-range commutes to work. We need to get out of the automotive rut. Consider leaving your car in the garage and pedaling to your job.

Point-by-Point Essay

Introduction

Thesis

The commute to work is a daily event for us. Too often it's a ritual we dread as we sit stuck in traffic jams while our tempers flare. Riding a bike is a better way to commute than driving a car.

1st Point of Contrast

First consider the costs. A bike can be purchased for a hundred dollars. It uses no gas or brake fluid. The tires, should they need replacing, are less than five dollars if you change them yourself. There is no mandatory insurance for bike riders. A car, even a used one, costs thousands of dollars. Gas costs, oil, fluids, and tires will set you back hundreds of dollars each year. The mandatory insurance can be as high as a thousand dollars or more a year.

2nd Point of Contrast

Body

The speed of the commuter's trip is another important concern. A bike can pass by cars stalled in snarled traffic. Riding a bike allows the commuter to take off-road short cuts, through a park or a parking lot. Cars are restricted to the road, and though they can travel much faster than bikes, rush hour conditions reduce their speed to a crawl.

3rd Point of Contrast

The health of commuters can be related to their modes of transportation. Bike riders increase their heart rates and build cardiovascular conditioning and muscle tone. They burn calories, which helps keep unwanted pounds away. Auto commuters get no exercise driving to work. To make things worse, the tension of gridlock traffic can raise blood pressure and stress levels.

4th Point of Contrast

The environment is affected differently by bikes and cars. Bikes emit no emissions, smog-building pollutants, or noxious discharges. Cars, on the other hand, spew unwanted elements into the air. During the rush hour commute, the fumes are so thick they hinder breathing and visibility.

Conclusion

Clearly, the bike is a superior way to make short-range commutes to work. Get out of the automotive rut. Consider leaving your car in the garage and pedaling to your job.

Free Sample Compare/Contrast Questions

1. In the Free Sample Chunk-by-Chunk essay, find places in Chunk B where the writer reminded you about what was said in Chunk A.

   _____

   _____

2. In the Free Sample Chunk-by-Chunk essay, point out transition words used in the Body.

   _____

   _____

3. Can you think of any advantages to using a bike that were not mentioned in the Free Sample essays? How about any disadvantages?

   _____

   _____

4. Would you ever commute to school or work on a bike? Why or why not?

   _____

   _____

Shrink-Wrap

Chunk-by-Chunk Paragraph

Riding a bike to work is superior to commuting in a car. A bike has very low operating costs. A bike is also surprisingly competitive in speed since it allows you to ride more quickly through traffic jams. Riding a bike helps build your muscle tone and keeps your heart healthy. And, finally, a bike doesn't hurt the environment. Unlike a bike, a car is expensive to run. Car owners have to pay for gas, oil, and tune-ups. While a bike rider can zoom past stalled cars, a driver in a car provides none of the health benefits of exercising the way riding a bike can. Finally, unlike the environmentally friendly bike, a car produces lots of pollution.

Point-by-Point Paragraph

Riding a bike to work is superior to commuting in a car. First let's look at costs. A bike needs your leg power and air for the tires. A car requires gas, oil, and mechanical tune-ups, all of which cost lots of money. In addition, the speed of your commute can actually be faster on a bike. A bike, unlike a car, can zoom through a traffic jam. Health benefits are another important advantage. Riding a bike keeps your muscles and heart in shape. Sitting in a car doesn't help your health at all. Finally, the environment is helped by riding a bike. The pollution-free bike differs greatly from the car, which releases toxic emissions and pollutes the air.

WE'RE GLAD YOU ASKED
COMPARISON AND CONTRAST Q&A

Q Can *any* two items be compared or contrasted in an essay?

A No, not successfully. The two items must have at least some significant degree of similarity or difference. Writing about an orange and the planet Jupiter won't yield a decent essay, even though they're both round. Likewise, writing about a size five running shoe and a size six and a half shoe won't produce a good essay, even though the shoes are slightly different.

Q Can I compare *and* contrast in the same essay?

A Of course. See our suggestion on page 99 about how to work in some differences if you're comparing or similarities if you're contrasting. It's usually a good idea to focus mainly on differences or similarities, though. This makes it easier to get and support a thesis. If the two items being discussed are alike just as much as they are different, it will be difficult for you to take a stand.

Q How much wood would a woodchuck chuck?

A We've never understood this one.

LEAVE ME ALONE.

Comparison and Contrast Topics Bank

Here are some topics you might use to practice writing comparison and contrast essays.

1. Myself now and myself five years ago
2. Going to the movies and watching movies on video
3. Two of your aunts, uncles, brothers, or sisters
4. High school and college
5. Two political candidates
6. My neighborhood now and my neighborhood ten years ago
7. Two kinds of popular music
8. Two friends
9. Two brands of automobiles, computers, soft drinks, athletic shoes
10. Two restaurants

20
CAUSE AND EFFECT

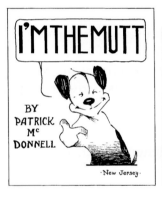

Cause/Effect Essay—When to Use It

In a *cause essay* you will present a condition and show what reasons (or causes) led up to it. In an *effect essay* you will present a condition and show what results (or effects) happened because of it. If you do both, you have a *cause* and *effect essay*. Most assignments won't allow you enough time to pay equal attention to cause and effect. It's usually best to emphasize one over the other.

You write cause and effect essays to explain what caused something to happen or to predict what effects will occur as the result of something that has happened or may happen. Suppose you are driving down the highway at 80 miles per hour. A cause essay would explain what led to your speeding.

105

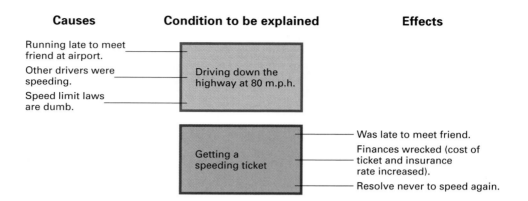

You're late for meeting your friend at the airport.

You see all the other drivers speeding.

You think speed limit laws are dumb.

Suppose a state trooper pulls you over and gives you a ticket. You now get to write an effect essay explaining what will happen as a result of your speeding:

You will be late to meet your friend.

Your finances are wrecked (cost of ticket and higher insurance rates).

You resolve to never drive above the speed limit.

ACTIVITY 20-1

Directions: Consider the subject in each shaded box below. Fill in the blanks to show which causes might have led to it. Then fill in the blanks to show what effects might happen as a result of it.

Causes _____

_____

_____

Being bored in Math class

Effects _____

_____

_____

Causes _____

_____

_____

↓

High school teachers going on strike

↓

Effects _____

_____

_____

Causes _____

_____

_____

↓

Bob and Marsha getting divorced

↓

Effects _____

_____

_____

Causes _____

_____

_____

↓

Flooding in a midwestern city

↓

Effects _____

_____

_____

Cause/Effect Essay—How to Build It

INTRODUCTION

You want to accomplish three things here:

1. Clearly identify your topic: speeding; the popularity of rap music; your nervousness about taking exams.

2. Mention the cause (or effect) that's not being emphasized: If you're writing mainly about causes, briefly tell your reader about the effects. If you're mainly talking about effects, briefly tell your reader about the causes. For instance:

   Because my speeding ticket cost me both time and money, it was helpful for me to see what factors led up to my driving down Main Street at 80 miles per hour.

   The factors that led me to drive down Main Street at 80 miles per hour seemed important at the time—the plane arriving at the airport, the other drivers setting the pace, my disregard for the law—but the drive resulted in disaster.

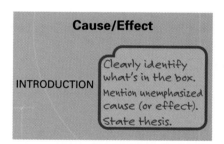

3. State your thesis: Here you point to the cause or characterize the effect. For instance, look at these cause essay thesis statements:

   The feud between my cousin and me happened because of a pileup of petty childhood resentments.

   The rise in gasoline prices at the pump can be traced to poor policy decisions at the federal level.

   The popularity of boy bands is due to the buying power of preteen girls.

Now look at these effect essay thesis statements:

As a result of our feud, my cousin and I have missed out on years of family fun.

The rise in gas prices at the pumps has dramatically changed my driving habits.

The popularity of boy bands has made preteen girls overly aware of sex.

BODY

This is the place in your essay where you identify and explain causes or effects. You may have a list of different causes or of separate effects. In either case, each cause or effect could be a separate paragraph.

Sometimes you may have to deal with a chain reaction, a more complicated situation in which each cause leads to an effect which in turn becomes a cause leading to the next effect, and so on. Let's see how this works. Remember the old nursery rhyme "For Want of a Nail"?

For want of a nail, the shoe was lost;

For want of the shoe, the horse was lost;

For want of the rider, the battle was lost;

For want of the battle, the kingdom was lost;

And all for the want of a horseshoe nail.

In this case, the cause and effect keep shifting. We start with a cause: the missing horseshoe nail. This causes an effect—the horseshoe falls off. The effect—the horseshoe falling off—then becomes the cause that leads to the next effect—the horse falls down and dies. And so on. A cause/effect chain reaction looks like this:

ACTIVITY 20-2

Directions: These are cause/effect chain reactions. Some steps in the chain have been left out. Fill in the blanks to complete the cause/effect chain reactions below.

1. A bad storm comes to town. ➔ _____ ➔ Lightning hits a transformer. ➔ _____ ➔ The food in Aunt Darlene's freezer goes bad.

2. Shoplifting increases in a local department store. ➔ _____ _____ ➔ The store hires extra security. ➔ _____ _____ ➔ The customers pay more for merchandise.

3. Neighborhood children tease the Baxter's puppy. ➔ _____ _____ ➔ The Baxters have to give their dog away when he is a year old.

CONCLUSION

The conclusion for a cause and effect essay should remind readers of your main point.

What Blueprint Should I Use?

Here's how the blueprints for a cause essay, an effect essay, and a cause and effect chain reaction essay might look.

BLUEPRINT 1: CAUSE

Introduction

◆ **Thesis:** Several incidents resulted in the speeding ticket I got on Friday.

Body

◆ **Cause 1:** Had to rush to get my friend to the airport.

◆ **Cause 2:** My alarm didn't go off.

◆ **Cause 3:** Other drivers were speeding.

◆ **Cause 4:** I didn't pay attention to speed limits.

Conclusion

◆ Sum up.

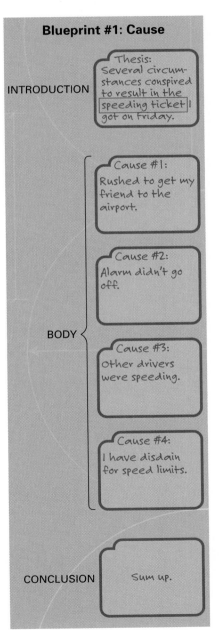

Blueprint #1: Cause

INTRODUCTION — Thesis: Several circumstances conspired to result in the speeding ticket I got on Friday.

BODY —
Cause #1: Rushed to get my friend to the airport.
Cause #2: Alarm didn't go off.
Cause #3: Other drivers were speeding.
Cause #4: I have disdain for speed limits.

CONCLUSION — Sum up.

BLUEPRINT 2: EFFECT

Introduction

◆ **Thesis:** The speeding ticket I got on Friday caused many problems.

Body

◆ **Effect 1:** My friend missed his plane.

◆ **Effect 2:** I had to pay $80.

◆ **Effect 3:** My insurance rates went up.

Conclusion

◆ Sum up.

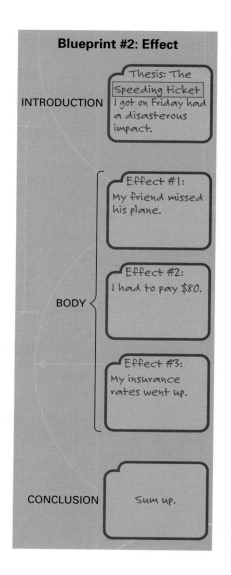

BLUEPRINT 3: CHAIN REACTION

Introduction

◆ **Thesis:** A simple nail led to the loss of a whole kingdom.

Body

◆ **Cause/effect 1:** A missing nail caused the horseshoe to fall off.

◆ **Cause/effect 2:** The missing shoe caused the horse to fall and die.

◆ **Cause/effect 3:** The falling horse disabled his rider.

◆ **Cause/effect 4:** The disabled rider was unable to deliver his message to the general.

◆ **Cause/effect 5:** The uninformed general lost the battle.

◆ **Cause/effect 6:** The lost battle caused the kingdom to fall to the enemy.

Conclusion

◆ Sum up.

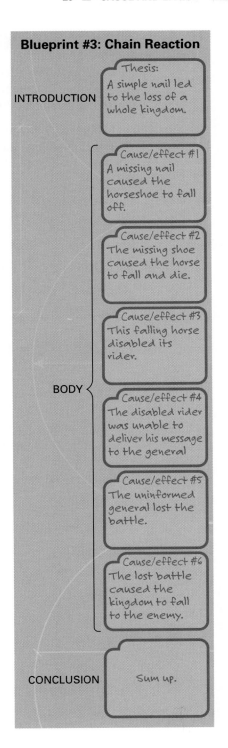

Blueprint #3: Chain Reaction

INTRODUCTION
Thesis: A simple nail led to the loss of a whole kingdom.

BODY

Cause/effect #1
A missing nail caused the horseshoe to fall off.

Cause/effect #2
The missing shoe caused the horse to fall and die.

Cause/effect #3
This falling horse disabled its rider.

Cause/effect #4
The disabled rider was unable to deliver his message to the general

Cause/effect #5
The uninformed general lost the battle.

Cause/effect #6
The lost battle caused the kingdom to fall to the enemy.

CONCLUSION
Sum up.

ACTIVITY 20-3

Directions: Insert chain reaction links that might follow in cause/effect 3, 4, or 5 described in Blueprint #3 on page 113. Here's an example of what you might do for cause/effect 2 (the horse falls and dies).

The horse fell, which caused him to break his leg.
The broken leg caused him to go into shock.
Shock caused the horse to die.

Cause/Effect Essay—Tips to Make It Work

❶ *Big deal or small stuff.* All causes and effects aren't created equal. There can be *major* effects and *minor* effects and major and minor causes. Be sure to make it clear to your reader which are which.

MR. PINGLE'S IN A
BAD MOOD

ACTIVITY 20-4

Directions: Label each of the causes below major or minor.

The mayor is removed from office.

Causes

_____ He was caught stealing city funds.
_____ He frequently has bad table manners.
_____ He divorced his wife and married an exotic dancer.
_____ The city council disagreed with his policies and proposals.
_____ He lost his temper when making public appearances.
_____ He forged documents to sell city-owned property to business associates.

❷ *Be logical.* Look at the logical fallacies, especially the post hoc fallacy on page 181. You don't want to mislabel causes.

Machinery Inc. went bankrupt after Mayor Platitude took office. The mayor's administration caused the business to fail.

❸ *Make sure you have not skipped any links in a cause/effect chain reaction.* If you skip from the missing horseshoe to the disabled rider, your readers may become confused.

Free Samples

Cause Essay

Introduction —
Thesis —

Cause #1 —

Body —

On Friday morning at 8:00, I thought my day was going well. By 8:30, I was standing by the side of the road with an angry state trooper who had just given me a speeding ticket. Several things had conspired to result in my getting a speeding ticket.

My friend Bob was visiting from Chicago. I was giving him a ride to the airport. The alarm clock didn't go off, so I got a late start. I raced out of my house at 7:45 instead of 7:15.

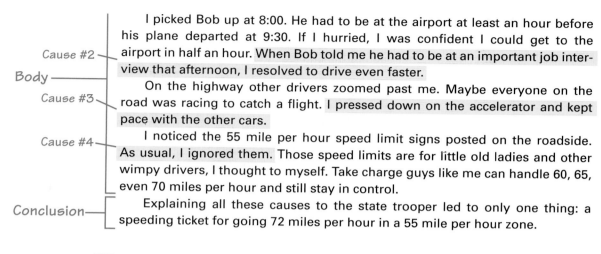

Cause #2

Body

Cause #3

Cause #4

Conclusion

I picked Bob up at 8:00. He had to be at the airport at least an hour before his plane departed at 9:30. If I hurried, I was confident I could get to the airport in half an hour. When Bob told me he had to be at an important job interview that afternoon, I resolved to drive even faster.

On the highway other drivers zoomed past me. Maybe everyone on the road was racing to catch a flight. I pressed down on the accelerator and kept pace with the other cars.

I noticed the 55 mile per hour speed limit signs posted on the roadside. As usual, I ignored them. Those speed limits are for little old ladies and other wimpy drivers, I thought to myself. Take charge guys like me can handle 60, 65, even 70 miles per hour and still stay in control.

Explaining all these causes to the state trooper led to only one thing: a speeding ticket for going 72 miles per hour in a 55 mile per hour zone.

Effect Essay

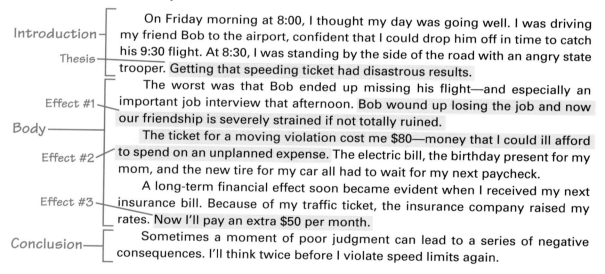

Introduction

Thesis

Effect #1

Body

Effect #2

Effect #3

Conclusion

On Friday morning at 8:00, I thought my day was going well. I was driving my friend Bob to the airport, confident that I could drop him off in time to catch his 9:30 flight. At 8:30, I was standing by the side of the road with an angry state trooper. Getting that speeding ticket had disastrous results.

The worst was that Bob ended up missing his flight—and especially an important job interview that afternoon. Bob wound up losing the job and now our friendship is severely strained if not totally ruined.

The ticket for a moving violation cost me $80—money that I could ill afford to spend on an unplanned expense. The electric bill, the birthday present for my mom, and the new tire for my car all had to wait for my next paycheck.

A long-term financial effect soon became evident when I received my next insurance bill. Because of my traffic ticket, the insurance company raised my rates. Now I'll pay an extra $50 per month.

Sometimes a moment of poor judgment can lead to a series of negative consequences. I'll think twice before I violate speed limits again.

Chain Reaction Cause and Effect Essay

Introduction

Thesis

Cause/Effect #1

Body

How can a tiny, insignificant nail lead to the loss of an entire kingdom, with all its land and riches? Let's look at the tale of the Battle of Bodelia to find out how important seemingly insignificant events can be.

The farrier shoeing the horses for King Joe's soldiers had consumed too much grog the night before. Awakening bleary-eyed and hung over, he forgot to put a nail in the front shoe of Dobbin, a horse used by couriers to deliver messages. Dobbin was put in his stall in the royal stables where he waited to be pressed into service.

Otto was entrusted with an urgent priority message from King Joe to take to the head general at Bodelia. Since it was a Priority Message, overnight delivery was guaranteed, and Otto went immediately to the royal stables where he saddled up Dobbin and galloped off to speedily deliver the message. As Dobbin raced through the forest, his front horseshoe became looser and looser. Finally, as they reached the edge of the forest, the loose shoe fell off.

Without the shoe, Dobbin lost his footing, tripped over a tree branch, and crashed to the ground. Sad to say, the fall killed Dobbin instantly, and Otto, temporarily trapped under the horse, suffered a broken ankle.

Still acutely aware of his Priority Message responsibilities, Otto said a quick and tearful farewell to Dobbin and set out toward Bodelia to deliver the king's note. His progress, understandably, was hampered by his broken ankle. Even using a tree branch as a crutch, he was only able to inch along. Nightfall came and went, and the sun rose with Otto still en route and the message still not delivered.

The head general waited at Bodelia for word from King Joe. Without instruction from the king, he was left to his own, somewhat limited devices. The general decided to attack at noon, when there was lots of bright sunlight, and so ordered his troops into battle.

The decision to attack at noon proved to be decidedly unwise. Since the enemy could see the sun reflecting off their shields for miles in advance, the head general and his army were soundly defeated. This loss at Bodelia was a costly one; enemy soldiers soon occupied the entire kingdom and King Joe was forced to abdicate his throne, abandon his castle, and move to an efficiency apartment.

And all of this resulted from the loss of one, simple nail, something you could pick up at the hardware store for less than a dime.

Cause/Effect #2

Body

Cause/Effect #3

Cause/Effect #4

Cause/Effect #5

Cause/Effect #6

Conclusion

Free Sample Cause/Effect Questions

1. In the Free Sample Cause essay can you find any mention of effects?

   _____

   _____

   _____

2. In the Free Sample Effect essay can you find any mention of causes?

   _____

   _____

   _____

3. Can you distinguish between major and minor causes or effects in any of the three Free Sample Cause/Effect essays?

_____

_____

_____

4. Have you ever gotten a speeding ticket? What were the causes and effects associated with your experience?

_____

_____

_____

Shrink-Wrap

Chain Reaction Cause/Effect Paragraph

A simple missing nail marked the beginning of the end for King Joe. A farrier with a hangover neglected to put a nail in the front shoe of Dobbin, one of the royal horses. When Otto, the courier, received an urgent Priority Message from the king, he promised to take it to the head general at Bodelia, overnight delivery guaranteed. Otto galloped off on Dobbin and sped toward Bodelia. Because of the missing nail, Dobbin's front shoe fell off, which caused him to lose his footing and fall. Dobbin was killed instantly and, as a result of the fall, Otto broke his ankle. Although Otto made a crude crutch from a tree branch and continued, painfully, on his way to Bodelia, he was not able to deliver the message on time. With no word from King Joe, the head general had no choice but to rely on his own judgment and so decided to attack at noon when the sunlight would be bright. The enemy forces saw the head general's army advancing miles away. King Joe's soldiers were soundly defeated, enabling the enemy to occupy the whole kingdom. King Joe lost his castle and his country, all because a simple nail was forgotten.

CAUSE AND EFFECT ESSAYS Q&A

Q Can you write an effect essay about results you think may happen if an event comes to pass?

A Yes. You don't have to report only on effects that historically have come to pass. Just remember to make it clear to your readers that you're writing about presumed effects. And be sure not to jump to illogical conclusions.

Q Is there a certain number of causes or effects I need to include?

A No. You can discuss one cause or effect at great length. But usually situations you're writing about will be complex enough that a single cause or effect won't be sufficient.

Q If a tree falls in the forest and no one hears it, does it make a noise?

A What? Speak louder. We can't hear you because of all the noise from one hand clapping.

Cause and Effect Topics Bank

Here are some cause and effect topics you might use to practice writing essays.

1. The popularity of tattoos
2. Violent video games
3. Graphic lyrics in popular music
4. A bad habit (of yours or someone you know)
5. Teenage rebellion
6. Illiterate athletes
7. Your fondness for (dislike of) a celebrity
8. Intolerance 不能容忍
9. Teenage parents
10. The change in clothing styles

21

DIVISION AND CLASSIFICATION

Division/Classification Essay—When to Use It

Let's start by saying you may almost never be asked to write *division essays*, where you must take one whole unit and divide it into its separate parts. A car, for instance, can be divided into the engine, trunk, passenger compartment, tires, etc. A shirt can be divided into the collar, sleeves, cuffs, buttons, etc. Writing a division essay is usually a simple exercise. However, it doesn't tend to make for very interesting reading. The separate parts of a whole unit are usually obvious, and it's not necessary to devote an essay to explain them.

On the other hand, you may often be asked to write classification essays, where you must take a big group or a general concept and arrange it into smaller groups or categories. Instead of dividing a car into its engine, trunk, tires, etc., you classify the various categories of cars: SUV's, minivans, sedans, convertibles, station wagons, etc. This is a good time to flip back to page 70 and read again about categories—a group of things with something in common. To do a good job of classifying, you have to be very clear about what the items in each category have in common. Think about a laundry bag. (Remember the laundry bag on p. 76?) This is another time that the laundry bag will prove useful. If we asked you to sort the clothes in a laundry bag, there are several ways you could do it:

◆ **You could sort the clothes by type:**

All the t-shirts in one pile
All the pants in one pile
All the socks in one pile
All the sweaters in one pile

◆ **You could sort the clothes by material:**

All the cotton in one pile
All the polyester in one pile
All the wool in one pile

◆ **You could sort the clothes by owner:**

All of Newton's clothes in one pile
All of Juanita's clothes in one pile
All of Aunt Darlene's clothes in one pile
All of Coco's clothes in one pile

The way you decide to sort the clothes is your principle of classification (P.O.C.), the rule you use to set up your categories.

If you don't have a clear P.O.C., you won't have a successful classification essay.

ACTIVITY 21-1

Directions: Come up with a P.O.C. for each of the following:

1. A deck of playing cards

_____

_____

_____

2. Television shows

_____

_____

_____

3. Vacations

_____

_____

_____

4. Restaurants

_____

_____

_____

5. Desserts

_____

_____

_____

Classification Essay—How to Build It

INTRODUCTION

This is where you identify the big group to be classified. After clearly stating your P.O.C., make sure you have a thesis that says more than simply stating there are four kinds of politicians or three categories of ice cream. (Remember you need to have an opinion.) You can state that one category is superior to the others. You can point out similarities and differences in the categories. But be sure that your thesis goes beyond just classifying.

ACTIVITY 21-2

Directions: Place a check mark in the blanks next to the good classification essay thesis statements.

_____ 1. There are four main kinds of superheros.

_____ 2. Only a few required courses in college are useful.

_____ 3. A liberal arts degree offers a wide variety of career opportunities.

_____ 4. Most team sports are not pursued by student athletes after graduation.

_____ 5. Many children's TV shows encourage violence.

_____ 6. Politicians come in three varieties.

_____ 7. The mall has a wide variety of stores.

_____ 8. Drug abusers come in many types.

_____ 9. Football teams need different kinds of skilled players to succeed.

_____ 10. Hobbies can be broken down into three categories.

BODY

This is pretty clear. Usually each category gets a separate paragraph in the body. Be sure to stick to your P.O.C.

ACTIVITY 21-3

Directions: Identify the P.O.C. for each of the classifications below; then cross out the items that do not fit with the grouping.

1. Students: P.O.C. _____

   freshmen   juniors
   sophomores   seniors
   honor roll students part-timers

2. Politicians: P.O.C. _____

   local   national
   state   crooked

3. Religions: P.O.C. _____

   Catholic   Muslim
   Protestant   Priest
   Jewish

4. Doctors: P.O.C. _____

   pediatrician   concerned
   obstetrician   ophthalmologist
   surgeon   wealthy

5. Dogs: P.O.C. _____

   herding   trained
   sporting   aggressive
   terriers   hounds

CONCLUSION

Sum up and, as usual, be sure to remind the reader of your thesis and your main points.

What Blueprint Should I Use?

Introduction

◆ **Thesis:** Successful horror movie villains scare us because their evil comes from powers beyond our control.

Body

◆ **P.O.C. 1:** Horror films based on supernatural evil present villains whose powers come from sources outside of the real world.

Dracula

The Exorcist

Stir of Echoes

Wolf

◆ **P.O.C. 2:** Science-gone-awry horror movies, where evil results from misguided technology or experimentation.

Frankenstein

Them

Soylent Green

◆ **P.O.C. 3:** Psycho-killer horror movies, where an evil being has a relentless drive to kill.

Jaws

Friday the 13th

Halloween

Alien

Conclusion

◆ Sum up.

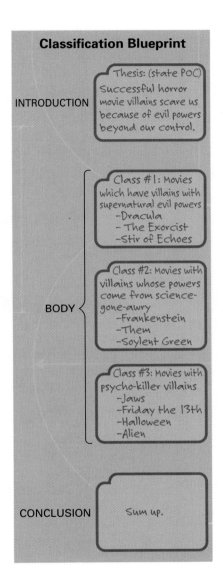

Classification Blueprint

INTRODUCTION — Thesis: (state POC) Successful horror movie villains scare us because of evil powers beyond our control.

BODY
Class #1: Movies which have villains with supernatural evil powers
–Dracula
– The Exorcist
–Stir of Echoes

Class #2: Movies with villains whose powers come from science-gone-awry
–Frankenstein
–Them
–Soylent Green

Class #3: Movies with psycho-killer villains
–Jaws
–Friday the 13th
–Halloween
–Alien

CONCLUSION — Sum up.

Classification Essay—Tips to Make It Work

❶ *Remember to stick to your P.O.C. Don't start out classifying the laundry by color and then switch to size. A classification essay can only work if you have the same P.O.C. from beginning to end.*

❷ *Try to account for all the laundry in the basket.*

It's better not to have categories of classification with only one item. You certainly don't want to end up with items left in the bottom of the laundry basket unclassified.

red clothes	plaid boxers
white clothes	unclassified—polka-dot shirt
blue clothes	striped tie

ACTIVITY 21-4

Directions: If you are sorting laundry by color, you might have a pile of red clothes, a pile of white clothes and a pile of blue clothes as well as a purple and white polka-dot shirt, a pair of plaid boxer shorts, and a green and yellow striped tie. Which system of classification would work best? A or B?

A

red clothes
white clothes
blue clothes
purple and white polka-dotted
green and yellow stripes

B

red clothes
white clothes
blue clothes
printed clothes

❸ *Avoid resorting to "etc." or "miscellaneous" to take care of leftover items.*

Free Sample

Classification Essay

Introduction—
Thesis—

Moviegoers love a good scream. Settling down in their seats, holding onto their boxes of popcorn, they eagerly wait for horror movies to scare them silly. Successful horror movies are scary because the evil that possesses their villains comes from powers beyond anyone's control.

1st Category—

Some horror villains get their evil powers from supernatural forces outside of the rules of nature. Dracula, and all other vampires, for that matter, defy death and then can transform themselves into bats and mist. In some vampire movies, the villains can fly. *The Exorcist*, a classic horror movie, presents a villain who is none other than Satan himself, possessing the body of a young girl. In *Wolfman*, a mild-mannered regular guy is transformed into a lupine killer. Movies like *Stir of Echoes* and *The Sixth Sense* scare us because ghostlike presences from otherworldly sources intrude into everyday life.

Body—

2nd Category—

In science-gone-awry horror movies, it is misguided technology that gives rise to evil. In the 1950s, botched scientific experiments (usually involving radiation) created giant ants (*Them!*), a killer vegetable (*The Thing!*), a fifty-foot tall man (*The Amazing Colossal Man*) and other mutant villains. Frankenstein, the classic horror villain, is created by a mad scientist. Most of the villains typical of the creature-feature genre have been created by malevolent scientists who force them to behave in monstrous ways.

3rd Category

Body

Psycho-killer horror movies give us evil beings who are motivated by a relentless desire to kill. (That the victims are often scantily clad teenagers only seems to up the ante.) These psycho killers can assume many forms. Consider the ravenous shark in *Jaws*, and the reptilian creature in the *Alien* series. When the villain is in human form, the same bloodthirsty compulsion to kill remains. Jason in the endless *Friday the 13th* movies and Michael Meyers in the *Halloween* series slaughter victims without tiring. Nothing more than a lust to kill sends them on their mindless killing sprees.

Conclusion

Supernatural, scientific, or murderous forces—all beyond the control of the average moviegoer—put the horror in horror movies. Moviegoers, safe in their plush seats, can relax and enjoy screaming.

Free Sample Classification Questions

1. What is the P.O.C. in the Free Sample Classification essay?

_____

_____

_____

2. Do the categories of classes given in this essay account for all of the items in the big group (horror movie villains)? Why or why not?

_____

_____

_____

3. Which class of horror movie villain is most frightening to you? Why?

_____

_____

_____

4. Using the P.O.C. used in the Free Sample Classification essay, can you add a horror movie villain to one of the categories?

_____

_____

_____

Shrink-Wrap

Classification Paragraph

The horror movies we love scare us because their villains come from sources beyond our normal control. The supernatural produces unearthly horror villains. In *Dracula* we see a vampire; in *The Exorcist*, the devil; in *Wolfman*, a werewolf. Some horror movies rely on villains created by science-gone-awry. The giant ants in *Them!*, the killer vegetable in *The Thing!*, the monster in *Frankenstein*, and a slew of accidentally irradiated creatures from the Black Lagoon and elsewhere sprang to life when technology backfired. The psycho-killer villains are propelled by an insatiable desire to kill. Whether in human form—Jason in *Friday the 13th* or Michael Meyers in *Halloween*—or in such incarnations as the shark in *Jaws* or the space creature in *Alien*, these evil beings are just relentless killing machines, seemingly preferring to prey on scantily clad teenagers. Whatever the source of their evil, these horror movie villains scare us because they are created from powers beyond our control. They give us just what we want when we settle down in our plush theater seats—a reason to scream our heads off.

WE'RE GLAD YOU ASKED
DIVISION AND CLASSIFICATION ESSAYS **Q&A**

Q How do I know if I can classify a group?

A One good guideline is to think about how broad a group you're looking at. Being asked to classify "People" is too big a task. (There are too many items in your make-believe laundry bag.) Likewise, a group like "Games" is too broad. If you can narrow down the group "People in my neighborhood" or "Board games") you'll have better luck.

Q What are the biggest problems I might have in writing a classification essay?

A There are two problems to watch out for: (1) A list that is too simple. (There are three kinds of teachers.) (2) Classification essays that have no opinion. Remember that the classes you come up with aren't ironclad (Even friendly teachers may be hostile at times). Don't be too rigid.

Q Whazzup?

A We're tired of hearing this one. Don't ask us again.

Division and Classification Topics Bank

Here are some topics you might use to practice writing division and classification essays.

1. Attitudes toward the environment
2. Politicians
3. Car dealers
4. Television news programs
5. Jobs for teenagers
6. College students
7. Rap stars
8. Waiters
9. News anchors
10. Concerts

22

PROCESS

Process Essay—When to Use It

A process essay gives readers step-by-step instructions about how to do something:

How to build a tree house

How to set up a computer desk

How to organize a neighborhood watch program

How to choose a college

How to change the oil in your car

Most of us are familiar with the simplest kind of process: a recipe. If you follow the steps, you'll end up with interesting results (the perfect birthday cake or chicken enchiladas). Although the writing you'll be doing in school will be more complicated, keep the format for a good recipe in mind.

Process Essay—How to Build It

INTRODUCTION

Your introduction needs to perform some special functions here. Think about how a recipe works. Often it will begin with information like this:

> This delicious cake has been a favorite in our family for all special occasions. It's not difficult to make, it stays fresh for days, and its unique blend of flavors makes it unforgettable.

One thing your introduction needs to do is motivate readers to master the process. Unless there's a reason to go through all the steps you're giving, why would readers want to waste their time? You need to convince them that this is a process worth going through. Keeping a recipe in mind as a model, think about other processes you could write about. Here are some examples of thesis statements that can work well in process essays:

Changing a tire is an important skill for car owners.

Changing a tire is not as easy as you think.

Changing a tire is easier than you think.

Changing a tire is a messy, time-consuming, and boring job.

Changing a tire can be quick and neat.

You get the idea. Have a point of view and let the reader know it in your introduction.

ACTIVITY 22-1

Directions: Come up with a possible thesis for each of the following process topics:

1. How to dress for a job interview

_____

2. How to have a successful blind date

_____

3. How to clean an attic (or garage)

_____

4. How to buy a used car

_____

5. How to do research on the Internet

_____

ACTIVITY 22-2

Directions: Choose a thesis from the last activity and write a short statement why it's worth mastering the process.

ACTIVITY 22-3

Directions: Define the task involved in each of the following activities.

1. Preparing for an exam

_____

2. Applying to college

_____

3. Washing your car

_____

4. Repotting a plant

_____

5. Planning a family reunion

_____

BODY

The most important things to remember in the body of a process essay are these:

❶ *Give the steps in chronological order.* Think about a recipe again. Would the following list of steps work if you were trying to bake a chocolate cake?

Get eggs, milk, and flour. Put pan in the oven when it's 350 degrees. Make sure you mix everything well. Have a big bowl on hand. Try to use high-quality chocolate. Beat the eggs 3 minutes before adding them to the flour. Bake for 30 minutes. Grease the pan well.

If you followed the steps in the order given here, your cake would be a disaster. You need to locate that big bowl before you beat your eggs, right? You need to grease the pan before you bake the cake, right? Make sure the steps in your process essay are written in the order that they will be performed.

❷ *A tip is not a step,* so don't confuse a tip with a step. Like a recipe, your process essay must present a sequence of steps. Don't give the reader a collection of useful tips: "Use the freshest ingredients. Know the exact temperature of your oven. Measure carefully." While this information may appear in a recipe, it isn't really a recipe because it doesn't matter which tip comes first.

ACTIVITY 22-4

Directions: Determine whether each of the following are steps in a process or just helpful tips. Insert "S" for step and "T" for tip in the space provided.

Getting Ready for Running a Marathon

_____ 1. Before beginning training, consult a doctor for a thorough check-up.

_____ 2. Stay focused on your goal.

_____ 3. Start with a three-mile run four times a week during week one of your training.

_____ 4. Eat a healthy, well-balanced diet.

_____ 5. For week two, substitute a five-mile run for one of your three-mile scheduled runs.

_____ 6. During week three, cut back to running three times a week, making two of your runs ten miles in distance.

_____ 7. The night before the race, eat a high carbohydrate meal of pasta and bread.

❸ *Use steps in the process to form the building blocks for the body of your essay.* If you have a few steps (say five or less), you can let each step be a paragraph in your body. The topic sentence for each paragraph in the body can define the step. For example, in a process essay about changing a tire, this could be a topic sentence:

First, make sure your car is in a safe place away from traffic.

It is likely that your process may have lots of steps. If so, try to group them into categories. Each category will be a paragraph containing the steps in that category. If all else fails, you can create categories such as Part 1, Part 2, and Part 3. But other more informative categories may occur to you.

Since chronological order is so important to a process essay, time divisions are often helpful categories. If you are writing about applying to college, you may want to use the following categories:

Fall: Talk to high school counselors, write for applications, work on financial statement

Winter: Go for interviews, fill out application forms, visit campuses

Spring: Compare offers, make decisions

For training a dog you may use these categories:

Week 1: Sit

Week 2: Stay

Week 3: Come

Week 4: Heel

Week 5: Down

ACTIVITY 22-5

Directions: For each of the following processes, number the steps in chronological order, beginning with step 1.

1. Participating wisely in an election

   _____ Vote on election day.
   _____ Research the candidates by reading newspapers and magazines.
   _____ Register to vote.

2. Getting your college schedule

   _____ Register in your college office or by phone.
   _____ Get a copy of the schedule bulletin.
   _____ Find out which classes you need to complete your major.
   _____ Look for classes at times that fit your work schedule.
   _____ Read about courses in your college catalog.
   _____ Ask friends for recommendations of teachers and courses.

CONCLUSION

There are no special requirements for your conclusion, although you may want to suggest that your reader try out the process that you've just discussed.

What Blueprint Should I Use?

A process essay needs clearly defined steps in a clear chronological sequence. Here is a blueprint for you to follow.

Introduction

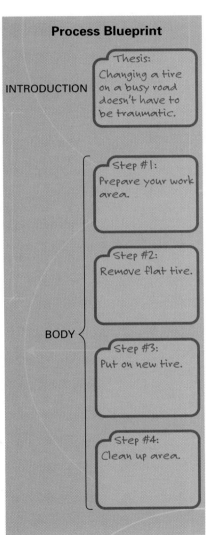

Process Blueprint

◆ **Thesis:** Changing a tire on a busy road doesn't have to be traumatic.

Body

   1. Prepare work area.

      a. Turn on flashers.

      b. Set up cones.

      c. Spread out drop cloth.

      d. Assemble tools.

   2. Remove flat tire.

      a. Loosen lug nuts.

      b. Jack up car.

      c. Remove lug nuts and place in hubcap.

   3. Put on new tire.

      a. Replace lug nuts and tighten.

      b. Secure hubcap.

   4. Clean up work area.

      a. Place all tools carefully in your trunk.

      b. Pick up cones, drop cloth.

Conclusion

◆ Sum up.

Process Essay—Tips to Make It Work

❶ *Become a troubleshooter.* Use your experience to help readers foresee potential problems that may arise. When explaining the process of making a cake, for example, you might offer someone this advice:

Be sure to sift the flour thoroughly. If you have lumps, the cake will not rise.

Include this troubleshooting advice in the step where the information will be useful.

❷ *Don't forget any steps.* Like a recipe, a process should include all the steps. If you leave out a step when it's needed, the results can be disastrous. If your cake is in the oven and you've forgotten to add the eggs to the batter, you're heading for nothing but problems.

❸ *Know whom you're talking to.* Like a recipe, a process essay needs to be aimed at an appropriate audience. If you opened a cookbook to make a chocolate cake and discovered you needed a special high-powered convection oven to bake it, you'd be disappointed. Don't present a process to beginners that's too technical, needs highly specialized equipment, or involves expertise only available to profes-

"I'll be in, honey, as soon as I rake the leaf."

sionals. An essay on "How to Perform Successful Neurosurgery" only has one appropriate audience: neurosurgeons. If you use an occasional unfamiliar term, define it.

❹ *Don't forget that spatula!* Be sure to list all the necessary materials and equipment. It would be a shame to have the batter all mixed up, only to discover you need a special spring-loaded cake pan. Let your reader know at the beginning of any process what materials and equipment will be needed—just the way a recipe lists the ingredients up front.

ACTIVITY 22-6

Directions: Make a list of the tools and equipment you might need to mention in essays on the following topics:

1. How to wash a car

2. How to cook an omelet

3. How to set up a successful lemonade stand

❺ *Don't be afraid of "you."* You've probably heard that it is not correct to write an essay in the second person (addressed to "you"). In some cases, it just seems too personal. What if you were reading an essay and the writer said, "You know how awful chocolate chip cookies are." You might think, "Hey, wait a second, I love chocolate chip cookies!" That's just the problem. When you use "you," you run the risk of making your readers feel uncomfortable. In a process essay, though, "you" is appropriate because the best way to communicate directions is directly.

❻ *Don't hesitate to guide your readers through the process by giving them timely advice.* Statements like "now here is the most difficult part of the process," "after this step, finishing this project will be easy" and "you'll enjoy this" will give your readers valuable insights that will help them complete the task at hand.

Free Sample

Process Essay

Introduction — Thesis —

    It's happened to everyone. Your car is rolling along the highway. Traffic is flowing freely, everything is fine. Suddenly a tire blows out and your happy times roll to an abrupt halt as you pull your car off to the side of the road. The key here is not to panic. Changing a tire on a busy road doesn't have to be traumatic. If you know a few easy steps, you can be on your way without a hassle.

First Stage — **First, prepare your work area.** Turn on your emergency flashers. This will alert on-coming traffic to your presence and keep you and your car from harm. Next, set up traffic cones (which you should have in your trunk) to further ensure that you will be visible to other drivers. When you've set up your cones, spread out a drop cloth by the flat tire. This will keep your clothes clean and help you keep track of your tools (lug wrench and jack). Once your work area is organized, you're ready to tackle the flat.

Second Stage — **You can begin by removing the hubcap and loosening the lug nuts**—top and bottom and then right and left (even before you jack up your car). Use your wrench to turn the lug nuts counterclockwise. If a nut is stuck, keep trying. When the lug nuts are loosened, do not remove them. (You don't want the tire to fall off before you're ready to remove it.) Put your jack together, place it under the car, and ratchet it up until the flat tire no longer has contact with the ground. Once the car is jacked up, remove the lugs and place them in the hubcap so that you will not lose them.

Body —

Third Stage — **Now it's time to take your spare from the trunk** and lift it up onto the bolts. Tighten the lug nuts in the same order you used to loosen them and make sure the hubcap is fastened securely.

Fourth Stage — **It's finally time to clean up your work area.** Place all the tools carefully in your trunk, first replacing the flat and then your wrench and jack. Next load your drop cloth and cones. Once back in your car, keep your emergency flashers on until you've safely merged into traffic and head to the nearest gas station to get your tire fixed.

Conclusion — Changing a flat tire is a dirty job and it can be dangerous, but it really isn't difficult. If you stay calm and focus on the task at hand, you can be back on the road in no time, ready to roll on with your busy day.

Free Sample Process Essay Questions

1. Can you identify the separate steps within the four main stages of the Free Sample Process essay?

_____

_____

2. Why did the writer choose to make a paragraph for each main stage of changing a tire instead of devoting a paragraph to each step in the process?

_____

_____

3. Can you think of any step in this process which needs to be explained in more detail?

_____

_____

4. Where in the essay has the writer anticipated a possible difficulty and warned the reader about it?

_____

_____

Shrink-Wrap

When you develop a process paragraph, your topic sentence makes your point and the steps for completing the process are your main supports.

Process Paragraph

Taking good notes in a college class isn't difficult. The first thing you need to do is purchase a notebook that you will be writing in. You'll also need to be sure to have several pens so that you don't run the risk of running out of ink. When you sit down in class, be ready to write as soon as your professor begins talking. As your professor lectures, don't feel that you need to write down everything she says. Be sure to write down everything she repeats or obviously slows down long enough for you to record. Also be sure to write down anything that you find written on the blackboard. After class, read through your notes, adding anything you didn't have time to write in class that you believe is important.

WE'RE GLAD YOU ASKED
PROCESS ESSAY Q&A

Q How can I find a good topic for a process essay?

A Think about things you do especially well or things you've done many times. Activities you do well are often activities you've mastered over a long period of time. When you train someone else to do them, you can share all the tips and shortcuts you've picked up to make the process go faster and easier. The more fun and/or important the activity is, the better your essay will be.

Q How can I tell if I've left something out?

A The best way to double-check is to go through the process mentally or to actually go through the process and test it out.

Q What's the difference between an elephant and a pachyderm?

A There is no difference!

Process Topics Bank

Here are some topics you might use to practice writing a process essay.

1. How to keep television from taking over your life
2. How to buy a computer
3. How to make your neighborhood the best in town
4. How to save money at the grocery store (or department store, etc.)
5. How to succeed in school when you have a full-time job
6. How to house-train a puppy
7. What to do if you lose your wallet
8. How to stop smoking
9. What to do if there's a fire in your house
10. How to plan a surprise party

23

NARRATION

Narrative Essay—When to Use It

Narration or storytelling, is as old as time. Even before the written word, we have told each other stories. The power of storytelling has lasted through the ages because stories interest people. A good, strong story can have the reader in the palm of your hand.

In narrative essay, you will be telling a story to make a point, using narration to support your thesis. You won't be telling a fictional tale with imagined characters and events. Instead you'll be telling the story of something that actually happened in order to convince your readers that your thesis is true.

Narrative Essay—How to Build It

INTRODUCTION

This is where you'll state your thesis. Whatever point you make in your thesis will need to be illustrated by the story you tell. Keep this in mind: Make your point in the introduction; then dramatize the point through a story.

BODY

The bulk of the story will take place here. Unlike more structured essays, the narrative essay allows for a lot of freedom in the way a story unfolds. But remember that paragraphs can signal a new narrative development, a change

A I was so tired – night time drive highway 30 mins everyday finish exam over night
B moist , no light , too fast , want to sleep
B not concentrate , so close , stop suddenly , bump her to be frightened by accident
  call ambulance and stay at car

learn :
not too close
concentrate
not too fast
full of animation

of location, or a passage of time. The events of the story provide the main building blocks of the body.

CONCLUSION

If you've done a good job of storytelling, you won't need to spoon-feed your reader a conclusion at the end of your essay. Rather than being a separate section, the conclusion can simply be the end of your story.

ACTIVITY 23-1

Directions: Write down a possible thesis for a narrative essay written on each of the following topics:

1. My first trip to the dentist

   Thesis: _____

2. Senior year

   Thesis: _____

3. Alcohol use on college campuses

   Thesis: _____

4. A concert I attended

   Thesis: _____

5. A family vacation

   Thesis: _____

6. My biggest rival

   Thesis: _____

What Blueprint Should I Use?

The blueprint for a narrative essay reflects huge variations in the structures of stories. Here's what a blueprint for a narrative essay might look like.

Introduction

- ◆ **Thesis:** What goes around, comes around.

Body

1. My grandfather died.
2. I had to leave school, missing homecoming weekend, to drive 300 miles to his funeral.
3. On the road, my car broke down.
4. A man stopped and helped me charge my battery.
5. I offered to pay him, but he refused to take anything and just asked me to do a good turn for someone else.
6. After the funeral, I stopped to help a stranded motorist and made the same request to her.

Conclusion

- ◆ **Maybe you don't need one.** (Doesn't the story you've told make its own point?)

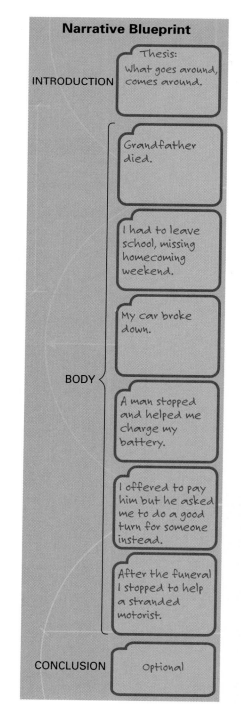

Narrative Blueprint

INTRODUCTION — Thesis: What goes around, comes around.

BODY
- Grandfather died.
- I had to leave school, missing homecoming weekend.
- My car broke down.
- A man stopped and helped me charge my battery.
- I offered to pay him but he asked me to do a good turn for someone instead.
- After the funeral I stopped to help a stranded motorist.

CONCLUSION — Optional

Narrative Essay—Tips to Make It Work

*food
don't know what
I like to eat
salad
olive oil
pasta*

❶ *Think about what makes a story a story.* There might be dialogue; there might be suspense or humor. Let your own attitude prevail. Be entertaining. Make your reader want to hear what happened next. Try to get your reader caught up in the events you are dramatizing. Remember that summarizing a story isn't the same as telling it.

❷ *Tell your readers enough so they get a feel for what's going on.* Details are everything! Don't overlook sounds, smells, and feelings.

❸ *Make sure your readers understand what's at stake.* In every good story, something is on the line for a character.

❹ *Show, don't tell.* Remember that in a good narrative essay, the story will show—not tell—your reader why the thesis is true. Don't preach. Tell your story and let the readers figure it out for themselves.

*my mother
annoy me
correct my feeling
at homestay.*

Free Sample

Narrative Essay

Thesis — Introduction —
Sometimes seemingly unconnected events can become connected in unexpected ways. What began as one of the worst weekends in my life ended up revealing something important to me about the surprising way the world works. As my grandfather always told me, what goes around comes around.

① went to Kenya
   excursion   too see refugee

② escape from other country
   drought
   camp   bad
   lack of materials

③ have diseases
   - baby, lack of vitamin thin
   - conservative notion
   - not allow foreign doctor
     to cure
   - believe their god to cure
                        them

use my knowledge to help
them   **Body**

abolish their conservative
notion

become a doctor, go to
the third world to
help people

During the fall of my sophomore year in college, I was making plans with my friends for homecoming weekend when I got a call from my mother. Grandpa Wilson had died of a sudden heart attack. Since my parents' divorce when I was three, my mother and I had lived with Grandpa Wilson. He and I were very close. When I was growing up, he took me fishing. We went for long walks in the woods. He told me all about the world, and his kindness to everyone was a constant example.

Amidst the sadness I felt for my grandfather, I also was angry that I would miss all the parties and good times I had been planning for the weekend. But I knew I had to leave school, my friends, and the parties and drive 300 miles back home to be with my Mom to attend Grandpa Wilson's funeral.

I left campus in a foul mood. As I drove along the interstate I fumed about the unfairness of the world. My grandfather was gone. I would be left out of the biggest party weekend at school and probably return a social outcast. Just when I thought my mood couldn't get any blacker, my car began sputtering and the engine stopped.

I managed to coast to the shoulder of the road. As I sat in the gathering darkness, watching the cars zoom past me, I finally resigned myself to trying to walk or hitchhike to the nearest exit, twenty miles away. Just then an old, blue Ford pulled up behind me. The driver was a middle-aged man wearing jeans, an old T-shirt, and work boots that had holes in the toes. Several of his front teeth were missing. I thought he looked like a real loser at best, or a serial killer at worst. However, he knew about cars and he had a pair of jumper cables, and in no time he had my car running again.

I offered to pay him, although my funds were limited. He just smiled and said that doing a good turn for someone else would be payment enough.

After I made it home, my mom and I planned the funeral. The minister talked about my grandfather, his love of nature and for his family, and reminded me again of how Grandpa Wilson tried his best to be kind to everyone.

Driving back to campus, I saw a station wagon pulled to the side of the road. I never had to think twice about stopping to help the young mother change her flat tire while she looked after her baby. As I pulled in front of my dorm, I wasn't really surprised to discover that missing the Homecoming weekend, the parties and the beer, really didn't matter much to me.

Free Sample Narrative Essay Questions

1. What are the main events in the story told in the Free Sample Narrative essay?

   _____

   _____

wake up lately
no mom call me
to wake up
forgot to wash
clothes

2. What details does the writer use to make the experience more vivid?

_____

_____

3. Is the writer's change of attitude justified? Why or why not?

_____

_____

4. Can you remember a time when an encounter with a stranger changed your way of thinking?

_____

_____

Shrink-Wrap

nobody help me to
clean up bedroom

lose thing
forgot to pay

guardian

Narrative Paragraph

When my sister went off to college I thought I'd died and gone to heaven. I no longer had to share my room! The first night she was gone, I played all my favorite CDs. I watched the shows I liked on TV and never had to fight with her for control of the remote. The closet space was all for me, and I didn't have to beg my sister to return sweaters or jeans of mine that she had borrowed. Because I'm a lot neater than my sister, I arranged things just the way I wanted and everything stayed in place. My schoolbooks were neatly stacked; my pens were laid out in a line; my jewelry box was orderly. Then, when I turned out the lights and climbed into bed, there was no one to gossip with, no one to say goodnight to, no one breathing across the room. For the first time in my life, I felt alone.

WE'RE GLAD YOU ASKED
NARRATIVE ESSAY Q&A

Q How can I find my own style to use in a narrative essay?

A Use words and phrases with which you're familiar and comfortable. Don't try to sound older or more intellectual or sophisticated than you really are. Don't overuse slang, but be easy and conversational in your tone. Let your voice come through in your writing.

Q How can I find a story on which to base a narrative essay?

A Think about incidents, events, or occurrences in your life that made a deep impression on you. It's likely that these events will be memorable to your readers as well.

Q Is there any way to make tofu taste great?

A Not that we've discovered.

Narrative Topics Bank

Here are some topics you might use to practice writing narrative essays.

1. A shocking experience
2. A lesson I learned the hard way
3. A date I'll never forget
4. It's better to be lucky than good
5. Don't judge a book by its cover
6. A friend who came through for me
7. A friend who let me down
8. How the best-laid plans can go awry
9. Man's best friend
10. The best things in life are free

24

DEFINITION

Definition Essay—When to Use It

We've all used a dictionary to look up unfamiliar words. The dictionary definition gives us the denotation (starts with "d," as in dictionary) or literal meaning of the word. For instance:

skirmish: a brief battle

wine: an alcoholic beverage made from fermented grapes

spectacles: eyeglasses used to correct vision

When a dictionary definition alone is not enough to fully understand a topic, we write a definition *essay* that goes beyond the denotation of a word. Definition essays explain the connotation (starts with "c," as in context) or what the term being defined implies in a larger way.

Use definition essays to show your opinion about concepts that cannot be captured by simple dictionary definition. This kind of definition can be helpful when writing about unclear, complex, or controversial subjects. What do you think the terms shown below really mean?

Controversial Subjects

Pornography	Right to Life	Censorship	Generation gap
Animal rights	Healthy lifestyle	Conservative	Liberal

Clichés

Role model	The perfect mate	A happy home
Work-a-holic	A good teacher	Man's best friend

Complex Ideas

Love   Hate   Honesty   Compassion   Charity

As you can see, the denotation of a term is not enough. You'll need to rely on your opinion.

Definition Essay—How to Build It

INTRODUCTION

Since your opinion in a definition essay is a vital element, be sure to include your view in the introduction. A thesis for a definition essay could be any of the following:

A healthy lifestyle is the road to misery.

A role model is not really helpful to young people.

A good teacher is not your friend.

Honesty isn't always the best policy.

Fear can make you stronger.

As you can see, your thesis should offer something new to supplement the standard definition. In a definition essay your goal is to give your reader a new understanding of something that goes beyond what the dictionary can offer.

BODY

The body of your definition essay is where you'll explain your definition. You have a tremendous amount of flexibility to decide how you want to set up the body of your essay. You may want to use examples, comparison or contrast, narration, etc., to get your definition across.

CONCLUSION

This is the place where you should try to briefly restate the gist of your definition.

What Blueprint Should I Use?

In a definition essay there are many different blueprints to use. This is a mode of development that makes use of one or more of the other modes to prove its thesis. From paragraph to paragraph you might use examples, comparison and/or contrast, narration, or any other mode.

Definition Essay—Tips to Make It Work

❶ *Never use a definition essay to define something that a dictionary definition could adequately explain.*

❷ *Don't be afraid to deal with your subjective ideas.* This isn't a research paper. Good definition essays are often personal. Since you're going beyond the concrete definition the dictionary gives, your opinions and attitudes come into play. As long as you offer convincing support for your opinions, you'll be OK.

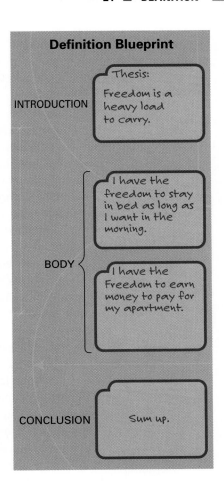

Definition Blueprint

INTRODUCTION — Thesis: Freedom is a heavy load to carry.

BODY —
I have the freedom to stay in bed as long as I want in the morning.

I have the freedom to earn money to pay for my apartment.

CONCLUSION — Sum up.

Free Sample

Definition Essay

Introduction

Thesis

When I was younger, I yearned for freedom. Every time my parents enforced my curfew or told me to turn off the TV and do my homework or reminded me it was time to set the table, I dreamed about being on my own and having the freedom to make my own decisions. Now that I'm away at college and living on my own, I'm finding freedom a heavy load to carry.

Topic Sentence #1

Because living in a dorm would be too confining, I opted to have my own apartment. Now I have the freedom to stay in bed as long as I want in the morning. Without my parents to wake me up, I am free to snooze through my 10 o'clock chemistry exam and to stay up until 2 A.M. watching movies which means that—when I do wake up, I stumble through my classes like a zombie.

Topic Sentence #2

Body

Living on my own also gives me the freedom to earn the money to pay for my apartment. My job as a waitress helps to pay the rent. I chose my hours—the dinner shift four nights a week. Although I am free to go out with my friends whenever I want, I often don't have the energy to party the way I used to after hours on my feet waiting tables.

Topic Sentence #3

Living on my own schedule frees me from the obligations of doing chores. Now I can let the laundry pile up into a mountain of dirty clothes. I never have to set the table or make my bed or wash and dry the dishes. I am free to eat leftovers out of a Tupperware container and I stand in my grungy jeans over the kitchen sink staring at the piled up dishes from long ago meals.

On my own, without anyone to boss me around, I find myself wishing for the restrictions of a good night's sleep, clean clothes, and a meal served on place mats with folded napkins.

Conclusion

Freedom takes some getting used to.

Free Sample Definition Essay Questions

1. What makes the tone of the essay ironic?

   _____

   _____

2. What does the writer achieve by repeating the word "freedom"?

   _____

   _____

3. What specific examples does the writer use to support the thesis?

_____

_____

4. In your life is freedom a blessing or a curse?

_____

_____

Shrink-Wrap

Definition Paragraph

When I was younger, I yearned to be free of the rules and responsibilities at home, where I had a strict curfew, a set time to study, and chores to do. Now I'm living in my own apartment and working my way through college. I have the freedom to sleep as late as I want—and to snooze through my 10 o'clock chemistry exam. I am free to pick my hours at work, waiting tables during the dinner shift, and free to go out with my friends after work. If I'm dead on my feet after carrying trays of food all evening, that's my choice. I don't have to lift a finger to wash dishes or do laundry if I don't feel like it. I am free to eat leftovers out of a Tupperware container as I stand in my grungy jeans over a sink piled high with dirty dishes. Freedom takes some getting used to.

WE'RE GLAD YOU ASKED

DEFINITION ESSAYS **Q&A**

Q Is it always a good idea to take time to define your terms for readers?

A Definitely. If readers don't understand how you are using certain terms, they won't be able to understand your point overall.

Q Will a good definition essay contain more than one mode of development?

A In most cases.

Q Is the glass half empty or half full?

A We always see it as half full, unless we're in a bad mood.

Definition Topics Bank

Here are some topics you might use to practice writing a definition essay.

1. Cowardice
2. A true friend
3. Pornography
4. Bravery
5. Christmas spirit
6. Punk rock or hip hop or rock and roll music
7. Faith
8. Intelligence
9. A good teacher
10. A successful party

25

DESCRIPTION

"He's about five feet six, has big brown eyes and curly blond hair, and answers to the name of Master"

Description Essay—When to Use It

Description is a tool we use every day. We use it when we speak:

"Which one of those boys is your brother?"

"That's him over there—the tall redhead wearing the faded blue T-shirt and the plaid shorts."

We use it when we write:

The delay in transporting the crops resulted in crates of brown, shriveled heads of lettuce and squished, blackened bananas.

When you use description as the basis of an entire essay, you give your reader sensory details to convey your attitudes about the subject about which you're writing. Description certainly calls to mind visual information, telling your reader the way something or someone looks. But don't forget that you have five senses, many of which may be useful to you. Besides sight, sound, smell, and touch, taste can also be used.

ACTIVITY 25-1

Directions: See how many of the five senses you can use to describe the following items:

1. A lemon

   sight _____

   sound _____

   touch _____

   smell _____

   taste _____

2. A penny

   sight _____

   sound _____

   touch _____

   smell _____

   taste _____

3. Gasoline

sight _____

sound _____

touch _____

smell _____

taste _____

4. Sand

sight _____

sound _____

touch _____

smell _____

taste _____

5. Toothpaste

sight _____

sound _____

touch _____

smell _____

taste _____

Description Essay—How To Build It

INTRODUCTION

One of the trickiest things about a description essay is to make sure you have a thesis. Your descriptive details have to add up, to point somewhere. Remember that the same basic rules that are true for all essays apply to *descriptive* essays as well: you must have an opinion on the topic about which you write. You need a thesis! Often descriptive essays are more personal than some of the other kinds of essays. Have you heard the old saying, "Beauty is in the eyes of the beholder?" That should give you a good idea how the thesis of a descriptive essay works. Often the thesis statement of a descriptive essay is subjective, coming from the way you relate to the descriptive details.

ACTIVITY 25-2

Directions: Circle the following statements that would make good thesis statements for a descriptive essay.

1. The Dalrymple's new house is a nineteenth century brick colonial.

2. The desert at night is beautiful in its barren stillness.

3. Cedric's grandmother is 98 years old, very thin and wrinkled.

4. When I look at my grandfather's weathered face, I see the most handsome man I know.

5. The industrial park is a scar, disfiguring the city's face.

6. The old house on Pine Street is terrifying.

BODY

The key here, as with all essays, is to provide your readers with information to convince them that your thesis is true. But with a descriptive essay, you have a lot more freedom as to how you set up the paragraphs in the body of your essay. You may want to borrow one of the blueprints for one of the other modes. You could describe your new car by comparing it with your old one. You could describe the members of the state legislature by classifying them according to the way they dress. You could describe a restaurant's decor by giving examples.

In a descriptive essay, there is no one way to set up your paragraphs. If you use comparison and contrast to describe something, you should, of course, follow the blueprint for a comparison and contrast essay. The same is true for any other mode you might use to write a descriptive essay. Whatever method you use to organize descriptive details, make sure that you stick with it throughout your whole essay.

CONCLUSION

There are no special requirements for the conclusion of a descriptive essay.

What Blueprint Should I Use?

There are many possible blueprints to use in a descriptive essay. This is a mode of development that often makes use of one or more of the other modes to prove its thesis. You might use examples and comparison/contrast or narration.

Description Essay—Tips to Make It Work

❶ *Don't overlook details.* The key to a good description is in the particular, specific details. Notice how the addition of specific details can help a description come to life:

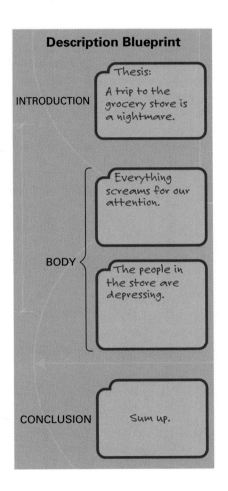

Description Blueprint

INTRODUCTION — Thesis: A trip to the grocery store is a nightmare.

BODY — Everything screams for our attention.

The people in the store are depressing.

CONCLUSION — Sum up.

A shabby old man was wearing a pair of faded blue disco pants, their wide bell bottoms frayed and covered with splatters of mud splashed up by passing cars.

❷ *Use metaphors to enrich descriptive language.* Comparisons, even unlikely ones, can help your readers clearly understand the nature of what you're describing:

Junked cars stood in the empty lot like disabled soldiers.

❸ *Remember that you're in the picture, that the description you're writing is yours.* Your essay is not just a photograph, capturing a factual dimension. It's more like a painting, interpreting your descriptive details. In other words, you're not just giving a description of the old house on the corner. You're giving *your* description. The objective facts (the boy is tall; the old wooden door squeaks; the sunlight shines in through the window) need to be given through your subjective impressions:

The tall boy reminded me of an awkward giraffe.

The persistent squeaking of the old wooden door frightened me.

The rays of sunlight streaming in through the window made the room warm and inviting.

Free Sample

Description Essay

Introduction —
Thesis —

Body —

Grocery stores are a necessary fact of life. We see them in every city, on every corner. We visit them all the time. A trip to the grocery store is a nightmarish journey.

The light in the grocery store is harsh and fluorescent, casting an unnatural, unflattering glow on everyone and everything. The pasty-faced shoppers trudging down the aisles, the pyramids of metallic cans, and the rows of the garishly artificially colored vegetables are all part of the atmosphere. Everything on the shelves is too bright, too big, too shiny. The labels scream out extremes: Super Giant Size! New and Improved! Tremendous Savings! Enriched with 25 Vitamins! No Fat! Low Fat! Sugar free! In a grocery store, nothing is subtle. Everything screams for attention.

> *Topic Sentence #1*

The shoppers look tired, their mouths set in a glum line, their eyes blank, their shoulders sagging as they roll down the aisle like robots. They all have someplace else to be. This is no place to linger. The employees, checkers, and baggers always seem to be distracted, looking right through the customers, ready to bolt the instant their shifts are finished.

> *Body*

> *Topic Sentence #3*

There is no escape from the constant background noises. The shopping carts, always in disrepair, clatter and squeak. The cash registers continually spit out shrill, electronic beeps. Some of the new-and-improved models have a nasal mechanical voice blankly announcing the price of each item in tones no human being ever uttered. A welcome relief from this unrelenting background noise is provided only by an irate mother loudly reprimanding a wailing child or a carelessly arranged display of canned soup crashing to the floor.

> *Conclusion*

We seem to be paying a high price indeed for our loaves of giant sized, vitamin enriched, super value bread.

Free Sample Description Essay Questions

1. In the Free Sample Description essay find words that apply to the five senses: sight, sound, smell, touch, and taste.

_____

_____

2. In the body of the Free Sample essay, the second paragraph does not have a topic sentence. What is the topic sentence implied by the details in this paragraph?

_____

_____

3. How closely does this essay match your attitude about shopping in a supermarket?

_____

_____

4. What descriptive details could be used to create a pleasant impression of a trip to the supermarket?

_____

_____

Shrink-Wrap

Description Paragraph

The supermodels gracing the covers of fashion magazines have nothing on my grandmother when it comes to beauty. Her skin isn't firm or smooth, but the wrinkles around her kind, blue eyes reflect smiles and laughter. Not once in her eighty-four years has she ever worn a Wonderbra or had silicone implants, but a hug from her is as soft and welcoming as a pillow. She's not one to work out in a gym, climb a stairmaster, or pump iron, but her ample waistline and full hips reflect the delicious cakes she's baked from scratch and the five children she birthed and raised. Sometimes beauty isn't flawless skin or a great figure; sometimes beauty is reflected in the mileage life wears on the face and body of a happy person.

WE'RE GLAD YOU ASKED

DESCRIPTION Q&A

Q If I'm writing a descriptive essay, should I use lots of adjectives?

A Since adjectives are words that describe nouns, you'll probably end up using more of them than usual, but don't overdo it. Every noun doesn't need an adjective, and you should definitely avoid using more than two adjectives next to any noun.

Q How do I know when I've described something enough?

A Put yourself in your reader's shoes. Imagine that you've never seen what you're describing, then read over what you've written. Can you see it?

Q Why does it always rain after I wash my car?

A We've wondered the same thing. Let us know if you figure this one out.

Description Topics Bank

Here are some topics you might use to practice writing description essays.

1. A place that makes you happy
2. A depressing place
3. The beach
4. An animal
5. A doctor's waiting room
6. A professional wrestler
7. A new or old car
8. A neighborhood you'd like to live in
9. The interstate at rush hour or at 5 A.M.
10. College jocks, professors, or cheerleaders.

PART
5

FIGHTING FAIR AND WINNING AN ARGUMENT

"My concession speech will be brief. You win."

26

WHAT IS CRITICAL THINKING?

Critical thinking produces ideas, opinions, and conclusions that can stand up to the test of logic. It's the kind of thinking that ensures your writing will actually make sense, especially to the college instructors who will be reading it. Let's take a look at some of the basic building blocks of critical thinking.

Induction

MOST OF US ARE TALL.

Induction—reaching a conclusion on the basis of incomplete evidence—is something you use every minute of every day. If we asked you to describe a giraffe, chances are you'd say "tall." You've seen a giraffe in the zoo. You've seen a picture of a giraffe in a book. You've seen some giraffes on a nature show on TV. But you haven't seen every giraffe in the world. In fact, you've only seen a tiny percentage of the planet's giraffe population. And yet you're convinced all giraffes are tall.

This incomplete evidence is called a **sample.** And on the basis of this sample, you can come to a broad conclusion about all giraffes. Most of the time such inductive reasoning is sound. (Short giraffes are in noticeably short supply.) But if the induction is to yield a valid conclusion, you must be able to say the sample is **known, sufficient**, and **representative.**

If someone says that the college faculty are controlled by space aliens, you can discount the conclusion because the sample isn't known. Which faculty? What aliens? If someone says that because Professor Smith is forgetful all professors are absentminded, you can discount the conclusion because the sample is not sufficient. One professor's behavior says nothing about a large group. If someone says that professors in England who wear robes show that State College professors are overly concerned with outdated and meaningless traditions, you can discount the claim because professors in England are not representative of the faculty at State College. The key to sound induction is to test the sample, the incomplete evidence upon which you're basing your conclusion.

ACTIVITY 26-1

Directions: Test the following claims to see if the sample is valid (V) or not valid (NV).

1. Scientists have proved that our cough syrup stops 95 percent of all coughs within minutes.

2. Blondes are dumb. My secretary is blonde and she is not very smart.

3. "Athletes are not healthy," said Dr. Smith, an orthopedic surgeon. "All of my patients are athletes."

4. A majority of cigar smokers prefer cigars to pipes.

5. I'm not going to see that movie. Cedric saw it and hated it.

ACTIVITY 26-2

Directions: Test the following inductive claims to see if the sample is valid (V) or not valid (NV).

1. If the government would release the evidence they're hiding, it would show conclusively that aliens landed in Roswell, New Mexico.

2. Eight out of ten top box office stars have recommended astrology as a key to success.

3. Pro athletes are violent. Look at O.J. Simpson.

4. The IRS is out to get us. Wait until you hear what they did to my neighbor.

5. Eighty-five percent of all inmates in prison came from divorced families, clearly showing that children of divorce are likely to turn to crime.

Deduction

Induction goes from a specific to a general conclusion. **Deduction** does the opposite: It goes from a broad, general statement to a specific conclusion. A deductive argument is constructed around something called a **syllogism**—a pattern in which two true statements are combined to make a new truth. Here is a trusty syllogism:

Truth 1: All giraffes are tall.
Truth 2: Cecil is a giraffe.
New truth: Cecil is tall.

Syllogisms can be sneaky. Sometimes one of the three parts is omitted. For instance:

The Petersons aren't invited, so they're not coming to the party. (Left-out Truth 1: Only invited guests can attend the party.)

Here is another sneaky syllogism:

All students will receive free I.D. pictures. Bob will get his on Friday. (Left-out Truth 2: Bob is a student.)

Sometimes syllogisms can sound convincing even if they are not valid. In order for a syllogism to be valid, three things must happen:

❶ *The two truths must in fact be true.* Truth 1 is usually a broad statement, reached through inductive reasoning. Check it using the three tests (see page 170) to see if the sample is valid.

Truth 1: Americans love football.

Truth 2: Byron is an American.

New truth: Byron loves football.

Truth 1 is based on an unknown sample. How many Americans were polled? Who says Americans love football? Since Truth 1 is not really true, all bets are off. The syllogism fails.

❷ *The terms of the syllogism must be clear.*

Truth 1: All lemons are yellow.

Truth 2: Bill's car is a lemon.

New truth: Bill's car is yellow.

"Lemon" has two meanings in this syllogism—a citrus fruit and an inferior product. The use of the term is not clear.

Truth 1: Animals have no moral sense.

Truth 2: Men are animals.

New truth: Men have no morals.

What do we mean by "animal" in this syllogism? Are we speaking strictly of the four-legged kind?

❸ *The syllogism must be in the proper form.* This means that the basic element in Truth 1 must also appear in Truth 2. See how logic falls apart when this rule is violated:

Truth 1: All sinners have lips.

Truth 2: All women have lips.

New truth: All women are sinners.

Sinners appears in Truth 1 but not in Truth 2.

Truth 1: The murderer wore a red coat.

Truth 2: Betty wore a red coat.

New truth: Betty is the murderer.

Once again, a basic element is missing. *Murderer* appears in Truth 1 but not in Truth 2. Note how seductive and misleading such faulty syllogisms can be:

Truth 1: The KKK favors private schools.

Truth 2: Joe favors private schools.

New truth: Joe belongs to the KKK.

Is Joe being fairly accused here? Why or why not?

ACTIVITY 26-3

Directions: Look at each syllogism below. If it works, write "W" in the space provided. If it doesn't work, write "DW."

_____ 1. Franco can't possibly get a promotion. He wasn't born in this country.

_____ 2. All alcoholics like beer. You like beer, so you must be an alcoholic.

_____ 3. Mr. Carmody saves half of his paycheck every week. He'll make a fine father.

_____ 4. The wind is real but we can't see it. So the Easter bunny must be real too.

_____ 5. President Bush wants to lower taxes. He'll go down in history as a great president.

ACTIVITY 26-4

Directions: Look at each of the syllogisms below. If it works, write "W" in the space provided. If it doesn't work, write "DW."

_____ 1. Ronald Reagan was a great president. He has Alzheimer's disease. Anyone with Alzheimer's disease would make a great president.

_____ 2. All good football players are heavy. Otto weighs 325 pounds, so he should be an All Star.

_____ 3. Alcoholics are often addicted to chocolate. Delia loves Hershey bars. She probably has a drinking problem.

_____ 4. Registered voters must be citizens. Carl is registered to vote, so we can assume he's a citizen.

_____ 5. The best things in life are free. It doesn't cost a penny to catch the flu. Having the flu is one of life's best experiences.

_____ 6. My brother is a doofus. He has freckles. People who have freckles are usually doofuses.

_____ 7. Legal drinkers in our state must be 21 years old. Karl can legally drink. I know Karl is 21 years of age or older.

_____ 8. Good things come in small packages. Benny gave his girlfriend a maggot in a velvet ring box. Maggots make good presents.

_____ 9. Low self-esteem can damage the immune system. Anyone with a lowered immune system must have low self-esteem.

_____ 10. Licensed drivers must pass a written test. Lola has her license; this is proof that she can read.

27

HOW DO I RECOGNIZE LOGICAL FALLACIES?

Objectivity and Subjectivity

Before we begin talking about fighting fair by avoiding logical fallacies, it's important to point out that there are some arguments that are just not worth having. You could be the most skilled debater in the world, but arguing about some topics is a waste of your time.

Imagine two students standing in the cafeteria line waiting to get lunch. The first student looks down the line into the vegetable selections and sees a vat of steaming broccoli. "Great," says student number one. "That broccoli looks delicious." Student number two looks down the line at the same broccoli. "No way," she says. "That broccoli looks gross." As the line inches along, the two students argue the merits of broccoli. "Broccoli is tasty." "Broccoli is nasty." "Broccoli is good." "Broccoli is bad." And so on, and so on, and so on.

These two silly students could argue on through lunch and dinner and breakfast the next morning and never come to a conclusion. The reason why is probably clear to you by now. Broccoli is good if you like the way it tastes. If you don't like the taste of broccoli, it's bad. The taste of broccoli is a matter of opinion. Arguments based totally on personal opinions don't usually lead to a conclusion. Statements based on opinion are **subjective.** They reflect the individual tastes, preferences, attitudes, and values of the speaker.

"Is it your intention to seethe for the next four years?"

At the other end of the spectrum are **objective** statements—statements that are based on facts. Suppose student number one says, "A four-ounce serving of broccoli contains your minimum daily requirement of Vitamin B." A quick glance at the broccoli package will decide whether or not this is true. Suppose student number two says, "Broccoli is not a good source of Vitamin C." Again, any debate over this statement would be quickly resolved.

You could argue about the nutritional merits of broccoli. You could agree about the proper time to plant broccoli seeds and when to harvest the plants. But it is a pointless exercise to argue about whether or not broccoli tastes good, or if broccoli is a pretty shade of green or an ugly one, or if broccoli florets do or do not look like the earrings your Aunt Buppa wore to the family reunion.

ACTIVITY 27-1

Directions: Can you argue the truth of the following statements? Put an "O" on the line next to objective statements and an "S" on the line next to the subjective statements.

_____ 1. The Lord loveth a cheerful giver.

_____ 2. Nobody doesn't like Sara Lee.

_____ 3. The statement "just between you and I" is incorrect grammar.

_____ 4. Cursing is a sin.

_____ 5. Michael Jordan was a better athlete than Shaquille O'Neal.

_____ 6. It's no use crying over spilled milk.

_____ 7. During the Monica Lewinsky scandal, President Clinton never once committed a crime.

_____ 8. Juanita looks pretty today.

_____ 9. Smoking cigarettes is bad for your health.

_____ 10. Money can't buy happiness.

_____ 11. Wally is the Beaver's older brother.

_____ 12. Dogs make better pets than cats.

_____ 13. Peanut butter and jelly sandwiches are the ideal school lunch for kids.

_____ 14. Absence makes the heart grow fonder.

_____ 15. Paris is the capitol of France and one of the world's most beautiful cities.

Well, you might be saying, if all you have to do is look up facts in a reference book somewhere, then what's the point of debate? Are all arguments about opinions useless? It all depends on **how** you argue. If you base your argument **only** on what you like or believe, then it will be pointless. But if you can show that your opinions are based on some **objective** information, then your arguments can be persuasive. Effective argument shows where opinions come from and how opinions are formed.

Fallacies

Not all arguments are fair fights. Some unfair forms of arguments are used so many times that they have been given specific names. Fallacies are forms of argument that are false, incorrect, and misleading. But this doesn't keep people from trying to use them to convince others about a point or issue. If you look closely, you'll notice many examples of fallacies in the arguments that advertisers, politicians, and others offer. Let's take a look at the most commonly used fallacies.

FALSE ANALOGY

When you use an analogy to argue a point, you compare two things that are alike in some way to show that they will be alike in other ways. A **false analogy** fails to do this. Analogy works well if the two things that you compare are actually similar. For instance:

> Juanita does a wonderful job taking care of kids in the day care center. Someday she will be a wonderful mother.

Is it reasonable to compare taking care of children in day care and taking care of children as a mother? How about this one?

> Bananas are good for your health. Try some banana pudding with each meal.

Is it reasonable to compare bananas and banana pudding? You can tell the difference between a fair analogy and a false analogy by finding the two items that are being compared and asking yourself if they are basically alike. Look at the analogy in this argument:

> The government requires fishermen to get licenses to catch fish. Why then shouldn't the government require parents to have licenses to have children?

What are the two items being compared here? Fishing and having babies? Is there enough similarity to make the analogy valid?

How about this one?

Bee stings kill more people each year than snake bites. Why then are we much more careful around snakes than around bees?

How are fatal bee stings and fatal snake bites alike? How are they different?

When you are making an argument in an essay, an analogy is often useful for giving an example to help support a point. If you find that you are extending the comparison on and on, take a good, hard look to make sure your analogy will hold up.

Comparing two items that aren't really alike is not fighting fair.

ACTIVITY 27-2

Directions: Label the items being compared in the following analogies as false analogy (FA) or valid analogy (VA).

_____ 1. Guns don't kill people. People kill people.

_____ 2. A woman needs a man like a fish needs a bicycle.

_____ 3. The college allows excused absences for football players who miss class because of away games. The same privilege should be granted to basketball players who miss class because of away games.

_____ 4. Every household has to balance the budget. The federal government should have to balance the budget too.

_____ 5. If cats and dogs can get along with each other, we should expect to learn to behave nonviolently in society. After all, people are smarter than cats and dogs.

_____ 6. We put beloved family pets to sleep when they get old. Why shouldn't it be legal to do the same thing for beloved members of the family when they get old?

ARGUMENT IN A CIRCLE

Have you ever heard a little kid try to argue about something? The conversation often goes like this:

Kid: I want a brand new bike!

Mom: We just bought you a new bike.

Kid: But I want a brand new bike!

Mom: There's nothing wrong with your old bike.

Kid: But I want a brand new one!

Mom: Why should we buy you another bike?

Kid: Because I want one!

Sometimes parents can present the same kind of argument.

Dad: Be home by 10:00.

Teenager: Why?

Dad: Because that's your curfew.

Argument in a circle occurs when a statement is supported simply by using the word "because" and then repeating a version of the original statement. For instance:

Only children are sad because happy children have brothers and sisters.

Smoking cigarettes leads to disease because cigarettes have a destructive effect on the body.

If the word "because" is suggested rather than stated outright, the argument may look a little better, but it's still circular:

Anyone who doubts Mayor Phillips' word should know just one thing: Mayor Phillips is not a liar.

You can avoid argument in a circle when you write by remembering to back up your argument with evidence. If you are attempting to convince your reader simply by repeating yourself, you're not fighting fair.

ACTIVITY 27-3

Directions: Put a circle by the statements below that are arguments.

_____ 1. The freeway is clogged with traffic because there are too many cars on the road.

_____ 2. Wild animals do not make good pets because they are not meant to be domesticated.

_____ 3. Harry has a bad temper because he cannot control his anger.

_____ 4. The freeway is clogged with traffic because the stoplights at the access ramps are not properly synchronized.

_____ 5. Wild animals do not make good pets because their temperaments are unstable.

POST HOC FALLACY

Derived from the Latin *post hoc, ergo. propter hoc*—which translates as "After this, therefore because of this—the **post hoc fallacy** states that because Event B happened after Event A, Event A caused Event B. Sometimes, on the surface, these post hoc arguments can seem convincing. But a closer look can tell whether the argument is valid or not. Take a look at this argument:

> Belinda walked into her closet and put on a green silk dress. Five seconds later Belinda fell over dead. Green silk dresses can be lethal.

You probably didn't fall for this one. Just because Belinda died after putting on her green silk dress doesn't mean that the green dress caused her death. This argument is a little more slippery:

> Students who own computers make better grades than students who don't.
>
> If you want your child to do well in school, buy her a computer.

Does simply having a computer cause better grades? Perhaps students who get computers were better students all along, before and after they became computer owners. Maybe parents who are willing to buy their children computers have a deeper interest in education for their children.

Often conspiracy theorists try to get a lot of mileage out of post hoc reasoning:

> President Clinton ate at a Chinese restaurant four times in the weeks before awarding Most Favored Nation status to China. He was influenced by Chinese-Americans in making this foreign policy decision.

Be careful about assuming that being linked in a time sequence is the same as having a cause and effect relationship. If you ignore other influences and focus only on the relationship in time between two events, you're not fighting fair.

ACTIVITY 27-4

Directions: Analyze the following arguments. If you find an example of the post hoc fallacy, write "PH" in the space provided.

_____ 1. The hailstorm dented many cars in my neighborhood. The dents in my car must have been caused by the hailstorm.

_____ 2. Rodney crashed his motorcycle while not wearing a helmet. His skull fracture is due to his failure to put on the proper safety equipment.

_____ 3. Betina got a promotion following her divorce. It looks like divorce was a good career move for her.

_____ 4. The day after Christmas always depresses me. I guess getting presents doesn't agree with me.

_____ 5. This roast beef must be spoiled. I ate some and now I feel sick.

_____ 6. The student body president should be removed from office. We elected him, and grade point averages immediately began to fall.

NON SEQUITUR

This fallacy is another Latin phrase; it means "It does not follow." A **non sequitur fallacy** happens when the arguer connects an event and its consequence on no real evidence or logic.

Mayor Phillips suffers from migraine headaches. He will not make a good political leader.

If we elect Mayor Phillips to another term, our city will be bankrupt within a year.

Here's an even more ridiculous one:

Mayor Phillips is of course a crook; if he weren't, he wouldn't be running for reelection.

To guard against such fallacies, just think about what you're doing. If you write without forcing yourself to examine the logic of your claims, you're not fighting fair.

ACTIVITY 27-5

Directions: Analyze the following statements. If you find any non sequiturs, label them "NS."

_____ 1. That building is too tall; the architect obviously doesn't care about people at all.

_____ 2. The pavement is slick with rain; cars are likely to skid.

_____ 3. My sister has a terrible temper. She needs to learn a foreign language.

_____ 4. General Motors has shown a profit this quarter. The CEO must be listening to advice from the Psychic Friends Network.

_____ 5. Those headlines are disturbing. I wonder why the newspaper editor wants to upset people.

_____ 6. If John Martin can score 35 points in a basketball game, imagine how well he'd do playing the piano!

_____ 7. The temperature is 96°. The runners in the Twin Cities Marathon will be very hot.

_____ 8. Traffic on the interstate is at a standstill. Why doesn't the city council propose a sales tax on tires?

_____ 9. Playing the stock market has created great prosperity. Money is the root of all evil.

BEGGING THE QUESTION

Begging the question is a fallacy that takes an unfair shortcut: basing an argument on a claim that has not been proved. This can appear as a question:

Has Mayor Phillips always been this unreasonable? *(Has it been established that Mayor Phillips is unreasonable?)*

Why do redheads have such bad tempers? *(Has it been established that redheads have bad tempers?)*

Sometimes begging the question can occur in a statement.

Mayor Phillips is no more dishonest than any other criminal in elected office. *(Who says Mayor Phillips is dishonest?)*

A particularly sneaky form of begging the question is asking someone to disprove an unproven statement.

How do you know that Mayor Phillips isn't an alien from outer space? *(Shouldn't it be proven that Mayor Phillips is an alien?)*

Can you prove that you didn't kill Colonel Mustard in the conservatory with the rope? *(Being innocent until proven guilty recognizes the injustice of begging the question.)*

When you write your essays, don't assume your argument is true before you prove it. If you ask your reader to accept your unproven argument, you're not fighting fair.

ACTIVITY 27-6

Directions: Analyze the following arguments. If you find an example of begging the question, label it "BTQ."

_____ 1. Have sociology professors always been politically radical?

_____ 2. Why is there so much controversy about abortion?

_____ 3. Have you ever wondered why people look so much like their dogs?

_____ 4. Because a new gymnasium would be a foolish waste of money, we should make-do with the old one.

_____ 5. The truth of the matter is that politicians know what's best for the city. We should follow their agenda.

_____ 6. Isn't it interesting that all serial killers were poor readers as children?

AD HOMINEM ARGUMENT

An **ad hominem argument** tries to attack the opposing debater rather than the argument at hand. In these situations, the character of the opponent has little to do with the question or issue being argued about. Consider the following argument:

> Mayor Phillips is in favor of gun control because he's afraid to defend himself against criminals. (*Does being a coward mean Mayor Phillips is wrong about gun control?*)

How about this one?

> Don't listen to Juanita's ideas about abortion. She isn't mature enough to be a good parent. (*Being a good or bad parent doesn't mean your ideas about abortion are valid.*)

You can avoid this fallacy by sticking to the issues. If you ignore the issues and, instead, run down your opponent, you're not fighting fair.

ACTIVITY 27-7

Directions: Analyze the following arguments. If you find an example of the ad hominem fallacy, label it "AH."

_____ 1. People who advocate antipollution laws are antibusiness.

_____ 2. How can we trust President Bush? His father has given him too much money.

_____ 3. Lucinda can't know anything about music. She never graduated from high school.

_____ 4. Don't believe what lawyers say. They're all crooks.

_____ 5. Lucas spent 5 years in prison. He is a convicted felon.

_____ 6. Mrs. Hadley has been divorced twice. There's no way she's a good role model for her students.

SLIPPERY SLOPE

The **slippery slope fallacy** slides an argument right past the question at hand, straight into a disastrous outcome. The problem is that the arguer has not provided evidence that the disaster will come to pass. Have you ever heard arguments like these?

If we register our guns, the government will take away all personal weapons and we'll be defenseless against tyranny. *(How do we know these events will occur?)*

Preventing corporal punishment in the classroom will lead to a generation of violent, out of control teenagers. *(Has this result been proven?)*

Smoking cigarettes leads to hard drug usage. *(Is this always true?)*

It's important to know if the predicted outcome is likely or unlikely. Since it's in the future, there's no way to tell for sure. But asserting horrible outcomes as certainties is the sign of lazy thinking. If you jump to extreme conclusions without evidence, you're not fighting fair.

ACTIVITY 27-8

Directions: Analyze the following arguments. If you find an example of the slippery slope fallacy, label it "SS."

_____ 1. If you're out late at night, you must be getting into mischief.

_____ 2. Marijuana can be addictive.

_____ 3. Experimenting with drugs leads straight to a life-long addiction.

_____ 4. If we lower the drinking age to eighteen, it won't be long until elementary school kids will bring beer to school in their lunch boxes.

_____ 5. Requiring gun registration is a move toward an inevitable police state.

EITHER-OR FALLACY

The **either-or fallacy** is for arguers who see things only in black or white. There are no shades of gray here. The arguers give you only two choices; their side or something terrible. Here are some examples:

You can either join my church or burn in hell for all eternity. *(Are there other choices?)*

Parents, you have a clear choice: Send your teenage son to military school or watch him turn to a life of crime. *(Maybe he could just be a regular high school kid.)*

Either join us in opposing tax increases or allow the government to take away all of our personal assets. *(Maybe we could just have a slightly lower bracket?)*

You can avoid making either-or fallacies by thinking carefully about all the possibilities at hand. If you narrow the choices only to your way or a terrible alternative, you're not fighting fair.

ACTIVITY 27-9

Directions: Discuss the possibilities not considered in the following either-or statements.

1. Criminals are the products of poverty or broken homes.

   _____

   _____

2. You can be an outstanding student or an outstanding athlete; the choice is yours.

   _____

   _____

3. If diplomatic talks break down, we should prepare for war.

   _____

   _____

4. Being a good parent means you'll have to ignore your responsibilities at work.

   _____

   _____

5. When a crisis hits, a family can either fall apart or grow stronger.

   _____

   _____

Conclusion

WRITING EFFECTIVE ARGUMENTATION

It's not hard to see that good writing is about more than coming up with specific examples and developing your ideas. Good writing is clear thinking on paper. You must take the time to evaluate the quality of your arguments and make sure you make your points without resorting to fallacious reasoning.

ACTIVITY 27-10

Directions: Look at each of the following arguments and decide whether it is sound or whether it uses a fallacy to try to make its point. Write "GA" beside the good arguments and "FA" beside the fallacious arguments in the space provided.

_____ 1. A defense attorney tells the jury in her opening argument, "You should not convict my client because he is not guilty."

_____ 2. Fred is a member of the choir, so he must be naturally musical.

_____ 3. A survey shows that 60 percent of senior citizens drink coffee, thereby proving that coffee prolongs a person's life span.

_____ 4. Workers with a high school diploma earn more money than workers who have not completed high school.

_____ 5. English courses in college should not be required because students shouldn't have to take courses they don't need.

_____ 6. Don't follow Dr. Burn's advice. He's had two heart attacks. What does he know about good health?

_____ 7. Whatever you do, please don't eat breakfast before driving to work. Ninety percent of commuters involved in fatal car accidents ate breakfast before leaving for work.

_____ 8. We trust doctors to prescribe medicinal drugs, so why not allow them to prescribe recreational drugs as well?

_____ 9. Will we vote for a raise for our teachers or allow our educational system to be destroyed?

_____ 10. Why is Tastee Cola the most refreshing soft drink you can buy?

_____ 11. If we allow the city to pass a curfew for teenagers, soon the city council will control our freedom to come and go as we wish.

_____ 12. George W. Bush did a good job as governor of Texas; he will do a good job as president.

_____ 13. We should vote for Governor Bush because he is the best choice for president.

_____ 14. It's obvious that the army is not well-equipped to defend the country; otherwise, why would so many enlisted men be playing golf?

_____ 15. Having children and having pets are both serious and expensive responsibilities. The government should allow tax deductions for pets as well as children as dependents.

ACTIVITY 27-11

Directions: Now go back and see if you can identify the type of fallacy in every argument labeled "FA." Write the type of fallacy in the space provided below each argument.

WE'RE GLAD YOU ASKED
FIGHTING FAIR AND WINNING AN ARGUMENT Q&A

Q If I don't agree with someone else's argument, does that mean the other person's argument contains fallacies?

A No. Arguments often have two reasonable sides. Of course, if you do find fallacies in your opponent's argument, that's going to make your argument that much stronger.

Q If I think I can get away with a fallacy, should I try to use it?

A No. Fallacies may be slick and easy, but they are never a substitute for clear thinking.

Q If advertisements are full of fallacies, why do I keep buying that stuff?

A Your guess is as good as ours.

P A R T

6

DEVELOPING STYLE

28

HOW DO I KEEP MY WRITING LIVELY?

Take a look around a college classroom. Observe students in the cafeteria. You'll notice that individuals stand out. Everyone is wearing clothes (of course!). Maybe many students are wearing jeans and T-shirts. But there are still differences to notice. Each student chooses clothes according to individual taste. Are the jeans dark denim or faded? Are they flares or straight legs? What color T-shirt? Individual choices in clothes, hairstyles, and jewelry all help to define style. The same is true of writing.

If you ask a group of students to write an essay on why they decided to attend college, not only will all of their answers be at least slightly different in terms of content, but they will all be written in different ways. Some will be written in long sentences; some will be written in short sentences, and some will combine both. Some will show off large vocabularies, and some will use basic, direct language. These qualities and others are part of the writer's *style*.

All writers have style from the moment they first put words on paper. What we want you to do is to become more aware of your own style as a writer and see what you can do to improve it. *What* you say when you are writing is very important, of course, but *how* you say it, your style, will affect how much your readers enjoy the experience and ultimately how much they take from what you've written.

Every essay is composed of paragraphs, and the paragraphs in turn are composed of sentences. The sentence is the basic unit of energy in your writing. Getting each sentence to work by itself and then with the sentences around it will help you to improve your style.

Imagine you walk into a party. The room is crowded with people. Who will attract your attention? You are likely to be drawn to someone interesting, someone who looks appealing, whose conversation is lively, who is entertaining. Essays work in much the same way. An essay that draws your interest, that's lively and entertaining, will stand out. Just as you might walk by someone at the party who is just standing around being nothing more than perfectly ordinary, you're likely to quit reading an essay that is nothing more than just words and paragraphs on paper. To help you to polish your style, keep the following three things in mind.

❶ *Sentence variety* (What kinds of sentences am I using?)

Look at the following paragraph:

I came to college because I wanted to get a better job. I wanted a chance at a better salary. I wanted the respect of the people I work with. I came to college because it was the right thing to do.

What the writer is saying is potentially interesting. The writer wants a good job, a bigger salary, and the respect of coworkers. Just about anyone can relate to these reasons. *How* the writer says these things slowly drains our interest though. Each sentence is constructed in the same pattern as the one before. By the time we reach the last word of the last sentence, we can almost hear a dull thud. Now look at the following paragraph:

I came to college because I was hoping to find a better job. I wanted a better salary and the respect of the people I work with. In the end, I decided to come to college because it was the right thing to do.

With a few minor changes (combining two of the sentences with a conjunction, adding an introductory phrase to the final sentence), four simple sentences have become three more interesting sentences. When we reach the last word, we feel interested in reading further. *What* the writer wrote didn't change; *how* she wrote it changed.

At this point, it would be a good idea to review the kinds of sentences all writers have at their disposal:

◆ **Simple**—one main clause and no subordinate clauses

We should recycle newspapers.

◆ **Compound**—two or more main clauses but no subordinate clauses

We should recycle newspapers, and we should find ways to dispose of motor oil safely.

◆ **Complex**—one main clause and one or more subordinate clauses

We should dispose of motor oil safely so that we do not pollute our water supply.

◆ **Compound-complex**—two or more main clauses and one or more subordinate clauses

We should recycle newspapers, and we should find ways to dispose of motor oil safely so that we do not pollute our water supply.

What kind of sentence do I have?

Simple	=	Main Clause			
Compound	=	Main Clause	and	Main Clause	
Complex	=	Main Clause	+	Subordinate Clause	
Compound-Complex		Main Clause	and	Main Clause	+ Subordinate Clause

As you can see, sentences can be simple or complicated. Successful writers use all types of sentences. They know that variety keeps their readers interested in what's going on.

ACTIVITY 28-1

Directions: Rewrite the following paragraphs with more sentence variety.

1.   This city needs to do something about all of the potholes. There are many potholes on the streets of this city. There are potholes at just about every intersection. Potholes line most of the side streets. Every day cars are ruined by all of the potholes in this city.

2.   All students should study a foreign language. Foreign languages teach them about their own language. Foreign languages give them insights into other cultures. Learning a language gives their brains a workout that they don't get from studying any other subject.

❷ *Sentence combining* (How can I put sentences together to make better ones?)

One of the best methods for coming up with more interesting sentences is sentence combining—looking for ways to connect smaller and/or repetitive sentences into longer, less predictable ones. If you're the kind of writer who writes simple sentences, this method may be especially helpful. Take a look at the following group of sentences:

The lawyer promised to sue on behalf of the accident victim.

The lawyer promised he would win the case.

The lawyer said the accident victim would receive a large settlement.

The lawyer didn't mention that he would be keeping over half of the settlement.

Notice the repetitive structure used in each sentence and how "the lawyer" is repeated in every one. Is there any way to shorten and combine these sentences? How about this?

The lawyer promised to win the case and receive a large settlement for the accident victim—although he didn't mention that he would be keeping half of it.

Your goal shouldn't be to write the longest sentences you can but to put ideas together when they make sense and avoid needlessly repeating words, ideas, and/or sentence structures.

ACTIVITY 28-2

Directions: Combine the following groups of sentences where possible to make fewer, more interesting sentences.

1. The climate here is too hot.
   The climate here is too muggy.
   It rains every day.
   The ground is always wet.

   _____

   _____

2. Raising children isn't easy.
   It is time-consuming.
   It requires patience.
   It requires money.

   _____

   _____

3. Many people are playing doctor in their own lives.
   They buy vitamins at health food stores.
   They buy natural supplements at health food stores.
   Some of these supplements include gingko and St. John's wort.
   They also buy echinacea.

   _____

   _____

   _____

4. Every New Year's Eve I make several resolutions.
   I plan to eat less.
   I plan to have more fun.
   I say I'll read a book every week.
   I say I'll watch less television.
   By the middle of the year, I've lost track of my resolutions.
   I'm back in my same old rut.

   _____

   _____

   _____

5. Abstract art confuses people.
Sometimes it frightens them.
They want to know the subject of the painting they are looking at.
They fee unsettled when they see only shapes and colors.

_____

_____

_____

❸ *Effective transitions* (How do I move from one idea to another?)

Transitions help to <u>tran</u>sport your reader from one idea to another. They help create smooth connections that take the reader from sentence to sentence and paragraph to paragraph. (Here are some things that transitions can do.)

◆ Show sequence by using such words and phrases as *first* (or *the first reason*), *second, third, to begin with, in addition, also, next, then, another reason, later, finally, last, in conclusion, to wrap up.*

There are many reasons I decided to become a doctor. First, I have always enjoyed helping other people. Second, when I was young, I had my tonsils out and become fascinated by life in a hospital. Third, I know that doctors make a good salary and are well respected by the communities they serve.

◆ Show another opinion through such words and phrases as *but, yet, although, on the contrary, on the other hand, in contrast, even though.*

Many people choose the field of medicine for the wrong reasons. They want to earn a very high salary or become really popular with the opposite sex. I, in contrast, have no such goals.

◆ Show examples by using such words and phrases as *for instance, for example, such as,* and *once.*

There are many specialties in the medical field. Some people, for example, choose pediatrics because they want to work with children.

ACTIVITY 28-3

Directions: Underline the transition words you find in the following paragraphs.

1.   Being married as a teenager isn't easy. First of all, there's the problem of the money you need. Teenagers usually can't compete for high-paying jobs. Also, it is difficult for people who are not twenty one to find housing. Landlords won't rent to teenagers unless someone over twenty one will be living on the premises. Finally, most teenagers are used to going out with their friends and having fun whenever they want. Teenagers who are married don't have that option.

2.   Cafeterias are, in many ways, superior to restaurants! At a cafeteria, customers can put together the exact meals they want—from a salad and soup, or neither, to a variety of desserts. At a restaurant, on the other hand, customers can only order the meal as it is described on the menu, and frequently they aren't allowed to make substitutions. As a cafeteria, customers can leave a small tip or no tip at all. On the contrary, at a restaurant, they are expected to tip between 10 and 20 percent. Cafeterias are informal and inexpensive whereas restaurants are frequently formal and high-priced.

Directions: Find a newspaper or magazine article you can clip and bring to class. Underline any transitions you see.

Transitions can be used in other ways. Here is a list of options.

◆ **Repeat an important word from the previous paragraph.**

Many renegade members of Congress rate their consciences without regard to their party's line on any given issue.

These renegade members are frequently lauded for their bravery but just as frequently lack party backing when they are up for reelection.

◆ **Using the same words, refer to a previous idea.**

. . . Sigmund Freud, in his psychological studies, identified what he called the id, the ego, and the superego.

Freud's belief in the id, the ego, and the superego led him to draw certain conclusions about the best way to treat patients with emotional problems.

◆ **Using a pronoun, refer to a person or idea just mentioned in the previous paragraph.**

After a closed-door meeting, many members of the city council urged the mayor to resign. In an announcement to reporters, however, he made it clear that he has no intention of resigning and openly dared the council to try to force him out of office.

29
DANGER ZONES IN DEVELOPING YOUR STYLE

Successful writers know that a piece of writing is never really finished and can always benefit from another look. So, after working on your sentences in the writing and revising stages, you will still have other areas where you can polish your writing—especially in the danger zones, the areas described in the following sections.

Clichés

One simple way you can make your writing more effective is by avoiding **clichés**—expressions that were once fresh and interesting ways to say things but through years of use have become stale. Look at the following sentences:

> When Cedric received first prize at the custom car show, Juanita was green with envy. He reminded her that he'd earned his success by the sweat of his brow.

Do you see any familiar phrases? How about "green with envy" and "by the sweat of his brow"? Just about everyone has used these expressions, and it is boring to see them again and again. Just stating the facts simply works better.

> When Cedric received first prize at the custom car show, Juanita was jealous. He reminded her that he'd earned his success by hard work.

The best way to eliminate clichés from your writing is to become more aware of them—and to wipe them out when you see them. How many of the following common clichés have you used in your writing?

add insult to injury
after all is said and done
beyond a shadow of a doubt
busy as a bee
calm before the storm
clear as a bell
depths of despair
easier said than done
few and far between
in no uncertain terms
in this day and age
last but not least
make a long story short
momentous decision
ripe old age
sadder but wiser
twist of fate
viselike grip
white as a sheet

ACTIVITY 29-1

Directions: Find five clichés to add to the list above.

1. _____

2. _____

3. _____

4. _____

5. _____

ACTIVITY 29-2

Directions: Cross out the clichés in the following sentences and replace them with direct, simple language.

1. I hope to live to a ripe old age.

2. The president was in the depths of despair after the defeat of his tax bill.

3. Babysitting for two five-year-olds keeps Mr. Waylon as busy as a bee.

4. In a cruel twist of fate, Juanita lost her purse on the same day that her rent was due.

5. Enrolling in college was a momentous decision for me.

Wordiness

When you're writing, and especially when you're revising, it is important to eliminate wordiness—the use of unnecessary words that take up space and slow your reader. Look at the following sentences:

> As the architect of large, tall skyscrapers, Louis Sullivan was a man who had no peers.

> As the architect of skyscrapers, Louis Sullivan had no peers.

Which of these sentences works the best? The second one is better because it is simple and direct and contains no unnecessary words. Isn't "skyscraper" by definition "large" and "tall"? Do we need to be told that Louis Sullivan was "a man"?

When an instructor assigns you an essay of a certain number of words, it may be tempting to pad your writing to make the count. But trust us, this isn't a good idea. The reader can always tell if you are adding unneeded words. When you use just the words you need, your writing is tight and energetic. Compare the following sentences:

Personally, in my opinion, I believe that crime is on the rise due to the fact that more people are abusing drugs. (22 words)

I believe that crime is on the rise because more people are abusing drugs. (14 words)

In the second sentence, the writer uses eight fewer words to say the same thing that the first sentence says. The writing is clear and direct and will keep readers reading (the ultimate goal of any writer!).

Some wasted words crop up regularly, and you should familiarize yourself with them. Here is a list:

Wasted Words	Better to Say
due to the fact that	because
in the modern society we live in today	today
I mentally thought to myself	I thought
my heart beat in my chest	my heart beat
at this point in time	now
personally, in my opinion	I think
he is a man who likes	he likes
the reason is because	the reason is *or* because

ACTIVITY 29-3

Directions: Cut the wasted words from the following sentences.

1. The coach is a man who likes players who are people who don't give up.

2. When Aunt Darlene didn't call, Juanita mentally thought to herself that there must be a problem.

3. The doctor said there is a reason to be optimistic at this point in time.

4. The museum contains many ancient old artifacts.

5. People in today's society do not know how to save and conserve money.

ACTIVITY 29-4

Directions: Which sentence of the following pairs of sentences is better? Think about wasted words when you make your choices. Circle the better of the two sentences.

1. When the figure skater failed to win a medal, the reason was because she fell on the wet, slippery ice during her routine.

   The figure skater failed to win a medal because she fell during her routine.

2. Investors in the modern society we live in today want profitable investments that make a lot of money.

   Today's investors want profitable investments.

3. When I saw the accident, I mentally thought to myself, I wonder whether someone has called the police.

   When I saw the accident, I wondered whether someone had called the police.

4. The company is now reevaluating its hiring policies because a former job applicant sued them.

   The company is reevaluating its hiring policies at this point in time due to the fact that a former job applicant sued them.

5. Personally, in my opinion, I think that no one should play tackle football without a helmet.

   I think that no one should play tackle football without a helmet.

Repetition

No one likes to hear the same thing over and over again. If you really want your reader to stay involved with what you are saying, you will need to cut out any needless repetition. Look at the following sentences:

It's great having an extended family. My extended family includes aunts and uncles and cousins. These aunts and uncles and cousins live in a two-block radius around my house. We've started to call this two-block radius "the family compound."

Notice how the writer picks up a phrase in each sentence and carries it on to the next one. This may be a good way of staying focused in the early draft of an essay, but for a final draft, it is unnecessarily repetitious. The writer appears to be struggling to come up with the next sentence, trying to stretch out a small amount of content. Ideally, your writing will appear to be effortless.

> It's great to live in an extended family. Mine includes uncles, aunts, and cousins—all of us living in a two-block radius around my house that we call "the family compound."

In the revised example, all of the needless repetition has been cut, and the writing now seems less labored—effortless. Every time you cut an unnecessary word, your sentences become lighter and move better.

Sometimes repetition can be used for dramatic effect. "Give me liberty or death" just doesn't have the same power as "Give me liberty or give me death." Sometimes repetition sets up a rhythm that pleases the ear and eye of the reader. The trick is to be aware that you are repeating something and know why you are doing it.

ACTIVITY 29-5

Directions: Eliminate any unnecessary repetition you find in the following sentences.

1. Aunt Darlene walked over to the post office and walked over to the library before returning home.

2. My writing is better than my writing used to be.

3. Learning to make stained glass windows or learning to make lampshades can be very rewarding.

4. Children in today's world must face all of the problems of today's world.

5. Photographs tell us about the values of the people in the pictures and how they felt about each other.

ACTIVITY 29-6

Directions: Rewrite the following paragraphs to remove needless repetition.

1. Violent video games should be outlawed. These video games contain images that stimulate players into wanting to commit violent acts in real life. These violent acts don't seem to have any consequences in the video games, so the players think they don't have any consequences in real life.

2. Sunday morning is my favorite time of the week. On Sunday morning I slowly read the morning newspaper. The newspaper always contains the most interesting stories on Sunday morning. After I read the Sunday morning newspaper, I fix myself a large breakfast. This large breakfast consists of eggs, grits, toast and coffee—all of my favorites.

Passive Voice

Successful writers know that it is generally better to use **active** verbs and avoid using **passive** verbs. What do we mean by this? Verbs are in the *active* voice when they express an action performed by their subjects:

The old man paid his bills.

Verbs are in the *passive* voice when they express an action performed on their subjects or when the subjects are the result of the action:

The bills were paid by the old man.

When you think about it, it just makes sense that writing sentences in the active voice will make your writing livelier and more interesting to read. The passive voice can lead to monotonous and awkward sentences. Look at the following sentences:

A good time was had by everyone. (passive voice)

Everyone had a good time. (active voice)

Bridge was played by the residents of the retirement home. (passive voice)

The residents of the retirement home played bridge. (active voice)

In each case, the active voice sentence is more energetic (and expressed in fewer words). The action is expressed directly (Bill throws the ball.) instead of indirectly (The ball is thrown by Bill.)

Read over the following paragraph and notice how the passive voice causes awkwardness:

When she graduated from college, a new Mazda was purchased by Kim and a new car trip to California was taken by her. This month-long trip was enjoyed very much, but then her job was about to begin. The car was sold by her and a flight back to Chicago was booked. The real world was entered by Kim on the first Monday in August.

The use of passive voice makes the writing in this paragraph monotonous and difficult to read. Notice how the paragraph changes when the verbs are expressed in the active voice:

When Kim graduated from college she purchased a new Mazda and took a trip to California. She enjoyed this month long trip very much, but then her job was about to begin. She sold the car and booked a flight back to Chicago. Kim entered the real world on the first Monday in August.

ACTIVITY 29-7

Directions: Rewrite the following sentences changing the verbs from passive voice to active voice.

1. New laws regarding national parks were passed by the Senate.

_____

_____

2. The team's final games were played at the old stadium.

_____

_____

3. The computers had been fixed by the technicians.

_____

_____

4. Last week's test results were explained by the teacher and new lab partners were assigned.

_____

_____

5. The lyrics of the song had been forgotten by the choir members, so they were made up as they went along.

_____

_____

Misplaced Modifiers

A modifier is a word or group of words that describes something. When modifiers are misplaced, they alter the writer's meaning. Take a look at the following sentence:

Tasting delicious and creamy, Aunt Darlene wanted a recipe for the candy.

What is delicious and creamy, Aunt Darlene or the candy? The candy is, of course, but by misplacing the modifier ("tasting delicious and creamy") the

"Wearing a leather harness, my grandmother takes our dog for a walk."

Misplaced modifiers can be confusing

writer leaves the meaning in doubt and has written a potentially embar-
rassing sentence. Since it is the candy that tastes "delicious and creamy"
and not Aunt Darlene, this information needs to be repositioned next to
the candy:

> Aunt Darlene wanted a recipe for the candy that tasted delicious and creamy.

In thinking about modifiers, remember one basic rule: Keep related
words together. An "*ing*" phrase ("basking in the sun," "running down St.
Charles Avenue") at the beginning of a sentence should refer to the *subject* of
the sentence.

> Basking in the sun, my brother forgot about his troubles.
>
> Running down St. Charles Avenue, the streetcar picks up many passengers.

Also be sure not to put words in the wrong place, as in this example:

> The new principal wants to eliminate dances at Willow Grove South.

The writer of this sentence wants to say that the principal has eliminated
all dances. Is that what he has said? Doesn't it sound like the writer is saying
that the principal wants to eliminate dances held on school grounds? By
rearranging the words of this sentence, the meaning becomes clear:

> The new principal at Willow Grove South wants to eliminate dances.

To catch problems with misplaced modifiers, you need to read your work
over carefully and think about what you mean to say.

ACTIVITY 29-8

Directions: Rewrite the following sentences to eliminate all misplaced modifiers.

1. The senator asked her constituents full of gratitude and respect to vote for
   her again.

_____

_____

2. Playing the stock market wisely, the investments made by the Parkers grew quickly in value.

_____

_____

3. Designed for today's road surfaces, consumers are eager to buy the new tires.

_____

_____

4. Reigning as king of carnival, the parade was led by Mr. Waylon.

_____

_____

5. The gardener began mowing the lawn happy to get the job.

_____

_____

Nonparallel Construction

In your math classes you have probably talked about parallel lines—straight lines that are equidistant and will never intersect. The concept of parallelism can also be applied to writing, especially writing where you end up listing things. The rule of parallel construction simply states that these items must "match" in the way they are expressed. Look at this sentence:

Before we left the laboratory, we were given the jobs of sweeping the floor, washing test tubes and to lock up.

Does this sound right to you? What if we wrote the sentence this way?

Before we left the laboratory we were given the jobs of sweeping the floor, washing test tubes, and locking up.

Does this sound better to you? It should. In this second example, the activities are listed in a parallel way. Each activity is expressed as an *"ing"* word (sweep*ing*, wash*ing*, lock*ing*). In the first example, two were "ing" words and one ("lock") was not. When you express your ideas in a parallel way, you make your reader's job easier.

Parallelism is something to check for as you revise. Make sure that each sentence is as clearly and smoothly written as it can be. If you come across a sentence that doesn't sound right, check and see if a parallelism problem is the cause.

ACTIVITY 29-9

Directions: Look for problems in parallel construction in the following sentences. Rewrite them in the space provided.

1. Entering college meant making my own schedule, buying my own books, and I got my own apartment.

_____

_____

2. Over the years she had many summer jobs including being a lifeguard at a country club, leading raft expeditions in Colorado, and aerobics instructor at a health club.

_____

_____

_____

3. Coco has always admired Juanita for her excellent study habits, her courage, and playing fair.

_____

_____

4. Good nutrition means eating fruits and vegetables, taking vitamins if necessary, and to avoid too many snack foods.

_____

_____

5. My next car will get fifty miles to the gallon, a leather interior, and chrome wheels.

_____

_____

DEVELOPING STYLE **Q&A**

Q   What is the easiest way to improve my style?

A   Make all of your choices carefully as a writer. Think about each word you choose and each sentence and paragraph you write. Believe in your ability to write well and take the time to do it. In general, your style will develop over time. The more reading and writing you do, the more effective and engaging your style will be.

Q   How can I develop a style that's distinctive?

A   Be natural. Use words and phrases that you're comfortable with, as long as they're appropriate to your audience (see p. 9). Avoiding clichés is one way to keep your writing different from everyone else's.

Q   Why do fools fall in love?

A   Apparently they can't help it.

PART 7

AVOIDING THE FATAL FOUR

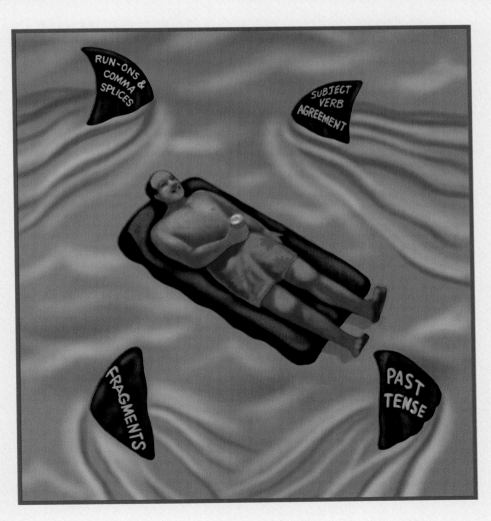

30
THE FATAL FOUR

Mistakes happen. Every writer who has ever lifted a pen or pencil or placed hands on a computer keyboard has made a grammatical error. Most of us make lots of them as we draft what we want to say. Before we show our work to other people, though, we want to clean up our manuscripts as much as we can. That means being able to recognize grammatical problems and knowing how to correct them.

After you've finished drafting a piece of writing, you should read it over several times and one of these times should be devoted to the most serious grammatical problems, what we call the *Fatal Four:*

❶ Fragments

❷ Run-ons and comma splices

❸ Subject/verb agreement

❹ Verb tense

These are the errors that can cause the most problems. Your readers may not understand what you have to say, and they may lose confidence in your ideas. Read on and find out how to protect yourself from the Fatal Four.

31

HAVE I WRITTEN A COMPLETE SENTENCE OR A FRAGMENT?

Proofreading is something you should do only after you've finished writing an essay, letter, or anything else you expect others to read. If you worry too much about grammar and spelling while you write, it can keep you from coming up with your best ideas and expressing yourself fully and most convincingly. But once you have finished your draft, you need to sweat these details. We've just covered the process of writing a paper from generating ideas to writing clear, convincing development paragraphs, from writing introductions that will grab the reader's attention to powerful conclusions. Now it's time to turn our attention to the very important final step in writing successfully: proofreading for grammar problems.

Is It a Sentence?

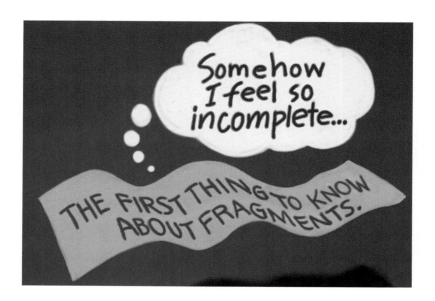

Most everyone knows what a sentence is: a group of words that starts with a capital letter at the beginning and a period at the end. What could be more simple? Actually it's not so simple. A capital letter at the beginning and a period at the end could also describe a fragment. Sentences are the basic element of your writing, and you need to know everything you can about how they work. When you proofread your writing, you're going to need to check your sentences first.

WHAT IS A FRAGMENT?

A *fragment* is a group of words with a capital letter at the beginning and a period at the end. It looks like a sentence, but it's not. You may have heard fragments described as: an incomplete thought, a dependent clause, or missing a subject or verb. We believe there's an easier way to identify fragments and correct them.

There is only one way to find a fragment: You must be able to determine for sure whether or not you have a *sentence*. There is no "almost" or "kind of" as far as sentences are concerned. A group of words is either a sentence or it's not. Here are some rules that will help you determine whether you've written a sentence.

◆ **Every sentence must have a subject and verb.**

This is a simple rule, but it won't help you if you don't know how to find a subject and verb. The verb is a word that expresses action or helps to make a statement. Look for it first when deciding whether you have a fragment or a sentence. Here are some tips to follow in locating the verb of a sentence.

Finding the Verb

❶ Ask yourself if the word expresses what someone or something *does* in the present or *did* in the past.

The cat jumped over the fence.

What did the cat do? The cat "jumped."

❷ Keep an eye out for the following words in a sentence. They're almost always going to be verbs.

am	can	did
are	could	do

does	might	should
had	must	was
has	seem	were
have	seemed	will
is	seems	would
may	shall	

❸ Don't be fooled by *-ing* words. Despite the fact that they might seem to convey actions, they are never verbs when used by themselves, no matter how much action they seem to show. Words like *kicking, cooking, swinging, tasting* can only be verbs if you add a form of the verb "to be" (*is* kicking, *was* cooking, etc.) which is known as the progressive tense. No *-ing* word used by itself can function as the verb in a sentence. You have no choice but to keep on looking for a verb.

The cat tries jumping over the fence.

The verb in this sentence is "tries," not "jumping."

❹ Don't be fooled by infinitives ("To" plus a verb—*to kick, to cook, to swing*—got it?). They will never funciton as the verb in a sentence.

The cat tries to jump over the fence.

Can "to jump" be the verb? No, it's still "tries."

❺ Watch out for the word "be" by itself. It will almost never be the verb in your sentence.

The cat be trying to jump over the fence.

"Be" cannot be the verb because it is by itself and "trying" cannot be the verb because it is an *-ing* word. In spite of the capital letter at the beginning and the period at the end, this is not a sentence. It's a fragment because it doesn't have a verb.

ACTIVITY 31-1

Directions: Try the rules out on these to see how many verbs you can find. Underline them.

1. To walk or to run. (to + verb rule)

2. Dancing on the ceiling. ("ing" word by itself)

3. We should go home now. (verb)

4. The teacher talking a long time after the bell.

5. Juanita and Cedric went bowling last weekend.

Finding the Subject

Once you've found the verb in your sentence, you're ready to find the subject. The simple thing to do is to ask yourself who or what does the action in the present or did it in the past. Who or what *is* something or *was* something in the past?

Mr. Waylon sang a lullaby to his pet turtle.

Tourism is good for our city.

Keep in Mind

The subject of a sentence will never be part of a prepositional phrase. (In case you don't remember, a *preposition* is a word used to show the relation of a noun or pronoun to another word in the sentence, and a *prepositional phrase* is a group of words that begins with a preposition.)

<u>on</u> the house	<u>in</u> the house	<u>with</u> the house
<u>upon</u> the house	<u>within</u> the house	<u>at</u> the house
<u>above</u> the house	<u>inside</u> the house	<u>by</u> the house
<u>over</u> the house	<u>beside</u> the house	<u>of</u> them
<u>below</u> the house	<u>under</u> the house	<u>among</u> them
<u>behind</u> the house	<u>from</u> the house	<u>without</u> them
<u>beneath</u> the house	<u>to</u> the house	<u>except</u> them
<u>around</u> the house	<u>into</u> the house	<u>during</u> winter
<u>past</u> the house	<u>toward</u> the house	<u>before</u> winter
<u>across</u> the house	<u>against</u> the house	<u>until</u> winter
<u>through</u> the house	<u>like</u> the house	

Read this list over several times and familiarize yourself with it, but don't worry about memorizing it. There's a copy of it on the verb card you will find at the front of the book.

ACTIVITY 31-2

Directions: Locate the subjects of the sentences below. Put parentheses around any prepositional phrases (so you can eliminate them); then put a "V" under verbs and an "S" under subjects.

1. The new houses on this street are made of brick.

2. Teachers give tests on a regular basis.

3. One of my uncles decided to go to graduate school.

4. Cedric and Juanita started to look for a present to give Aunt Darlene.

5. The governor plans to propose a new holiday called Governor's Day.

Another guideline to keep in mind when searching for the subject is that when a sentence begins with "there" or "here," the subject comes after the verb. For example, look at the following sentence:

There is a bowl of apples on the table.

Now ask yourself who or what is on the table. Since "bowl" follows the verb "is," then "bowl" is the subject.

There is a tricky situation you should know about. The only time you can have a sentence without a subject is when the subject is understood—in other words, when the subject is "you." This is called the "You Understood Rule."

Look at these sentences:

Bring the kids.

Take your time.

Get out of here this instant!

To whom are they addressed? To *you*. Sentences that use the You Understood Rule must be a command or request (Bring the kids), and the "left out" subject can only be the word, "you."

So let's review what we know so far: *Every sentence must have a subject and verb.* But that's not all there is to it. There's a second part to the rule, and that is that *the subject and verb cannot be cancelled out by converter words.*

Converter Words

Converter words are words that convert, or change, sentences into fragments. They take perfectly good subjects and verbs and turn them into subjects and verbs that don't work on their own. This is how it works:

Juanita began skydiving.

Is this a sentence? Yes. Definitely. It has a verb (*began*) and a subject (*Juanita*). Look at what happens, though, when we add one little word:

When Juanita began skydiving.

You still have your subject (*Juanita*) and your verb (*began*). There's a capital letter at the beginning and a period at the end, but is it a sentence? No. Words like *when* and the other ones you see on the list below turn a perfectly good sentence into a fragment.

after	unless
although	until
as, as if	what, whatever
because	when, whenever
before	where, wherever
how	whether
if, even if	which, whichever
in order that	while
since	who, whom
that, so that	whose
that (can be hidden)	why

This is another list you need to be familiar with but don't need to memorize. You can find this list on the card at the front of this book whenever you want to review the rules.

A converter word cancels out the subject and verb. You can still see them in the sentence, of course, but for all intents and purposes you don't have a subject and verb.

When Juanita began skydiving.
       S   V

In the previous example, "Juanita" and "began" have been cancelled out by the converter word "when." This means you have to look elsewhere for a subject and verb. While "skydiving" could be a subject, is it the subject here? If so, is "when" the verb? Of course not. So . . . "When Juanita began skydiving" is not a sentence.

In order to make "When Juanita began skydiving" into a sentence, you'll have to add a subject and verb. Remember your rule: *Every sentence must have a subject and verb that are not cancelled out by converter words*. How about this:

When Juanita began skydiving, her mother cried.

Have you added a verb? Is there a word that tells what someone did? Yes, the word "cried." Who cried? Jaunita's mother.

Take the time to check any suspicious-looking words against your list of converter words. In this example, is "skydiving" a converter word? No, it's not on the list. So do you see any word that would cancel out the subject and verb "she cried?" No. Therefore, the example (When Juanita began skydiving, her mother cried) is a complete sentence—guaranteed. You can always check a sentence out to be sure it's a sentence: If a group of words has a subject and a verb that are not cancelled out, it's a sentence. *Note*: A converter word cancels out only what it is connected to in meaning. For example:

After Cedric ate lunch he took a nap.

("After" means after Cedric ate, not after he took a nap.)

or,

After lunch Cedric took a nap.

(Does "after" mean after lunch or after Cedric took a nap. Because "after" isn't connected to Cedric in meaning, it doesn't cancel out the subject and verb.)

ACTIVITY 31-3

Directions: Look at each of the following groups of words. If it's a sentence, put "S" in the blank. If it's a fragment, put an "F."

_____ 1. Parents make mistakes.

_____ 2. Although they try hard.

_____ 3. Not knowing how to listen.

_____ 4. When they talk to you.

_____ 5. They are just too busy.

The Hidden "That"

Now that you have your basic rule (*every sentence must have a subject and verb that are not canceled out by converter words*), is that all you need to know? Not exactly. One of the converter words, "that," doesn't even have to appear in the sentence to cancel out the subject and verb. It sounds pretty weird, doesn't it? It won't be so strange once we explain it.

The clothes they bought.

Is this a sentence or a fragment? Let's go through the process step by step. Is there a verb—a word that tells what someone does or will do? (Yes, the word "bought.") Who or what "bought?" ("They" bought.) Is "clothes" a converter word? (No.) Looks OK, doesn't it? You've found your subject and verb and there's no converter word to cancel them out. Looks good, but there's one more thing you need to check.

The clothes that they bought.

Is this a sentence or a fragment? Keep in mind that a hidden converter word works the same way as one that appears in the sentence. It cancels out the subject and verb that follows it.

The clothes ^{that} they bought.
             S   V

ACTIVITY 31-4

Directions: Find the hidden "that" in the following examples. Insert it where it belongs.

1. The car I rented.

2. A book I want to recommend.

3. The stuffed panda the little girl left at school.

4. One vacation he never forgot.

5. A computer she built by herself.

Now that you've located the hidden converter word "that," how can you turn these fragments into sentences? There are two possibilities:

❶ *Add something to the end.* Keep in mind that whatever you add, you must end up with a subject and verb that aren't canceled out.

The clothes they bought look great.
    S   V

The clothes they bought were bargains.
    S   V

The clothes they bought feel comfortable.
    S   V

Note: The subject and verb don't have to be next to each other.

❷ *Add something to the beginning.* We have the same warning for you here—no matter what you add, you need to wind up with a subject and verb that aren't canceled out.

Cedric laughed at the clothes they bought.
  S   V

They returned the clothes they bought.
  S   V

I filled my closet with the clothes they bought.
S V

Exception to the rule: Watch out for "that" when it is the subject of the sentence.

That is the shirt he bought.

How can you tell when "that" is a converter word and when "that" is used as a subject? Here's a simple method. If you can substitute "this" for "that" and it makes sense, then "that" is **not** a converter word; it's a subject. Let's see how this works.

The cookies that he baked.

Can you say, "The cookies this I baked?" Of course this makes no sense, so "that" is a converter word. Now look at another example:

That cookie is burned!

Can you say, "This cookie is burned?" Yes you can, so "that" is a subject. Okay, before we do some practice, let's review our basic rule: *Every sentence must have a subject and verb that aren't cancelled out by converter words.* When you're checking for fragments, keep the following tips in mind:

❶ There are certain words that are always verbs. (Use the list on p. 219).

❷ No *-ing* words by themselves will function as verbs.

❸ The word "to" plus a verb is never a verb.

❹ A verb is the word in the sentence that tells what someone or something does in the present or did in the past.

❺ The subject of a sentence will never be part of a prepositional phrase.

❻ The only time you can have a sentence without a subject is when the sentence is a command and the subject left out is the word "you."

❼ The converter word "that" can be hidden.

❽ "That" is not a converter word when it is the subject of a sentence (when "this" can be used in its place).

ACTIVITY 31-5

Directions: Look at each of the following groups of words. If it's a complete sentence, put an "S" in the blank. If it's a fragment, put an "F."

1. _____ Before the last game of the season.

2. _____ Singing in the shower.

3. _____ Because Juanita's hard drive crashed.

4. _____ Watching cartoons and eating waffles on Saturday morning.

5. _____ If Cedric finds his keys before lunch.

6. _____ Behind the teacher's desk.

7. _____ The three main reasons I applied to college.

8. _____ Listening to my favorite CDs.

9. _____ After the subway train arrived at the station.

10. _____ A mayor who will balance the budget.

11. _____ That cake is delicious.

12. _____ My brothers came over to play basketball.

13. _____ Aunt Darlene racing to the grocery store for a loaf of bread.

14. _____ Believing that the enemy was about to attack.

15. _____ When Cedric invited Juanita to go bowling.

16. _____ Those buildings over on Market Street.

17. _____ Reading folktales from many different countries.

18. _____ Where the bridge crosses the river.

19. _____ The kind of apples I love.

20. _____ Timmy called out to the waitress at the counter.

21. _____ To find solutions to the school's problems.

22. _____ A beautiful new car with all of the luxury options.

23. _____ Shopping for new clothes.

24. _____ The house I remodeled two years ago.

25. _____ She began to write the story of her whole life.

26. _____ Choosing the best paint for Timmy's Restaurant.

27. _____ Because he didn't have a map, he got lost.

28. _____ While Mr. Waylon thought about running for a seat on the city council.

29. _____ Excellent videos I always enjoy.

30. _____ Walking is good for your health.

ACTIVITY 31-6

Directions: Look at each of the following groups of words. If it's a complete sentence, put an "S" in the blank. If it's a fragment, put an "F." Keep your fragment card out and review as necessary.

1. _____ Watching the Olympic trials on a hot July afternoon.

2. _____ Being a professional athlete isn't easy.

3. _____ Before the next presidential election takes place.

4. _____ If genetics research can't find an answer.

5. _____ Beneath my apartment, there are two other apartments.

6. _____ To forget his past and make a new start.

7. _____ Finding out the teacher's attendance policy.

8. _____ Driving to Oak Park to look for Frank Lloyd Wright's architecture studio.

9. _____ An incredible neighborhood where beautiful homes line both sides of the street.

10. _____ When I forgot my history book, I called my brother and asked him to bring it.

11. _____ Laughing at the dancing bear.

12. _____ Because it was crowded, Juanita left the party early.

13. _____ Because Juanita left early.

14. _____ Surfing the Internet for fun and profit.

15. _____ We the people of the United States.

16. _____ How delicious the chocolate was.

17. _____ While the magician completed his last trick.

18. _____ Where caves are plentiful.

19. _____ Since the rate hike was approved.

20. _____ Living in this city gets more expensive every day.

21. _____ Unless the president changes his mind.

22. _____ Although there are two new antipollution bills in Congress.

23. _____ If Cedric can't make it, Juanita will go in his place.

24. _____ The textbook I need.

25. _____ Whether or not global warming is a problem.

26. _____ Eating baby carrots with ranch dressing.

27. _____ How I learned to stop worrying about things I can't change.

28. _____ Playing by the rules.

29. _____ After dialing the number of the psychic hotline, I hung up.

30. _____ Raising children in today's world isn't easy.

ACTIVITY 31-7

Directions: Underline any fragments you find in the following paragraphs.

1. When you are lost or stranded. Building a fire should be your first order of business. A fire will give you confidence. It can be used for signaling help. Cooking food. Repelling dangerous wild animals. It can also be used to make useful tools.

2. Table lamps have changed over the years. Because the light source has changed from kerosene to gas to electricity. The first light bulbs were invented in 1879. Using electric lamps. Became popular in the 1890s.

3. People today are working more than ever. Using computers, fax machines, and telephones. Which should make life easier. It is amazing how technology has changed our lives. Filling our time rather than saving it.

4. That is an excellent class. The professor knows everything about art history. Can answer any question. She shows slides of important paintings. The kind of paintings that changed the art world. Her lectures are funny and interesting. The reading assignments open your eyes. Definitely not boring.

5. More and more senior citizens are returning to work. Sometimes because they need money. Sometimes because they are bored. Many companies are seeking these older workers because older workers are dependable. And happy to have a job.

WE'RE GLAD YOU ASKED
FRAGMENTS Q&A

Q Why do I see fragments in the writing of published authors?

A Sometimes writers use fragments for dramatic effect. They know when they are using them and use them in a way that enhances their writing.

Q Are fragments always short?

A No, fragments can often be quite long. Just because the writer has strung many words together doesn't mean that he or she has written a complete sentence.

Q What's the difference between a duck?

A One of its leg is both the same.

32

HAVE I WRITTEN A RUN-ON SENTENCE OR USED A COMMA SPLICE?

Now that you know more about what is and is not a sentence, you're ready to proofread for a problem that is known by many different names: CS—comma splice, RO—run-on, and FS—fused sentence. This problem occurs when the writer reaches the end of a sentence and starts another one without using punctuation correctly to show the reader what is

happening. There are two basic ways a writer can fail to separate sentences correctly:

◆ **Problem 1:** "<u>Sent Sent</u>" (Sentence no punctuation Sentence). (Run-on or Fused Sentence). In this case you see two sentences with no mark of punctuation in between:

Bill won the election he received 55 percent of the votes.

To check for this problem, you will need to identify the subjects and verbs just as you did in the last chapter. Remember the rule: *Every time you have a subject and verb that are not cancelled out by a converter word, you have a sentence.*

<u>Bill</u> <u>won</u> the election <u>he</u> <u>received</u> 55 percent of the vote.
　S　V　　　　　　S　　V

In this example, we see two subjects and two verbs—a very confusing situation.

235

32 ■ HAVE I WRITTEN A RUN-ON SENTENCE OR USED A COMMA SPLICE?

◆ **Problem 2:** <u>Sent, Sent</u> (Sentence comma Sentence). (Comma Splice)
In this case you see two sentences with a comma in between:

Bill won the election, he received 55 percent of the vote.

In order to proofread for this problem, you need to notice every subject and verb and to check carefully for converter words that might cancel them out.

So now that you know how to tell if there's a problem, what can you do about it? You have three choices to correct sentence end punctuation mistakes:

❶ <u>SENT. SENT</u> (Sentence period Sentence). Here you separate the sentences with a period.

> Bill won the election. He received 55 percent of the vote.

❷ <u>SENT, conj SENT</u> (Sentence comma conjunction Sentence). Here you separate the sentences with a comma plus a conjunction. (Examples of conjunctions include *and, but, or, for, nor, so,* and *yet.*)

> Bill won the election, and he received 55 percent of the vote.

❸ <u>SENT; SENT</u> (Sentence semicolon Sentence). Here you separate the sentences with a semicolon. Use them only when the two sentences are closely related in meaning.

> Bill won the election; he received 55 percent of the vote.

Be careful with your use of semicolons. Some people become addicted to them. They begin to think they are just the same as periods. Think of semicolons as softer, less final than periods. Use them sparingly and only when two sentences are strongly related in meaning.

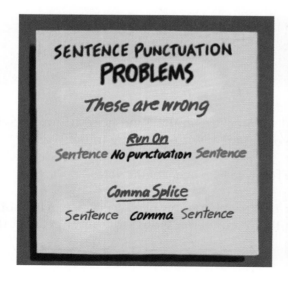

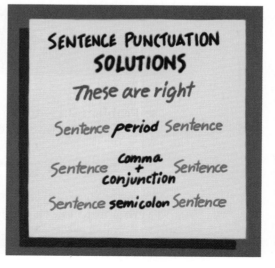

237

32 ■ HAVE I WRITTEN A RUN-ON SENTENCE OR USED A COMMA SPLICE?

Don't forget the You Understood Rule (see p. 223). You can have a sentence even though the subject doesn't actually appear.

You Bring your dancing shoes we plan to have a party.
S   V   S   V

Since in this instance we have two subjects and two verbs, this is a SENT SENT situation, and we must use one of the three methods we just discussed to correct it: We plan to have a party, so bring your dancing shoes. Before we get some practice, let's review our rules. Look at the following:

Because I had no money, I couldn't go to the movies.

How many sentences do you see here? One? Two? (Remember that "because" is a converter word.) The answer is one. Also note the correct use of the comma. Now look at the following:

I had no money. Then my father loaned me ten dollars.

How many sentences do you see here? One? Two? This time, the answer is two because "then" is not a converter word. And finally:

I had no money, then received a loan.

How many sentences do you see here? One. There's only one subject.

ACTIVITY 32-1

Directions: Make any necessary corrections in the following sentences. If the sentence is correct as it is, place "C" beside it.

1. We have several reasons they are all good ones.

2. I am repairing the house myself, it's not easy.

3. Cedric collects butterflies he thinks they're beautiful.

4. Winter is my favorite season the cold weather makes me feel alive.

5. Those oranges are delicious they just arrived from Florida.

6. My nephew walks to school every day it's about five miles.

7. Aunt Darlene knits sweaters for everyone I'm getting one next.

8. I've studied management for two years I'm very qualified for the job.

9. Juanita plans to go to law school she hopes to receive a scholarship.

10. Don't forget to call us when you get there, otherwise we'll be worried.

11. Here are the cookies you ordered I hope you like them.

12. Cedric left his Walkman on the bus Juanita found it.

13. Every summer I plant vegetables I can hardly wait for them to come up.

14. I love economics it's my most interesting class.

15. The planet Mercury is closest to the sun Pluto is the most distant.

16. Parents need to spend more time listening to their children it will make a real difference.

17. The basketball team lost every game the coach accused them of giving up.

18. Because I was late, I lost my chance to get a ticket.

19. Come over on Friday night we'll have a blast.

20. Aunt Darlene loves chocolate there's no such thing as too much as far as she's concerned.

21. Bring a jacket, don't forget your gloves.

22. Cedric and Juanita get a student discount at the theater luckily they remembered to bring their ID cards.

23. That's a great movie, it's a favorite of mine.

24. Mr. Waylon knew a good mechanic he told Aunt Darlene to call him.

25. After World War II ended, many houses were built across the United States.

26. My car broke down therefore I have no way to get home.

27. I don't drink coffee, but I still manage to get plenty of caffeine.

28. The house is very bright inside there are many windows.

29. Though Coco isn't engaged yet, she has already planned her wedding.

30. Recycling is good for our environment it just makes sense.

ACTIVITY 32-2

Directions: Make any necessary corrections in the following sentences. If the sentence is correct as it is, place a "C" beside it.

1. Having a yard sale isn't difficult, you just need to know a few tricks.

2. Set up your sale near the street if you want people to see what you've got, flaunt it.

3. Using price tags doesn't make sense yard sale shoppers know what they are willing to pay and will tell you.

4. The sale will go more smoothly if you have help you shouldn't hesitate to ask a relative or friend to join in.

5. Yard sale shoppers will buy more if the seller is friendly and helpful a successful yard sale is full of laughter and ideas on how to use all that junk.

6. If you want people to buy, be sure to organize your goods neatly, don't forget that your customers will expect to bargain.

7. Shoppers at yard sales should let the seller speak first; the seller may ask for less than you would have offered.

8. Some modern credit cards are imbedded with a computer chip, they give the consumer more security when purchasing items online.

9. These credit cards also allow consumers to gain access to private information the Internet is now a safer place.

10. All over the country parents are rediscovering the benefits of day care centers being with other children and a variety of caregivers is stimulating.

11. Parents used to prefer having their children cared for by relatives or in a neighbor's home now a majority of them are choosing day care centers.

12. Even families who can afford nannies are choosing day care centers, they see clear benefits for their children.

13. This shift to day care centers reflects the blurring line between education and caregiving parents want the educational benefits offered by day care.

14. After last month's gas bill, Coco decided to insulate her attic, she realized it would save money in the long run.

15. Coco caulked around all of her windows and doors when she realized glass storm windows would be too expensive, she made her own out of plastic.

16. A man from the gas company told her to be sure to lower her thermostat whenever she left the house this would save additional dollars.

17. Coco is pleased with this month's gas bill all of her efforts really made a difference.

18. When Timmy, the owner of Timmy's Restaurant, enrolled in cooking school, his customers rejoiced as a chef, Timmy had nowhere to go but up.

19. Timmy learned how to make beef Stroganoff, chicken Kiev, and other Russian favorites most of the time, though, his customers ordered hamburgers.

20. There are fewer than 1,000 giant pandas in existance some conservationists think we should begin cloning them.

21. Since 1996, the number of critically endangered mammals has risen from 169 to 180 the number of primates alone has risen from 13 to 19.

22. If conservationists could wave a magic wand, they would halt habitat destruction and hunting these activities continue to endanger more species every year.

241

32 ■ HAVE I WRITTEN A RUN-ON SENTENCE OR USED A COMMA SPLICE?

23. When Aunt Darlene retires, she plans to attend clown school in Florida her dream is to join a small traveling circus.

24. Aunt Darlene has begun to think about how she'll dress in a baggy suit covered with multicolored buttons and a bubble gum pink wig would be perfect.

25. When Aunt Darlene told Mr. Waylon about her dream, he laughed then he revealed that he dreamed of working as a tour guide in a cave full of bats.

26. At one time, most towns had a locally-run bookstore these stores catered to the tastes and needs of the people who lived in the town.

27. The owner of the bookstore would get to know his customers and make recommendations the owner would always keep a close eye on what books were selling and keep them in stock.

28. These bookstores were very different from each other each one reflected its owner's and a town's reading tastes visiting the town bookstore used to be a way of finding out important information about a town.

29. Chain bookstores have changed the way books are sold every mall has one, and they all look the same.

30. Small independent bookstores still exist you should make every effort to seek them out and support them by buying your books from them.

ACTIVITY 32-3

Directions: Correct any run-ons and comma splices you find in the following paragraphs.

1.   When you remember the name of a person you've recently met, you make him or her feel important you add a large measure of personal warmth to a conversation. This new acquaintance feels that you are listening. When you know someone's name, this person is no longer a stranger there is nothing like feeling you've made a new friend. Learning someone else's name is the first step.

2.   New Orleans is a great city for tourists. The French Quarter gives visitors a unique glimpse into the past they will see an extraordinary group of buildings dating from the 1700s to the present day. The food is sumptuous and extraordinary in its variety. Delicious seafood, Cajun specialities and first-rate Italian dishes can be found everywhere it is difficult to find a bad meal in this city. A perfect day in the city would include visits to the aquarium, the D-Day museum, and the Audubon Zoo, capped off by a ride on the St. Charles streetcar.

3.   Back in the 1950s no one paid for television it was commonly believed that once viewers had had TV for free, they would never pay for it. Pay cable television started very slowly HBO was the only channel. Over the years it has become increasingly popular most homes in areas served by cable are hooked up. The fees for cable television have gone up considerably in the past ten years. Many people alive today can't remember when TV was free paying for TV has become a way of life for them.

4.   Children should not have television sets in their rooms. If parents don't monitor what their children are watching, they will watch shows they shouldn't watch they will see too much violence. Television interrupts valuable study time it also keeps kids up too late. The best plan is for parents to keep the television centrally located and to control when it is turned on and off.

ACTIVITY 32-4

Putting It Together I

Directions: Correct any fragment, run-on, or comma splice errors you find in the following paragraph.

Over the years, I've encountered three kinds of teachers, the Devoted, the Divided, and the Dispossessed. And survived. Devoted teachers do their jobs with love and the best interests of their students always at heart they really get you excited about learning. Divided teachers, while pretty good at what they do, always make you feel like they're not completely into it. They arrive late and

243

32 ■ HAVE I WRITTEN A RUN-ON SENTENCE OR USED A COMMA SPLICE?

leave early. Forget your name the second the semester is over. Dispossessed teachers don't belong within ten miles of a classroom. They are bored by the subject they are teaching and bored by you.

WE'RE GLAD YOU ASKED

RUN-ONS AND COMMA SPLICES **Q&A**

Q Are there any tricks I can use to catch run-ons and comma splices?

A Try reading your work out loud. Listen for places where your voice drops in pitch, then check to see if you've come to the end of a complete sentence and whether what follows is complete as well.

Q Is one method of correcting run-ons and comma splices better than another?

A No one method is technically better than another, but semicolons are most effective when the sentences are closely related in meaning.

Q Does eating chocolate make you happy?

A Yes.

33
DO MY SUBJECTS AND VERBS AGREE?

"Sometimes I think you guys don't want peace."

Look at the following pairs of sentences:

A. He run all the way home.
B. He runs all the way home.

A. They is going to the store.
B. They are going to the store.

Which of the sentences above sound right to you? If you chose B in each case, you have a good "ear" for subject/verb agreement and can go on the basis of what sounds right in most cases. What about these?

A. One of the boys is my friend.
B. One of the boys are my friend.

A. Neither of the cars has been washed recently.
B. Neither of the cars have been washed recently.

If you chose A in both cases, you're on your way to being an expert on subject/verb agreement. Even if your ear doesn't tell you the right answer, you can become an expert by learning the rules and following three easy steps.

How to Check for Subject/Verb Agreement

❶ *Find the subject and verb in the sentence.* You've already had lots of practice with this, but don't hesitate to go back and review pages 219–222. Keep in mind that the subject is what the sentence is about, and the verb tells you what the subject does. Also remember that the subject of a sentence is never in a prepositional phrase. (See p. 222 for information on prepositional phrases.) And finally, recall that the following look like verbs but aren't really verbs:

-ing words by themselves (*rowing, waltzing, eating*)

to + verb (*to play, to write, to fall*)

be by itself

❷ *Match the subject to one of the following categories.* This rule is important because the subject tells the verb what to do. In other words, the verb will change to agree with the subject.

I

you

we

they

he, she, it

Your subject will either be the word *I, you, we, they, he, she,* or *it,* or you can match the subject with one of the following: we, they, or he, she, it. Let's see how this works:

◆ If the subject is "I" plus anyone or anything, it goes in the **we** category.

 ◆ my dog and I = we

 ◆ my best friend and I = we

 ◆ my parents and I = we

 ◆ my classmates and I = we

◆ If the subject is more than one of anything, it goes in the **they** category.

 ◆ potato chips = they

 ◆ mom and dad = they

 ◆ those CD-ROMS = they

 ◆ Mr. Waylon and Aunt Darlene = they

 ◆ her dreams = they

◆ If your subject is one of anything (one person, idea, object, feeling, place, or one whatever), it will be a **he, she,** or **it** subject.

 ◆ trash can = it

 ◆ his uncle = he

 ◆ teacher = he or she

 ◆ my desk = it

- ◆ jealousy = it
- ◆ mother = she

Keep in mind that a word can be plural without having an "s" at the end. Words like people, mice, and children don't end in "s" but they are plurals.

ACTIVITY 33-1

Directions: Match each of the words below with one of the following categories: we, they, he, she, it. Write your answer in the space provided.

1. street _____

2. pine trees _____

3. my father, my uncle, and I _____

4. pink elephants _____

5. the minister's wife _____

6. fire and ice _____

7. cereal _____

8. summer job _____

9. two summer jobs _____

10. my mechanic and I _____

11. a clarinet and two saxophones _____

12. three silly puppets _____

13. Coco's sister _____

14. singing _____

15. bouquet _____

OK, let's review what we know. To make sure that your subject and verb agree, you need to find the subject and verb and match the subject with I, you, we, they, or he, she, or it. If you're with us so far, you're ready for the third and easiest step.

❸ *Read the chart below and find the right form of the verb.*

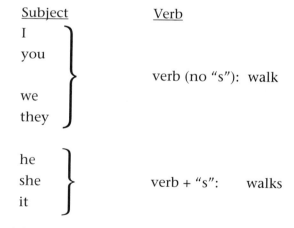

Subject	Verb
I you we they	verb (no "s"): walk
he she it	verb + "s": walks

Problems with subject and verb agreement happen in the present tense (except for "was" and "were" mistakes)—especially when you need to decide whether to add an "s" to the verb or not. If you add it where you don't need it, you have as big a problem as the place where you need it and forget to add it. Even if your "ear" tells you when to add it and when to leave it off, it helps to know why. If you follow the three steps we've been talking about, you'll always have subjects and verbs that agree.

Take a look at the following sentence:

One of the houses in my neighborhood need/needs to be painted.

Now let's go through the steps to ensure correct subject and verb agreement.

❶ *Find the subject and verb.* Is the subject "houses"? Is the subject "neighborhood"? Remember to look out for prepositional phrases! (See p. 222 to refresh your memory, or use your verb card.)

One (of the houses) (in my neighborhood) needs to be painted.

After we eliminate the prepositional phrases and discover that the subject can't be "houses" or "neighborhood," it becomes clear that the subject has to be "one."

❷ *Match the subject.* If "one" is the subject, how many things are we referring to? This one couldn't be easier:

one = one

So we match the subject up with the *he, she, it* category: One house = *it*.

❸ *Read the chart.* When you do this, you see that when the subject is *it*, you add an "s" to the end of the verb. So . . .

One of the houses in my neighborhood need<u>s</u> to be painted.

The verb now "agrees" with the subject.

ACTIVITY 33-2

Directions: Underline the correct verb in each of the following sentences.

1. The president of the company make/makes a speech.
2. That hat look/looks good on you.
3. The boy in the back of the room start/starts to cough.
4. Mr. Waylon and Coco go/goes grocery shopping every Saturday.
5. My friends and I play/plays football after school.

Group Nouns

Be ready to practice subject/verb agreement some more at the end of the chapter, but first we need to let you know about two more things that will help you make the right choices. The first thing you need to consider is **group nouns**—words like "everyone" and "everybody." Here's a list:

everyone
everybody
anyone
anybody
someone
somebody
each
either
neither

When one of these words is your subject, it matches with the *he, she, it* category.

Though "everyone" may sound like a lot of people, it actually refers to every *individual* one or one person at a time. Therefore, it matches with the *he, she, it* category. Look at *everybody*—it means "one body"—the same is true for "somebody" and "anybody." All mean one body. "Each" means "each one," and either means "either one." No matter how big the group may be in all, when one of these words is your subject, think of it as one thing and match it up in the *he, she, it* category. And that, of course, means you need an "s" on the end of the verb.

Everyone plans to be back before midnight.

Neither parent wants to take responsibility.

ACTIVITY 33-3

Directions: Underline the correct verb in each of the following sentences.

1. Anybody know/knows as much about computer repair as I do.
2. Each of the children bring/brings a bag lunch.
3. Someone has/have taken out the book I need.
4. Everybody take/takes math and English in the fall semester.
5. Neither of the teachers give/gives difficult tests.

The Verb "To Be or not To Be"

Another thing you need to keep in mind is the verb "to be," a verb unlike any other. The only way to make sure you know it will be to *memorize* the chart shown here.

To Be

If your subject is . . .	. . . your verb is	
	Present tense (now)	Past tense
I	am	was
you we they	are	were
he she it	is	was

ACTIVITY 33-4

Directions: Underline the correct verb in each of the following sentences.

1. Aunt Darlene and Juanita was/were out shopping for Cedric's present.
2. Many people be/are greedy.
3. The new civic center was/were dedicated last Thursday.
4. We was/were minding our own business.
5. One of the new girls at work is/are already my friend.

ACTIVITY 33-5

Directions: In each of the following sentences, underline the form of the verb that agrees with the subject. While you're at it, put parentheses around any prepositional phrases you find, and draw a box around the subject.

1. The magazines is/are piled up on my bedside table.

2. Juanita and Coco has/have planned a surprise party for Cedric.

3. He wants/want books and CDs for his birthday.

4. Timmy cooks/cook a platter of cheeseburgers for the party.

5. Every one of the guests brings/bring a small gift and a donation to Cedric's favorite charity.

6. The guests makes/make their own sundaes with ice cream, hot fudge, strawberry topping, whipped cream, and candy sprinkles.

7. All of the presents is/are piled on the table.

8. Cedric thanks/thank all the guests for coming.

9. Each of the guests leaves/leave with a bag of leftovers.

10. Juanita and Coco hugs/hug each other before saying goodnight.

11. My boss insists/insist that we arrive at work on time.

12. The teacher places/place the books on the table.

13. After the trial, the judge asks/ask the jury for its verdict.

14. Most of the girls plays/play soccer on Saturday afternoon.

15. Many of the boys is/are good cooks.

16. The new computers was/were paid for by the parents' association.

17. The bowl of apples is/are on the table.

18. Every one of my friends likes/like pizza.

19. Playing games is/are fun.

20. That hat belongs/belong to me.

21. My uncle and my brother invests/invest in the stock market.

22. Cedric and Coco sends/send E-mail to each other.

23. My sister and I laughs/laugh at the same jokes.

24. The library and the science building is/are right next to the student union.

25. That bank charges/charge a fee if you overdraw your account.

26. My brother and I both has/have red cars.

27. Each of my pens is/are out of ink.

28. The theater company plan/plans to present a musical this spring.

29. The band always marches/march in the 4th of July parade.

30. Both of those stores sells/sell jeans.

ACTIVITY 33-6

Directions: In each of the following sentences, underline the form of the verb that agrees with the subject. While you're at it, put parentheses around any prepositional phrases you find, and draw a box around the subject.

1. One of the main things I like about the Super Bowl is/are the commercials.

2. The other thing I like about the Super Bowl is/are all the snacks my father brings/bring.

3. Either of those books is/are perfect for reading to a two-year old.

4. That bookstore has/have books for all ages.

5. Debussy and Rachmaninoff is/are two great composers.

6. The parents' group is/are going to vote on the budget for the coming year at this week's meeting.

7. My grandparents was/were four of the kindest people I ever knew.

8. A good schedule consists/consist of courses you need in order to graduate.

9. Most of those video games involves/involve violence.

10. Whenever he's lonely, my brother asks/ask me to come over to watch a movie.

11. Missing work due to illnesses has/have been a problem for me over the past year.

12. Migratory birds fills/fill the trees at the state park.

13. Every year I takes/take some kind of arts and crafts course because I loves/love to make things.

14. The football and basketball teams has/have their own workout areas.

15. The university has/have set aside more funds for athletic programs.

16. Successful athletic programs helps/help raise funds from alumni.

17. At homecoming, the chancellor always gives/give a speech promoting school spirit.

18. The best part of the movie is when the main character loses/lose his mind.

19. Power outages is/are an increasing problem in our electricity-devouring society.

20. Two reporters from the city's newspaper was/were on the scene before long.

21. Each of my uncles has/have donated to my college fund.

22. Every time a witness testifies/testify, the jury listens/listen carefully.

23. When Juanita asks/ask him to help with the dishes, Cedric always says/say no.

24. Junk mail piles/pile up on tables all over my house.

25. Mustard and mayonnaise is/are Aunt Darlene's favorite condiments.

26. That Rolls Royce fills/fill my garage, so I will have to sell it.

27. All of the nurses believes/believe that conditions at the hospital must be improved.

28. Neither of those horses is/are friendly.

29. Figuring out your income taxes isn't/aren't easy.

30. The university pep band marches/march across the football field.

ACTIVITY 33-7

Directions: Correct any subject/verb agreement errors you find in the following paragraphs.

1.   Sunday is Juanita's day to relax and have fun. She begin by getting up late. She have a leisurely breakfast and reads the newspaper. In the afternoon, Juanita go bowling or to a movie and pick up lunch at a fast food place.

On Sunday night, she usually make spaghetti or pizza and have some friends over.

2.   Our campus need several improvements. First of all, we needs more parking. Many students has to park off campus. Secondly, we needs a cafeteria that serve decent food. The one we have now is not good. Finally, this campus be ugly. We has to do some more landscaping.

3.   Cell phones is better than traditional phones. A cell phone go with you anywhere. It fit in your pocket and is right there when you need it. If you has an emergency of some kind, all you needs to do is pull it out and make your call. With a traditional phone, you has to stay in one place if you wants a phone nearby.

ACTIVITY 33-8

Putting it Together II

Directions: Correct any problems with fragments, run-ons, comma splices, or subject/verb agreement that you find in the following paragraphs.

1.   The race begin with a one-mile swim. Piece of cake. Then you rides a bike for eighteen miles. Riding almost entirely off road. Crashes happen every few miles if your bike or your neck isn't broken, you get up and keep going. The race end with a six-mile run. If you come in first, you'll have won the Xterra World Championship.

2.   The perfect apartment for a single person have a bedroom, a living room, and a kitchen. With all of the appliances. It have a lot of storage. And plenty of electrical plugs. It's always good to have lots of windows light just make people feel good.

SUBJECT/VERB AGREEMENT **Q&A**

Q Do subject/verb agreement errors ever occur in the past tense?

A Only with "was" and "were."

Q If I can't identify the subject and verb of a sentence, will I ever be able to solve my subject/verb agreement problem?

A We're afraid not. If you have questions about how to identify subjects and verbs, see page 219.

Q Does the rain in Spain fall mainly on the plain?

A Last time we checked.

34

AM I USING THE PAST TENSE CORRECTLY?

Writers use the *past tense* to talk about anything that happened before they began writing. Whether it happened ten years, ten minutes, or ten seconds ago, it needs to be expressed in the past tense. There are a couple of basic rules you need to keep in mind in order to form the past tense of verbs:

❶ Either add *-ed* to the end of the verb or change the way you spell the verb.

She plays basketball on the school team. *(present)*

She played basketball last January. *(past—add -ed)*

He writes mystery stories in his spare time. *(present)*

Two years ago he wrote his first mystery novel. *(past—change "write" to "wrote")*

They are investing in the stock market. *(present)*

They were investing in war bonds back in the forties. *(past—change "are" to "were")*

I remember back when I was a kid.

Notice that to form the past tense you add -ed or change the spelling. There's no such word as "wroted." There's no such word as "ared." If you suspect that a verb may require a spelling change in the past tense, look it up in the dictionary. If you look up the verb "write," the dictionary will show "wrote, written" right after the word "write."

ACTIVITY 34-1

Directions: Fill in the blanks below with the correct form of the verb shown in parentheses.

1. *(to buy)* Yesterday, I _____ a basket of blueberries.

2. *(to ask)* The teacher _____ if Friday should be test day way back in December.

3. *(to bring)* Last Christmas, Mr. Waylon _____ his famous green bean casserole.

4. *(to draw)* When I was five, I _____ people with stick arms and legs.

5. *(to play)* Last summer, the children _____ in Aunt Darlene's backyard.

How are you doing? If you're not ready to go on, go back and review this material from the beginning. If you are, let's talk about another kind of past tense: the helper past (the past perfect).

❷ In the helper past, use a "helper" (*has, have,* or *had*) to show the past tense of a verb.

She bakes gingerbread men. *(present)*

Last Sunday she baked gingerbread men. *(past)*

She has baked gingerbread men every Sunday for the past three years. *(helper past tense)*

In the helper past, some past tense verbs stay the same. You just add the helper when necessary.

She watched her son's little league baseball game.

She has watched her son's little league baseball games all summer long.

Some past tense verbs take a different form in the helper past. Take a look at the list below:

been
done
drawn
gone
gotten   Only used with a helper
seen   *(has, have, had)*
taken
thrown
written

Below you will find a chart where you can look up any verbs you might be confused about. The verbs marked with an asterisk (*) are the ones that don't follow the rules. You'll want to memorize the ones you don't already know.

Verb	Present	Past	Helper Past
to be	am, is, are	was/were	been
to cut*	cut, cuts	cut	cut
to do	do, does	did	done
to draw	draw, draws	drew	drawn
to get	get, gets	got	gotten
to go	go, goes	went	gone
to have	have, has	had	had
to lay*	lay, lays	lay	laid
to lie*	lie, lies	lay	lain
to put*	put, puts	put	put
to see	see, sees	saw	seen
to take	take, takes	took	taken
to throw	throw, throws	threw	thrown

If you keep the following rules in mind, forming the past tense correctly shouldn't be difficult.

❶ To form the past tense, either add -ed or change the spelling. Never do both!

❷ Get to know the verbs that have a special form in the helper past, and then use them only for the helper past. Don't switch between regular past and helper past. (Use your chart if you aren't sure.)

In addition to these rules, there are a few tips that can help you form the past tense. First, the helper agrees with the subject.

He has eaten his lunch.

They have eaten their lunches.

If you need any help, go back and review your subject/verb agreement rules. Second, if there's an "n" sound at the end of the verb *(shown, broken, taken)*, you almost always use a helper.

ACTIVITY 34-2

Directions: The following sentences are written in the present tense. Rewrite them in the space below so that all verbs are past tense.

1. Habitat for Humanity builds houses for people who don't have enough money.

2. Twenty volunteers arrive at the empty lot.

3. First they lay a foundation.

4. Then they build supporting walls.

5. Each week they perform new tasks.

6. After several months, the house is finished.

7. The volunteers give a party for the new homeowner.

8. The homeowner writes thank-you notes to each volunteer.

9. Owning a home makes her feel good.

10. When Habitat for Humanity begins building its next house, the homeowner joins in.

11. The weather is getting warmer.

12. The new theater complex opens on Friday.

13. The raid on the supply depot draws enemy fire.

14. Cedric goes on a major fishing trip every July.

15. Mr. Waylon has agreed to go with him.

16. The photographer takes pictures for the campus newspaper.

17. She does well for her age.

18. The car needs new spark plugs and an air filter.

19. I always get a cold right before my birthday.

20. They are looking for solutions to the city's budget problems.

ACTIVITY 34-3

Directions: Check the verb tenses in the following sentences. If the tense is correct, put a "C" in the space provided. If it's not correct, put an "X" and make the necessary changes.

_____ 1. She had not spoke to the teacher yet.

_____ 2. Cedric losted his new wallet.

_____ 3. The sisters buyed matching dresses.

_____ 4. Those new computers have broke down five times.

_____ 5. I didn't believe what she said.

_____ 6. Aunt Darlene has ask me to go to the Pretzel Museum with her.

_____ 7. Timmy's Restaurant has closed for the day.

_____ 8. The problems cause by gambling have gotten worse.

_____ 9. Jaunita use to make her pet cat wear a feathered hat.

_____ 10. The money for the stadium the city built last year come from our taxes.

ACTIVITY 34-4

Directions: Underline the correct verb in the sentences below.

1. Yesterday my lunch consist/consisted of two carrots and a celery stalk.
2. The cost of living went/gone up.
3. Cedric had threw/thrown a wild pitch.
4. I saw/seen some great paintings at the museum.
5. When the new boss came in, I ask/asked for a raise.

ACTIVITY 34-5

Directions: The following sentences are in the present tense. Rewrite them in the space below in the past tense.

1. Architects are studying how the school environment affects students.

2. Studies show that students' test scores increase in buildings that open to fresh air.

3. Lots of natural daylight also helps.

4. Students need school buildings that make them feel optimistic.

5. Studies reveal that parents who like the way their child's school looks become more involved.

6. Cedric's band plays at Café Bongo and wows the audience.

7. His solo receives a standing ovation.

8. The music critic for the local newspaper calls him "the next big thing."

9. The new governor thanks the voters for their support and asks for their assistance.

10. The legislature considers the governor's proposals and then rejects them.

11. The bill to raise property taxes fails to pass, and the governor becomes angry.

12. He tells the citizens that the taxes are going to be used to improve education.

13. He urges them to write or call their legislators.

14. The citizens respond, and on a second try the bill passes.

15. If my cough persists, I am going to see a doctor.

16. Every summer I take the ferry to Ship Island.

17. It takes courage to admit it when you make a mistake.

18. Juanita climbs the stairs to her apartment.

19. She opens her door and sets down her groceries.

20. She falls back when Cedric and Darlene jump from the shadows and shout, "Surprise!"

ACTIVITY 34-6

Directions: Rewrite the following paragraphs in the past tense.

1.   Aunt Darlene is a Habitat for Humanity volunteer. She helps in the building of three houses. Her job consists of nailing trim work and painting window frames. She suggests that Juanita and Cedric join her on one of the projects. She believes that Habitat for Humanity is making a difference in her community.

2. The new landscaping really improves this neighborhood. Grass grows along all of the sidewalks. Redbud and silver maples shade the streets and there is now a bubbling fountain at the corner. All of the residents love walking and riding their bikes down the new gravel path.

3. The CEO of the appliance company is in town for the stockholders' meeting. He attends several presentations and delivers a speech. He announces the company plans to diversify in the coming year. He urges stockholders to stick with the company and promises increased dividends in the fourth quarter.

ACTIVITY 34-7

Putting it Together III

Directions: Look for any problems (subject/verb agreement, sentence end punctuation, run-ons, or comma splices, past tense, fragment) and correct them.

1. Homemade tapes and CDs make great gifts. Gifts that don't cost much. If you think about the person you are making the gift for, you can look through your music collection and make a list of songs he or she might like. Remember when you are back in high school and the songs you like then. When you have a list of about ten songs, make your tape or CD you will be amazed by how much this gift will touch the person you give it to.

2.   Detroit automakers feel proud of themselves After developing new safety features. Dual airbags is now standard equipment. The availability of antilock brakes. New and improved seatbelts. America's drivers are better protected than ever. they still need to drive more carefully.

3.   Yesterday was a disaster. When I woked up I couldn't find my homework, it wasn't anywhere. My key broke off in the lock of my car, so I had to take the bus. What a mess. I was late for my class. After class my friends lefted campus without telling me I had to eat that awful cafeteria food. No flavor whatsoever. Things wasn't any better in the afternoon. By the time I return home, I was read to go straight to bed. Just to put an end to that day.

VERB TENSE **Q&A**

Q Is it better to write essays in the present tense or in the past tense?

A There is no preferred verb tense. The important thing is to use the tense that is appropriate in each specific situation.

Q If I know I need to use past tense but I'm not sure whether the verb changes form in the past tense, is there anything I can do?

A Yes, look up the verb in your dictionary. It will list present, past, and helper past (past perfect) forms. If you look up the verb "run" for instance, you'll find "ran" and "run" right after it. "Ran" is past tense and "run" is the helper past.

Q Who let the dogs out?

A We were wondering the same thing.

35

SMALL STUFF
YOU NEED TO SWEAT

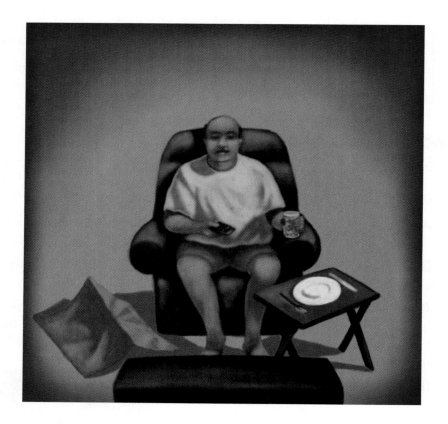

Many students worry a lot about the small stuff. They think their writing would be fine if they could only spell correctly or put commas where they are needed. While it is very important to pay attention to spelling and comma placement and to learn the rules that can help you, it's important to recognize their place in the grand scheme of things. If you have problems in the Fatal Four categories, no matter how perfect a speller you are or how well you know the comma rules, your writing still won't work. On the other hand, if your writing is generally free of Fatal Four and content problems yet contains a few spelling and comma errors, you'll usually be OK. All writers slip up from time to time.

What you need to do is to learn the rules and apply them carefully. Looking for these kinds of minor problems is the last thing you should do when you are proofreading. It's much more important to fix a fragment or subject/verb agreement problem than to fix a spelling mistake. If you do have time for a thorough proofreading for minor problems, and are able to catch some, so much the better. If you make lots of spelling mistakes and have other minor problems it can have a fatal effect. You want your readers to encounter as few problems as possible so that they will be able to concentrate on what you are saying and possibly end up convinced.

In the next sections, we will take a look at some of the most common minor problems.

JDLR

Security people have an acronym they like to use: JDLR—<u>J</u>ust <u>D</u>oesn't <u>L</u>ook <u>R</u>ight. Anything they see that looks suspicious and seems to require further investigation is described as JDLR. From experience, they know that things that just don't look right, probably aren't right. Whenever you are proofreading your writing, you need to be a detective combing the scene for anything that just doesn't look right. If it just doesn't look right, it probably isn't right and needs to be corrected.

Keep in mind, though, that sometimes when something just doesn't look right, everything turns out to be OK. Sometimes the dead body on the park bench is actually someone who is sleeping. Be careful with your writing. When something just doesn't look right, find out why it doesn't look right. Have a good reason for making the changes you make.

36

SPELLING

"We're reducing your royalties by ten
percent due to spelling errors."

Spelling is a problem for every writer to one degree or another. No one can
possibly know how to spell every word, so you're in good company if you
don't always know how to spell all the words you want to use. Now you

know one of the reasons why dictionaries were invented and why computer programs have spell checkers.

Spelling words correctly makes a difference. Imagine that you are an employer trying to fill a job vacancy and receive letters containing the following sentences:

I am writing to apply for the job you advertized in yestiday's newspaper.

I am writing to apply for the job you advertised in yesterday's newspaper.

Which applicant would you want to hire? Both applicants use exactly the same words and yet the second example makes a much better impression because the writer did not misspell any words. We might even come to the conclusion that the second writer is smarter than the first—all because the writer's words are spelled correctly.

That's the funny thing about spelling. If you spell words correctly, readers think positively about what you are saying. It gives you a little extra edge as far as convincing them that what you say is true and reasonable. If you're spelling your words correctly, readers won't even notice, but if you make lots of mistakes, it may become the *only* thing they notice.

If you want to improve your spelling (and we hope we've convinced you that it's a little thing that will make a big difference in how readers react to your writing), a good place to begin is by making a list of words that you've misspelled in the past. You may have noticed that words you have trouble with tend to haunt you.

Take a sheet of paper that is small enough to be folded into your paperback dictionary. (You do carry a paperback dictionary with you at all times for help with reading and writing, don't you?) Divide the paper into two columns. Read through previous papers that your instructor has marked, write down any spelling errors on the left, and the correct spelling on the right.

You can use this dictionary pullout for a couple of purposes. First, you can review problem words before you write and before you proofread. Second, you can quickly check spelling whenever you

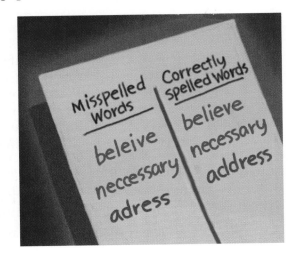

want to use one of these words. Let's take a look at some of the more popular misspelled words. We'll give you some tips and suggestions that will make solving this problem a little easier.

Words that Sound the Same but Are Spelled Differently

One of the mysteries of life is why the English language ended up with so many words that sound just the same to the listener but are spelled differently and mean different things. Life would certainly be easier for all of us if all words sounded as different as they look. Since this isn't the case, though, we need to acquaint ourselves with these words and learn the differences between them. Let's start with three of the most common ones.

their—shows possession, as in "their new car" or "their political views"

they're—contraction of "they are"

there—used in all other situations, as in "over there"

your—shows possession, as in "your dog" or "your writing skills"

you're—contraction of "you are"

two—the number 2

too—means *also*, as in "I saw my teacher in the cafeteria too," or *in excess*, as in "too much cheese" or "too many prerequisites"

to—used in all other situations, as in "to the store"

ACTIVITY 36-1

Directions: Underline the correctly spelled choices in the following sentences.

1. Bring (you're, your) favorite CD to the party on Friday night.

2. (Your, You're) (to, too, two) young (to, too, two) see that movie.

3. (There, Their, They're) (to, too, two) late (to, too, two) place (there, their, they're) orders.

4. (They're, Their) driving (to, too, two) fast.

5. (Your, You're) help is greatly appreciated.

6. (There, Their, They're) are (to, too, two) reasons for this.

7. They spend (to, too, two) much time playing video games.

8. The professor wonders whether (your, you're) planning to take the final exam.

9. (You're, Your) going to need to paint (you're, your) house this summer.

10. After (there, their, they're) graduation ceremony, the students went (to, too, two) the beach.

There are other sound-alikes that you should know about. We've included some short tips to help you remember the differences.

complement—helps to complete something else

compliment—praise or congratulations *("I" like compliments)*

con<u>science</u>—what helps us determine right from wrong *(make a "science" of knowing right from wrong)*

conscious—self awareness, deliberate, intentional

desert—a region lacking rainfall and vegetation

dessert—a sweet served at the end of a meal *(have an extra helping of "s" for dessert)*

hear—to listen *(has an "ear" in it)*
here—in this place, opposite of there

its—shows possession
it's—contraction of "it is" *(it is an apostrophe!)*

past—ended, finished *(ends in "t" like past tense)*
passed—past tense of "to pass"

peace—state of tranquility or quiet
piece—a portion of *(give me a piece of pie)*

plain—an expanse of level land *(the rain in spain stays mainly in the plain)*
plane—a flat surface

principal—the head officer of a school *(if he's nice, he can be a "pal")*
principle—a general truth or law *("le" like in "rule")*

threw—past tense of "to throw" *(has the same number of letter(s) as throw)*
through—into one side and out the other

weight—any quantity of heaviness *(you need to lose "eight" pounds)*
wait—to remain in expectation or readiness

whether—if it be the case that
weather—atmospheric conditions *(has an "a" like "rain")*

ACTIVITY 36-2

Directions: Underline the correctly spelled choice in each sentence.

1. One day I hope to be the (principle/principal) at my old high school.

2. It was (passed/past) midnight when Cedric finished his psychology paper.

3. The governor hasn't decided (whether/weather) to support the tax cut.

4. Your (conscious/conscience) will bother you if you borrow Aunt Darlene's book without asking her.

5. Most (principles/principals) have advanced degrees in education.

6. I can't (wait/weight) to get my own cell phone.

7. Listen, I found the information I needed (here/hear) on the Internet.

8. Juanita's favorite (dessert/desert) is strawberries topped with fresh whipped cream.

9. Let's have some (piece/peace) and quiet.

10. Do you like those cookies (plain/plane) or with nuts?

Spelling Rules That Can Change Your Life

If you haven't encountered these rules before, now's the time to memorize them and put them to work. As with any rule, there's occasionally an exception, but these should help you most of the time.

◆ **Rule 1:** "I" comes before "e"—except after "c" or when the sound is "a" (as in "neighbor").

brief, piece, reprieve ("i" before "e")

receive, perceive (after "c")

eight, weigh (the sound is "a")

◆ **Rule 2:** At the end of a word—add a vowel, lose the "e"; add a consonant, keep the "e." If a word ends in "e," drop the "e" if you add anything that begins with a vowel (a, e, i, o, u). If you add anything that begins with a consonant, keep the final "e."

bored + ed = bored, bore + ing = boring (lose the "e")

grace + ful = graceful, settle + ment = settlement (keep the "e")

An exception to this rule is made when a word ends in "ce" or "ge," in which case you keep the final "e" when you add anything that begins with "a" or "o."

irreplaceable

exchangeable

◆ **Rule 3:** Consonant to consonant is constant. If a word ends in a consonant and you add something beginning with a consonant, just add it. Nothing changes. There are no exceptions.

play + ful = playful, resent + ment = resentment

◆ **Rule 4:** Double up consonant when a vowel is coming. If a one—or two—syllable word ends in a consonant, double the final letter if you are adding something that begins with a vowel.

bat + er = batter, bat + ing = batting

An exception is made if the final consonant comes after two vowels, in which case it's not doubled.

sleep + ing = sleeping, sweet + en = sweeten

◆ **Rule 5:** Prefix changes nothing. Do not change the spelling of a word if you add something to the beginning.

mis + behave = misbehave, dis + appoint = disappoint

co + operate = cooperate

ACTIVITY 36-3

Directions: Put the spelling rules we've just given you to work. Underline the correctly spelled choice in the following sentences.

1. The politician was disappointed/dissappointed by the election results.

2. Aunt Darlene believes/beleives in the importance of taking vitamins.

3. Cedric is keepping/keeping an eye on his nephew.

4. We are hopeful/hopful that it won't rain the day of the outdoor concert.

5. Aunt Darlene's neighbors/nieghbors have a pet pig.

6. The placement/placment of the ball is important when kicking a field goal.

7. Some writers prefer pens with erasable/eraseable ink.

8. The new lab equipment weighs/wieghs a ton.

9. After awhile, watching television can get boreing/boring.

10. There's a cat creeping/creepping through the backyard.

Most Frequently Misspelled Words

Here is a list of the most frequently misspelled words. Get to know them.

a lot	committed	lose	sandwich
absence	complement	marriage	scissors
accept	compliment	medicine	seize
acceptable	conscientious	mischief	separate
achieve	consistent	misspelled	significant
achievement	courageous	muscle	soldier
address	courteous	neighbor	souvenir
affect	deceive	neither	sweat
all right	definite	niece	sweet
already	delicious	nuisance	temperature
angel	desirable	occasion	thorough
angle	enough	parallel	through
annual	especially	perceive	unnecessary
anxious	excellent	possession	wear
arrange	fourth	possible	Wednesday
assistance	further	potatoes	weird
assistant	grievance	prairie	
attendance	half	precede	
beautiful	healthy	prejudice	
believe	height	probably	
bicycle	independence	proceed	
breath	independent	psychology	
bureau	interest	quality	
business	interrupt	quiet	
calendar	it's	receipt	
ceiling	knowledge	receive	
cemetery	laugh	recipe	
changeable	likely	responsibility	
choose	loneliness	restaurant	
chose	loose	rhythm	

ACTIVITY 36-4

Directions: Underline any misspelled words you find in the sentences below, and then spell them correctly in the space above.

1. The judge is commited to teaching criminals to be courtious.

2. The labor union filed a greivance against the chief of police.

3. It's common knowlege that you shouldn't run with sissors in your hand.

4. I plan to minor in sychology.

5. The baby's temperture went up despite the medacine.

ACTIVITY 36-5

Directions: Underline any misspelled words you find in the sentences below, and then spell them correctly in the space above.

1. Scientists are studying the affects of lonliness on health.

2. Uncle Waylon's wierd nieghbor is at it again!

3. After marrige, it's important to maintain a degree of independance.

4. The asisstant told us to stay out of mischeif.

5. Doing excellant work is its own reward.

6. I want to complement you on the way the colors of your cloths compliment each other.

7. That psycology perfessor has a strict attendence policy.

8. Two paralell lines will never intersect.

9. She is related to Aunt Darlene by marrige.

10. If I loose ten pounds, my clothes will be lose.

ACTIVITY 36-6

Directions: Underline any misspelled words you find in the sentences below, and then spell them correctly in the space above.

1. Running a high temprature for a long time can be dangerous.

2. Cedric through the ball as hard as he could.

3. The rythm section propelled the band to new hieghts.

4. Dan Quayle no longer likes potatos.

5. This will probly be her last attemt to make the Olympic team.

6. The assistant coach is anxsious about the tryouts.

7. Its you're responsability to pay your taxes.

8. The soldures siezed the castle.

9. This house is often very quite.

10. If your having truble with a problem, procede to the next one.

ACTIVITY 36-7

Directions: Underline and correct any spelling errors you find in the following paragraphs.

1. The anual meeting of the Resturant Association will be held at Timmy's on Wensday, Feberary 12. Several significant issues will be discused. Separate commitees will analyze last year's profit margins, food qualitie, and new uses for the potato. Afterward, members will have a delishus dinner.

2.   People who live in hurricane zones must be throughly perpared. They should store water, food, and medacine and keep a flashlite handy. If a hurricane is approaching, they need to seize the moment and pack up there valuable possessions and procede to higher ground.

3.   If I could live anywhere, I would live in California. The whether their is beautiful. I love to go siteseeing in the diffrent nieghborhoods of Los Angeles and to sample the food a varius restaraunts. Everywhere in California I see and here exotic birds. For me, their can never be to much California.

Three Great Reasons to Carry a Dictionary

❶ To look up the meaning of words you don't know

❷ To check the spelling of words

❸ To check on verb parts (which will help you correct verb tense problems)

37

PRONOUNS AND THEIR ANTECEDENTS

Somewhere along the way you have probably learned what a "noun" is, though maybe at this point you're not quite sure. A noun is a person, place, or thing. What, then, is a pronoun? A pronoun is a word that stands for a noun and keeps the English language from boring us silly. Without pronouns, we'd have to write sentences like these:

The president vetoed the bill and then the president asked a group of senators to make a new proposal.

The women's soccer team won the game that the women's soccer team needed to win.

Because of pronouns, we can simplify our sentences.

The president vetoed the bill, and then he asked a group of senators to make a new proposal.

The women's soccer team won the game that it needed to win.

In the first sentence, "he" stands for "president." In the second, "they" stands for "women's soccer team." "He" and "they" are *pronouns*. The words they stand for ("president" and "women's soccer team") are called *antecedents*.

In order to use pronouns successfully, you need to know that they come in two forms: singular and plural.

Singular	Plural
he, she, it	they, we
him, his, her	their, our
I, me	you, us, them

The rule here is pretty simple. If the noun you are replacing is one of anything, then the pronoun must be *singular*. If the noun is more than one of anything, then the noun is *plural*.

The <u>scientists</u> have released <u>their</u> findings.

After <u>my cousin and I</u> left the concert, <u>we</u> went to my aunt's house for tamales.

If you want to make sure that your pronoun agrees with its antecedent (that the noun and pronoun are both singular or both plural), you will first need to locate the noun the pronoun is replacing. Look at the following example:

Every one of the bricklayers brought their tools.

Does this sentence sound correct to you? Maybe it does, but remember that your ear doesn't always tell you the truth. What nouns is the pronoun "their" replacing? Is it "bricklayers"? No, it's "one." Is "one" singular or plural? It's singular of course.

Every one of the bricklayers brought his or her tools.

ACTIVITY 37-1

Directions: Underline the correct pronoun in each of the following sentences.

1. The porcupines left his or her/their quills in the dog's nose.
2. Every boy on the team has his/their dreams of being a pro someday.
3. Don't tell the clowns that no one thinks their/its act is funny.
4. All of the scientists have his or her/their own methods of conducting experiments.
5. The students rented his or her/their own computer.

ACTIVITY 37-2

Directions: Underline the correct pronoun in each of the following sentences.

1. Each of the candidates has his or her/their own education proposals.
2. My two aunts brought her/their own bottles of apple juice to the party.
3. Every child should have his or her/their own books to read just for fun.
4. Those women have made her/their plans for the weekend.
5. Ask that man to bring his/their own bicycle next time.
6. Each lobbyist will plead his or her/their case before a vote is taken.
7. The company is going to ask the researchers to verify his or her/their data.
8. After lunch, Aunt Darlene and Juanita plan to wash his/their cars.
9. In the future, all of the students will have to provide his or her/their own text-books.
10. The boy and girl sit in the same room but play his or her/their own games.

ACTIVITY 37-3

Directions: Underline the correct pronoun in each of the following sentences.

1. Every one of the new recruits has been issued his or her/their own uniform.

2. At the end of summer, Cedric and Mr. Waylon will go on his/their vacation to a fishing camp in Minnesota.

3. All environmentalists have his or her/their concerns when it comes to how power is generated in the United States.

4. If anyone new calls, please tell him or her/them to try back in about an hour.

5. A developing nation must do what it can to spur its/their economy.

6. A director of health services is always going to have his or her/their own agenda.

7. Each of the children should have his or her/their own books.

8. All of the new cars have its/their special features this year.

9. Each of the automakers has its/their own design team.

10. If you are able to get the tickets on time, tell them not to forget his or her/their suitcases.

ACTIVITY 37-4

Directions: Underline the pronoun choices in the following paragraphs.

1. Ed Perkins, one of the new workers, forgot to bring his/their lunch. Everyone in the cafeteria shared some of his or her/their lunch and chipped in money for a drink. Ed has promised to bring his/their lunch tomorrow. He's very grateful to his coworkers for being willing to share his/their lunches with someone they'd never met before.

2. Kate Callahan, the senior archivist, is one of the women who will be saluted for her/their accomplishments. Each of the honorees has done first-rate work in her/their field. After they receive her/their awards, there will be a banquet.

38

WORD ENDINGS

Plurals and Words Ending in "-ed"

One of the things that successful writers learn to check for when they are proofreading is word endings like plurals and "eds." Sometimes when you're writing, you begin thinking about the next word you're going to write before you finish the one you're on, and this can result in your forgetting a letter or two. Sometimes writers leave letters off when they write because they write the same way they speak, and when they speak, they aren't always careful to pronounce their endings. Take a look at this sentence:

The mayor made two proposal at the city council meeting.

Do you see any problem? Yes. The mayor made more than one proposal, so you need to add "s."

The mayor made two proposal<u>s</u> at the city council meeting.

Look at this sentence:

The students brought their book to class.

Unless the students pooled their money to buy a single book, there is more than one book. If each student has his or her own book, then you need to say so.

The students brought their book<u>s</u> to class.

As you can see, "s" endings can affect the meaning of what you write.

ACTIVITY 38-1

Directions: Add "s" where necessary in the following sentences.

1. The citizens of the country have their opinion about these issues.
2. Camels store extra fat reserves in their hump.
3. Artists get a variety of inspiration from different everyday experience.
4. All of my relative took picture at the family reunion.
5. At the United Nations, every country has its flag on display.

"S" isn't the only letter writers sometimes leave off the ends of words. "ED" can also be a problem. Like "s" endings, we often leave "ed" endings off because we don't always say them when we speak.

What People Sometimes Say	*What's Right*
use to	use<u>d</u> to

I use<u>d</u> to spend more time with my friends.

| suppose to | suppose<u>d</u> to |

The president is suppose<u>d</u> to speak at 8 P.M.

| ice coffee | ice<u>d</u> coffee |

Please order an ice<u>d</u> coffee for me.

ACTIVITY 38-2

Directions: Add "-ed" endings where necessary in the following sentences.

1. I ate several pounds of spicy, boil shrimp at the picnic.

2. The bake potato tastes delicious when you melt cheese over it.

3. The police drove to the crime scene in unmark cars.

4. Unrefine behavior is not allowed at Miss Eleanor's Etiquette School.

5. A well-tune engine runs better.

"S" and "ed" endings may seem like small things, but as we've shown, they can affect the clarity of what you're saying and the conclusions readers may draw about how well you speak. Like apostrophes, a little awareness can be a dangerous thing. Sometimes when writers become aware of the problem, they begin to add "s" and "ed" endings where they aren't needed.

ACTIVITY 38-3

Directions: Add "s" and "ed" endings where necessary in the following sentences.

1. We have two car in our driveway but only one is freshly wax.

2. If you have been given good service, then you're suppose to give a tip.

3. Cedric's mother show him how to replace the three button that had fallen off his shirt.

4. When my brother was little, he persist in thinking that spaghetti originate in France.

5. A true collector will not be able to pass up all those cup and saucer.

ACTIVITY 38-4

Directions: Add "s" and "ed" endings where necessary in the following sentences.

1. Freshly brew coffee actually does taste better than coffee that has been sitting in the pot.

2. The girls said the boys were not allow in their clubhouse.

3. The gleaming wash floor startle the students.

4. Those lamp need shade.

5. The new director of customer relations was not use to dealing with irate customers.

6. Aunt Darlene put out bowls of mixed nut and potato chip.

7. More than one bakery has shown how to make a million dollar profit on glaze donuts.

8. You can find direction to my house on the Internet.

9. The amuse audience stopped the show three time with their wild laughter.

10. Cedric gave Juanita a hand-carve necklace and a bag of jelly bean.

ACTIVITY 38-5

Directions: Add or subtract endings where necessary in the following sentences.

1. He was looking for a furnish room to rent.

2. It will take two bolt to tighten the handrail.

3. Those tablecloth are not on sale this week.

4. A pair of glove makes a good gift for just about anyone.

5. Every good cook has a recipe for mash potatoes, and I have even heard of one that contains pure beets.

6. We spent the night at their recently purchase condominium on the Gulf Coast.

7. The clothes were full of stain and wrinkle.

8. The recently replace air filter needed to be changed again.

9. The two professor changed office at the last minute.

10. His sunburn skin began to bother him.

ACTIVITY 38-6

Directions: Add endings where necessary in the following paragraphs.

1.   The closet definitely needed cleaning. There were unlace shoe and old game piece scattered on the floor. Hangers in all size filled the rod, and the two shelf above were overloaded with boxes full of book. A closet is suppose to be more than a giant junk drawer, so I better get to work.

2.   Buying a use car is a good idea if you can find one of the good one. A good use car runs well, has all the necessary part—from hubcaps to smooth seat cover. An abuse car is a bad choice. If you find a good, reasonably price one, buy it.

39

ADVERBS AND ADJECTIVES

An adjective tells *what kind* of person, place or thing. An adjective modifies a noun.

Bubbles the clown is depressed.

(What kind of clown? A depressed clown)

The tiny beetle scuttled across the wide street.

(What kind of beetle? Tiny. What kind of street? Wide.)

ACTIVITY 39-1

Directions: Underline the adjectives in the following sentences.

1. The wilted flower drooped in the August heat.
2. The new senator is corrupt.
3. The police investigation has been progressing well.
4. The burritos in the new restaurant are delicious.
5. On our last vacation, we visited a national park in northern Minnesota.

An adverb tells us information about another adverb, adjective, or a verb.

The lawnmower cut easily through the long grass.

(How does it cut? Easily.)

He talks very loudly on the phone.

(How does he talk? Loudly. How loudly? Very.)

ACTIVITY 39-2

Directions: Underline the adverbs in the following sentences.

1. A chillingly scary face appeared in the window.
2. When I dropped her off at the railroad station, we said goodby sadly.
3. The engines of today's cars run more efficiently than the engines in older cars.
4. Time goes slowly when you are waiting for an important phone call.
5. The boy on the bicycle careened wildly through the neighborhood.

The problem with adjectives and adverbs for many writers comes when they confuse the two. You need to know which is which. An easy way to tell the difference between adjectives and adverbs is that adverbs almost always end in "ly." Remember that an adjective has a very limited role. It can only tell you what kind of noun is being talked about. An adverb never modifies a noun.

ACTIVITY 39-3

Directions: Underline the correct word to complete these sentences. If it's an adjective, underline it once. If it's an adverb, underline it twice.

1. The party ended quick/quickly.
2. Jobs in the medical field pay good/well.
3. Everyone in the movie theater applauded after the happy/happily ending.
4. The newspapers treated the new president fair/fairly.
5. Do careful/carefully work and you will be rewarded.

40

THE RULES OF CAPITALIZATION

Capital Letters

The first word you ever wrote was probably your name, and the first capital letter you ever put on paper was the one that comes at the beginning of your name. Whatever your name, everyone knows that you capitalize the first letter of every name, first or last.

This rule of capitalization is one of many, and it's essential that you master all of them if you want to keep your reader focused on what you have to say and not be distracted by mistakes.

Rules of Capitalization

❶ Capitalize the first word in a sentence.

When the time is right, Cedric will ask Betina on a date.

❷ Capitalize the word "I."

Although I knew the answer, my mind went blank.

❸ Capitalize the days of the week, months of the year, and holidays.

Today is Tuesday, January 12, National Remember to Feed the Squirrels Day.

❹ Capitalize the names of *specific* people, places, and things.

The Golden Gate Bridge in San Francisco, California, is an amazing feat of engineering.

❺ Capitalize people's titles.

General Eisenhower became President Eisenhower after his election in 1952.

❻ Capitalize a family member only if you use it as a name.

I wanted Mommy to buy me more candy.

❼ Capitalize compass directions (e.g., north, south, east, and west) *only* if they name a particular area of a city, country, or region.

Silver jewelry is a specialty in the Southwest.

❽ Capitalize the first word, the last word, and any important words in the title of a book, story, play, poem, or movie.

Many critics believe that <u>The Great Gatsby</u> is one of the best American novels ever written.

❾ Capitalize the first word in a line of dialogue.

Priscilla said, "Go home, Elvis."

❿ DO NOT capitalize the seasons of the year.

I enjoy snow skiing in the winter and waterskiing in the summer.

ACTIVITY 40-1

Directions: Make sure capital letters in the following sentences are used correctly. Make changes where necessary.

1. Whenever I'm asked, I tell people that thanksgiving is my favorite Holiday.

2. The next Election will be held on tuesday, November 5.

3. No trip to paris is complete without a visit to the eiffel tower.

4. While uncle waylon was in rome, he took many pictures of the colosseum and the trevi fountain.

5. Many people want to meet senator Clinton and ask her what it was like to be first lady.

ACTIVITY 40-2

Directions: Make sure capital letters in the following sentences are used correctly. Make changes where necessary.

1. The sultan of brunei is a very wealthy man.

2. My favorite southern rock band is called better than ezra.

3. One of the greatest children's books is <u>mike mulligan and his steam shovel</u> by virginia hamilton.

4. Last summer I took a tour of the white house, which is at 1600 pennsylvania avenue, washington, d.c.

5. When my Father said, "Merry Christmas Everyone," we all applauded.

6. I am a big fan of the Chicago cubs and attend as many games as I can at wrigley field.

7. If her name is mrs. Smith, where is mr. Smith?

8. This year's session of the supreme court began last monday.

9. This Spring I will be visiting the northwest for the first time.

10. Then Juanita turned to Aunt Darlene and said, "this letter is for you."

ACTIVITY 40-3

Directions: Make corrections in capitalization wherever necessary in the following sentences.

1. The mayor introduced chancellor parkinson to members of the news media.

2. Last Winter we stayed at mountain laurel lodge on lake Helen.

3. Come to the corner of forest and linden, and be sure to bring your sled.

4. Fresh Pumpkins will be available at the October fest being held in riley memorial park.

5. I don't think dad knew that I borrowed his buick.

6. I took history, french, and math 101.

7. Then she said, "happy valentine's day!"

8. My sister came here for easter before returning to oregon.

9. The new secretary of the treasury was approved by the u.s. senate.

10. The f.d.a. establishes rules regarding the food that the americans eat.

ACTIVITY 40-4

Directions: Make corrections in capitalization wherever necessary.

1.   The national park system offers everyone the opportunity to appreciate nature close up. At shenandoah state park in virginia, visitors can stay in a lodge and be treated every day to a view of the appalachian mountains that is unparalleled. If you enjoy water sports and bike riding in a beautiful wooded setting, lake itasca state park near bemidji, minnesota, is the place for you.

2.   I never considered a career in archaeology until i took anthropology 1000. In that class, professor linley took us on a dig in du page county. We found relics left behind by the illini tribe. I don't think I've ever taken a college class that was more exciting. I worked hard but it didn't feel that way; I've never earned an "a" more easily.

41

PUNCTUATION MARKS

Commas

When writers think about grammatical errors, they probably worry about spelling and commas more often than anything else. They worry about not using commas when they need them and using them when they don't.

Like most things connected to writing correctly, familiarizing yourself with the rules will take most of the mystery out of when to use and not to use commas.

EIGHT TIMES YOU REALLY NEED TO USE COMMAS

❶ Use a comma to separate the date from the year.

December 7, 1941

❷ Use a comma to separate the city from the state or country.

New Orleans, Louisiana

❸ Use a comma to separate every item in a series.

At the store Juanita bought milk, butter, peanuts, and orange juice.

❹ Use a comma to set off descriptive words that are not essential from the person, place, or thing being described.

Mr. Douglas, the senior member of the committee, voted to extend the meeting.

❺ Use a comma to separate adjectives that describe the same person, place, or thing *if* the word "and" can be used between them without changing the meaning.

The river is dirty, smelly, dangerous, and unfit for recreational activity.

❻ Use a comma to separate a dependent clause (fragment) from the sentence that follows:

After his most recent discovery, Dr. Waldren will make a report to the AMA.

❼ Use a comma to set off phrases that briefly interrupt the sentence.

Pigs, for instance, can easily be trained to walk on a leash.

⑧ Use a comma to separate a direct quote from the rest of the sentence.

"Give me liberty or give me death," said Patrick Henry.

ACTIVITY 41-1

Directions: Insert commas where they are needed in the following sentences.

1. Mardi Gras a spectacular celebration is held every spring in New Orleans Louisiana.

2. Mardi Gras is celebrated with parades where float riders throw beads cups plastic cigars spears rubber chickens stuffed animals and small coins called doubloons.

3. John Smith this year's king of Mardi Gras lives in a neighborhood called the Garden District.

4. After the parades are over on Mardi Gras Day the king goes to a ball and dances with the queen.

5. Looking at the crowd Mr. Smith makes a toast by saying "Happy Mardi Gras."

ACTIVITY 41-2

Directions: Insert commas where they are needed in the following sentences.

1. After killing off Sherlock Holmes in one book Sir Arthur Conan Doyle was forced by public outcry to bring him back in another.

2. That house the most run-down one on our block, is going to be renovated.

3. Former President Clinton was born in Hope Arkansas.

4. The new TV show premiered on September 2 1958.

5. Those hiking trails are dusty hilly and full of rocks.

6. Aunt Darlene's sister however does not like spicy food.

7. "Four score and twenty years ago" President Lincoln began.

8. Coco believe it or not was given an award for good behavior.

9. If you have trouble sleeping don't exercise or consume caffeine close to bedtime.

10. DVDs in addition to a movie often contain outtakes interviews with actors, and commentary by the director.

ACTIVITY 41-3

Directions: Insert commas where they are needed in the following sentences.

1. Our cruise began in Vancouver British Columbia and ended in Anchorage Alaska.

2. Please give your old still in good condition clothes to your favorite charity.

3. This is to confirm my reservation for dinner on March 17 2003.

4. Because Timmy was able to buy a bushel of tomatoes cheaply he decided to offer a stuffed tomato special that night.

5. The new proposal by comparison benefits people living in rural areas.

6. That new situation comedy is derivative boring and utterly false.

7. Mrs. Lovejoy the new crossing guard makes all of the children smile.

8. Before the soldiers made it to the beach a hard rain began to fall.

9. In the spring of 1977 millions were stricken with disco fever.

10. Cedric's favorite movies are *Citizen Kane Bonnie and Clyde* and *The Godfather.*

ACTIVITY 41-4

Directions: Insert commas where necessary in the following paragraphs.

1.   Firstborn children according to psychologists are more likely to be con-
forming and traditional. Because they identify with their parents' power and

authority, they are tough-minded, determined, and marked for success. Firstborn children unlike later children tend to be more responsible achievement-oriented, and organized.

2.   Later borns however are more likely to question parental authority. They are more likely to challenge the status quo and they may engage in rebellious activity. Later borns because they have to find their own place in the family while overcoming their elder sibling's tendencies to domineer may also be more easygoing cooperative and popular.

End Marks

There are a few simple rules regarding end marks—the period, the question mark and the exclamation point.

❶ Use a period at the end of every complete sentence.

The new supervisor arrived last Tuesday.

Cedric will give Juanita a ride to her guitar lesson.

❷ Use a question mark at the end of any question.

Did the new supervisor arrive last Tuesday?

Will Cedric give Juanita a ride to her guitar lesson?

❸ Use an exclamation point at the end of any exclamation.

Get over here immediately!

That's fantastic news!

ACTIVITY 41-5

Directions: Choose the correct end mark for each of the following sentences.

1. When will the soup be ready

2. The Supreme Court was divided on the issue

3. Don't look at me that way

4. The sound quality on the new DVDs is incredible

5. Does anyone care about the plight of endangered species

6. Can someone pick my brother up at midnight

7. It's none of your business

8. The conductor of the orchestra lifted his baton

9. Watch out for those sparking wires

10. Are there any other points to consider

Apostrophe

The apostrophe is a small mark of punctuation that can make a big difference in your writing. Apostrophes are used to perform two very different jobs. They fill in for a left-out letter in contractions, and they show possession.

Let's start with the easy one first. The apostrophe is used to show contraction. In English, speakers and writers run certain words together:

I am becomes *I'm*

could not becomes *couldn't*

did not becomes *didn't*

they are becomes *they're*

Juanita is becomes *Juanita's*

. . . and so on

We use the apostrophe to stand for the letter that has been left out.

In *I'm*, the apostrophe stands for the "a"

In *couldn't*, it stands for the "o"

In *didn't,* it stands for the "o"

In *he's,* it stands for the "i"

Exception: In *won't,* the apostrophe stands for "o" but "ill" is shortened to "o"

ACTIVITY 41-6

Directions: Write the contraction form of the following words.

1. cannot _____

2. should not _____

3. will not _____

4. have not _____

5. would not _____

The other situations where you need to use the apostrophe is when you are showing your reader who owns what.

If a football belongs to Gabi, it's Gabi's football.

If a microwave oven belongs to Sam, it's Sam's microwave.

If a vacation belongs to your mail carrier, it's your mail carrier's vacation.

When people are involved, it's usually pretty easy to remember to use the apostrophe. People own things, so it just makes sense. Sometimes, though, it's not so easy to remember to use apostrophes, but they are just as needed.

If the bowl belongs to the cat, it's the cat's bowl.

If the popcorn belongs to the movie theater, it's the movie theater's popcorn.

If the purple interior belongs to your car, it's your car's purple interior.

ACTIVITY 41-7

Directions: Add apostrophes where necessary in the following sentences.

1. Grandpas beard is getting too long.

2. The economys getting stronger every year.

3. The mayors from several cities will meet next week to discuss education.

4. The mayors driver got a speeding ticket.

5. The mayors going to be late to the meeting.

So now you know there are two situations where you use the apostrophe: to show ownership and to fill in for a left out letter in contractions. Here are some special cases, though, that sometimes cause problems.

◆ ***It's*** **vs.** ***its.*** If you say, "The cat played with its toy mouse on the porch," you would not use an apostrophe in the word "its." The possessive form for the word "it" never has an apostrophe. The apostrophe appears only when you mean "it is"—which is shortened to "it's."

It's raining men.

◆ **Plural words that don't end in "s"**—words like men, women, and children—all refer to more than one person but do not have "s" endings. If you want to show ownership, you must add an apostrophe and an "s."

the women's political caucus

the men's reading group

the children's theater company

◆ **The apostrophe goes <u>after</u> the word that is the owner.** If there are three kittens that share a bowl, it's the *kittens' bowl*. If two of the kittens run away, it will now be the *kitten's bowl*.

ACTIVITY 41-8

Directions: Add apostrophes where necessary in the following sentences.

1. The boys father treats all his sons equally.

2. The cattles constant grazing keeps the grass low.

3. Its going to be a long time until Halley's Comet returns.

4. Theres time for each idea to get its fair hearing.

5. Its lucky that the professors students were paying attention when he told them about the exam.

Putting apostrophes in the right places is a finishing touch that your readers will really appreciate. Some writers, though, make the mistake of using apostrophes almost every time they add an "s." They don't even think about the rules.

We ate hot dog's and hamburger's before the rally.

I believe in the Constitution and the Bill of Right's.

New invention's are changing the way we think about our homes.

None of the apostrophes above make sense because they are not being used in contractions or situations where possession is taking place.

ACTIVITY 41-9

Directions: Add or eliminate apostrophes wherever necessary in the following sentences.

1. Ten dollar's are missing from Friedas wallet.

2. The chair's leg need's to be repaired.

3. After a brief absence, the girls mothers returned to help them finish their research paper's.

4. The right to bear arm's is at the center of a controversial piece of legislation.

5. Scientist's work long hour's to come up with their discoverie's.

ACTIVITY 41-10

Directions: Add or eliminate apostrophes wherever necessary in the following sentences.

1. Average citizen's can do much to assist the cities clean-up initiatives.

2. The League for Women Voter's will be meeting at Aunt Darlenes this week.

3. The classrooms improvements included new desk's and chair's.

4. That restaurants turtle soup is the best in the state.

5. The basketball league has agreed to several new rule's and regulation's.

6. Cedrics car will need new spark plug's by the end of the year.

7. Our colleges art department has won several awards' and earned everyones respect.

8. President Roosevelts polio kept him in a wheelchair.

9. Chicagos Museum of Science and Industry is one of the most interesting museums' I've ever visited.

10. All of the Beatles number one hit's were collected on a single CD.

ACTIVITY 41-11

Directions: Add or eliminate apostrophes wherever necessary in the following sentences.

1. That movies ending was really unbelievable.

2. The actors last line made you wonder if the citys police department was completely corrupt.

3. The brake's and tire's on Anne's car needed to be replaced.

4. The television stations manager decided he would no longer put violent show's on the air.

5. Two dog's and six cat's were found in the old couples house after they moved to the nursing home.

6. A bakers dozen gives you a total of thirteen cookie's or doughnut's or whatever.

7. The womens volleyball team went to the state championship.

8. Once you taste Aunt Darlene's garlic bread, you won't want to stop eating it.

9. This semesters last day of classe's comes sometime in June.

10. The Empire State buildings elevator is amazingly fast.

ACTIVITY 41-12

Directions: Add or eliminate apostrophes wherever necessary in the following paragraphs.

1.   Among New Yorks many attractions is the Statue of Liberty. During the year's it has stood in New York Harbor, it has become one of Americas most powerful symbols. New immigrants to our shore's see it as representing their dream's of life, liberty, and the pursuit of happiness.

2.   Last years new computer model's are a thing of the past. This years are faster, more compact, and versatile. A computers shelf life seem's to be getting shorter and shorter as each companys new innovations inspire us to replace outdated equipment. Consumer's always assume that the new model's are better.

Quotation Marks

Quotation marks are a way of distinguishing words or groups of words from other words or groups of words. There are a few simple rules to remember.

❶ Use quotation marks before and after someone's exact words (direct quotation). You don't need to use quotation marks when you aren't using the exact words (indirect quotation).

Direct quotation: The instructor said, "Bring your first draft to my office."

Indirect quotation: The instructor told me to bring my first draft to his office.

❷ Use quotation marks to set off titles of chapters, short stories, arti-cles, poems, episode titles from TV shows, and song titles.

"Winter Dreams," a short story by F. Scott Fitzgerald, is a favorite of mine.

Cedric's favorite oldie is "Ruby" by Ray Charles.

ACTIVITY 41-13

Directions: Add quotation marks where necessary in the following sentences.

1. Your car needs a new battery, said the mechanic.
2. I love the <u>Mary Tyler Moore Show</u> episode called The Death of Chuckles the Clown.
3. The history professor assigned Chapter 19, Queen Victoria's Reign.
4. This newspaper article, Sick Humor, is really interesting.
5. The last song on the album, Moonlight Mile, is the best.
6. The tax cut, said the president, has not eaten up the budget surplus.
7. You really should read Richard Hugo's poem, Degrees of Gray in Phillipsburg.
8. The professor asked her students to analyze Four Summers by Joyce Carol Oates.
9. I'm exhausted, said my sister. I just couldn't get to sleep last night.
10. E. B. White's essay, Once More To The Lake, has a powerful conclusion.

Underlining or Italics

In handwritten or typed papers, underline titles of books, magazines, newspapers, movies, TV shows, and works of art (paintings, statues, major musical compositions). If you are using a word processing program, you may use the italics feature instead of underlining.

The New Orleans <u>Times-Picayune</u>
<u>Newsweek</u>, *Vanity Fair, Sports Illustrated, Time*
<u>Venus de Milo</u>, *Guernica*
<u>Schindler's List</u>, *Silence of the Lambs*

ACTIVITY 41-14

Directions: Underline whichever words should be italicized in the following sentences.

1. Shakespeare in Love was reviewed in Time.

2. Many people consider the New York Times to be an excellent newspaper.

3. Have you read The Color Purple by Alice Walker?

4. The symphony conductor decided that the Brandenburg Concertos would be performed during the next concert series.

5. I've decided to begin subscribing to PC Weekly and US News and World Report.

42

FORMAT FOR PAPERS

When you think you've got an essay that's good enough to turn in (you've checked out the content from start to finish and proofread every sentence diligently), you have one more thing to think about before you turn your essay in: how your paper looks. Some students get hung up on making their manuscripts, neat and clean from the start if they're writing by hand, but it's really not something to think about until you're satisfied with what you've said and how you've said it.

Coming up with a neat looking draft of your essay that is easy to read is definitely a good idea because it helps you to make a good first impression. Take whatever time you have to give your essay the following finishing touches.

❶ *Give it the professional look.* Use white notebook paper or printer paper that is 8-½ by 11 inches.

❷ *Make your writing easy on the eye.* Be sure to leave wide margins on all four sides (1 to 1-½ inches is good). Give your reader's eyes a chance to rest and some space to write a comment.

❸ *Keep it clear.* Use blue or black ink if you're writing by hand. Don't use pencil for a final draft! When you use a word processor, be sure your printer is in good working order with sufficient ink to print your essay clearly.

❹ *Make it easy to read line by line.* Be sure to double-space and indent the first line of every paragraph five spaces.

❺ *Get credit for your hard work.* Be sure to put your name on the paper as well as your course title and number, section, and the date. Your instructor will tell you where to put this information.

Some instructors care more deeply than others about how you present your work, but you know from your own experience that the neater a manuscript is the easier it is to read. Be sure to take the time to follow whatever personal rules or aspects of presentation your instructor particularly emphasizes. A writer wants to give his readers every reason to be impressed by his work.

Join the G.U.P. (Grammar Underground Police)

As you learn more about grammar, you begin to notice mistakes in the writing you see all around you. Do you ever see signs at your college or in stores that contain spelling and other grammatical errors? Next time you do, pull out a pen and make a corretion. If it's impractical or inappropriate to make the correction yourself, tell someone who can. Here are some signs we've seen recently and the corrections we've made:

Sign	The Correction
Wig's	Wigs
Not responsible for lost of money	Not responsible for loss of money
Pizza Night! Come and socialize with your fiends and teachers	Pizza Night! Come and socialize with your friends and teachers
Blue Ridge Mountains Gift's	Blue Ridge Mountains Gifts
Please be good to your lungs; the furnishings and futur guest by not smoking	Please be good to your lungs, furnishings, and future guests by not smoking

WE'RE GLAD YOU ASKED

SMALL STUFF YOU NEED TO SWEAT Q&A

Q Which should I focus on first when reading over my writing, major or minor errors?

A Major Errors. We hope that you'll catch all the places where you need to improve your work, but try to nail the big mistakes first.

Q Will I ever got to a point where my writing will be totally error free?

A Try to sharpen your proofreading skills. Remember that you will become more proficient with practice. But also remember that none of us is perfect.

Q How much DNA does a human being share with a banana?

A Fifty percent (and we're not kidding).

PART

8

PRACTICE AND MASTERY TESTS

"Forty-one years of marriage.
That's a long, long, long learning curve."

43

THINKING ABOUT YOUR WRITING

Moviemakers have a ritual called "dailies"—a process during which they watch what they film each day. This allows the director, actors, and production team a chance to evaluate the film in progress to see if changes need to be made in the filming process the next day. They might discover that a scene needs to be reshot because there wasn't enough light. They might decide that an actor needs to work harder on the accent he's using or that the set designer has cluttered up the scene with too much furniture. Watching dailies is a way the creators of the film learn how to make a better film.

In a similar way, writers can learn how to write better by examining their work and thinking about the process. If writers become aware of problem areas, they can apply what they learn to their next writing experience. Use the following questions to evaluate your writing process next time you write, and then return to them after each new writing experience. Improving your writing is an ongoing process—even the best, most successful writers constantly look for ways to sharpen and polish their work.

- What was your purpose in writing this essay? What did you hope to prove?

- Can you think or any questions readers might ask while reading your essay?

- Did you clearly state your ideas?

- Did you support your ideas with enough explanation (details and examples)?

- How would you now describe yourself as a writer?

- Which aspects of your writing are most successful? Which ones do you need to work on?

Let's take a closer look at some of these questions.

Writing for Different Purposes

WHAT'S MY ASSIGNMENT?

You can discover important clues when you look at an assignment carefully. If you pay attention, you can save yourself time and energy. And you can help ensure that the completed assignment will be done correctly.

How Long Should It Be?

Often your instructor will give you specific information about how long a successful assignment should be—for example, 10 pages or 1,500 words. A "page" usually refers to double-spaced text typed on one side of a sheet only. Regular type font usually yields one page for every 250 words.

There may also be indirect information to help you decide how long your assignment should be. How broad or narrow is your assignment? Do you have to discuss all the causes of the Revolutionary War or just the most important ones?

Look at the Fine Print

Many students waste valuable time and energy by simply reading the assignment too quickly. Are you asked to discuss the causes *and* effects of air pollution or to discuss the causes *or* the effects? Are you asked to compare *and* contrast two methods of crowd control during political protests or to compare *or* contrast? Are you asked to discuss the most important *qualities* or the most important *quality*? These little details can make a big difference in what you're being asked to write about.

ESSAY EXAMS

Remember what we just told you about looking at the fine print? Now do the same thing for any exam directions and essay questions you are faced with. Often instructors include information such as how long to spend on each question or how many of the questions students are required to answer. Many times students run out of time because they tried to answer four questions when the directions asked them to answer only two out of four questions. Think of the question itself as an assignment and pay attention to the fine print.

RESEARCH PAPERS

Research papers come in a wide variety of styles, but all of them call for you to gather information from outside sources. That's the "research" part. The "paper" part requires you to form an opinion on the given topic and to support it by using the information you gathered in your research. A research paper is really a variation on your basic essay blueprint (p. 3). Like an essay, a research paper has a thesis; an intro, body and a conclusion; and supporting details. However, a research paper also differs from an in-class essay in several ways. Unlike an in-class essay, a research paper always requires outside research involving materials you have at home, in libraries, or on the Internet. It must rely on objective information to support the thesis. And a research paper requires documentation. Documentation includes direct and indirect quotes; magazine, newspaper, book and direct interview sources; and Internet sources.

PLAGIARISM

Proper documentation is essential to writing a successful research paper. If you don't document the sources of your ideas carefully, you may find yourself violating your school's policy on plagiarism—presenting another person's words or ideas as your own. Plagiarism, in case you didn't know, is a very serious charge that can have a very harmful effect on your academic career. No matter where you have found your ideas (whether they're from a magazine or a book, a friend's paper, or a file at your fraternity, or whether you downloaded them from a Web site or purchased them from a writing service), not giving the source proper credit is the same as stealing.

There's an easy way to avoid plagiarism: always be sure to cite your sources. When you use someone else's exact words, put quotation marks around them and identify the source in a parenthetical citation on your "Works Cited" page. When you put someone else's words and/or ideas into your own words (which is known as *paraphrasing*), you also need to identify the source in a parenthetic citation and on your "Works Cited" page. Here are some examples:

Direct Quotation

In his essay "The Flaw in the Flaw," Russ McDonald argues that we should not think of Shakespeare's heroes as doomed by their tragic flaws but should instead "regard them as gifted, as possessing a surplus of talent that puts them into immediate conflict with a hostile world" (McDonald 9).

Paraphrase

When trying to understand Shakespeare's heroes, critic Russ McDonald argues, we should not rely on the idea of the "tragic flaw" but should instead see these characters as too idealistic, intelligent, or powerful to fit comfortably into the world in which they live (McDonald 9).

Plagiarism

Shakespeare's heroes aren't tragically flawed; they are just too talented for the rest of the world to appreciate.

Keep in mind that one of the ways your instructor is going to be evaluating your research is on how well you handle the documentation. An instructor who suspects plagiarism will compare your essay to the available sources and may ask you to show your rough drafts, define words you have used, or explain in writing what you meant in any passage that seems different from the way you normally write.

WHAT WILL HAPPEN IF I PLAGIARIZE?

Penalties for plagiarism vary from school to school, but most consider it to be a very serious offense that will affect your grade and possibly cause you to be suspended or expelled from your college. Ask your instructor what the rules are at your school. Most importantly, though, don't put yourself in a position even to be suspected of plagiarism. Document your sources with great care.

44

ADDITIONAL PRACTICE EXERCISES

In this section, we give you the chance to work on what you have learned about sentences and paragraphs.

SENTENCE PRACTICE

Directions: **Each of the following sentences illustrates a kind of problem you've worked on in this book. In the blank to the left, label the problem as fragment (F), run-on (RO), verb (S/V), comma splice (CS), subject/verb tense (VT), and then correct the sentence on the line below.**

_____   1. There is many reasons to pursue a postgraduate degree.

   _____

_____   2. Defending our country from international technology thieves.

   _____

_____   3. Cedric hadn't ate a good meal in over a month.

   _____

_____   4. Depression affect many people's lives.

   _____

_____   5. The latest poll results are in the president's disapproval rating is quite high.

   _____

   _____

_____   6. Don't believe everything you hear, the weather is about to change dramatically.

   _____

   _____

SENTENCE PRACTICE (continued)

_____   7. The hurricane that hit in 1967 flatten the entire downtown area.

_____

_____   8. Just before Louis Armstrong played his final concert.

_____

_____

_____   9. The shelves in the library needs to be dusted.

_____

_____   10. Timmy wants to franchise his restaurant, it's a way to make a lot of money.

_____

_____

_____   11. Let your friends know how you feel don't keep it to yourself.

_____

_____   12. Here is the lab reports the doctor asked for.

_____

_____   13. Forgetting how important it is to buy tickets in advance.

_____

_____

Name: _____   Date: _____

_____ 14. Road construction brought traffic to a stop I was late for my brother's wedding.

_____

_____

_____ 15. By the time the track meet was held, she had ran over sixty miles in about two weeks.

_____

_____

_____ 16. There is good reasons for the slowdown in the economy.

_____

_____ 17. Last week Aunt Darlene bringed her lunch to work.

_____

_____ 18. Drawing and painting is two of Cedric's favorite leisure time activities.

_____

_____ 19. "Don't forget about our allies," said the general then he left the room.

_____

_____ 20. Whether or not we are going to Chicago this year.

_____

PARAGRAPH PRACTICE

Directions: **Make corrections where necessary.**

Blind dates is no fun. Sometimes your friends want to fix you up they think they know the kind of person you might like. Because they've known you for awhile. Believe me, no one knows who you would like but you. I gone on a blind date and it was a complete disaster. No fun at all.

SENTENCE PRACTICE

Directions: **Make minor problem corrections in the sentences below. If the sentence is correct, put a "C" in the blank to the left.**

_____ 1. The governors assistant told the reporters to come back at 3 oclock.

_____ 2. Aunt Darlene returned from the store with eight bag of grocery.

_____ 3. Most of the people want his own cell phone.

_____ 4. The Smithsonian Institution houses many great collection's.

_____ 5. There are to many children living in violent home.

_____ 6. If you pay you're taxes on time, you will get your refund more quickly.

_____ 7. Coco watched Mr. Waylons house while he was on vacation.

_____ 8. The street department took it's time in preparing our street.

_____ 9. They wanted they're furniture made out of wood, not particleboard.

_____ 10. Kids today are learning thing in third grade that we didn't learn until sixth.

_____ 11. As far as I'm concern cable TV has to many channels.

_____ 12. Every one of those girls needs to bring their books.

SENTENCE PRACTICE (continued)

_____ 13. One clothing fad was acid-wash jeans.

_____ 14. Meteorologist have charted the principal whether changes of the last fifty

year.

_____ 15. There are many new innovation in this years cars.

_____ 16. All of the children have changed his or her clothes.

_____ 17. The principle asked if any of the student's wanted to go hiking in the

dessert.

_____ 18. Juanita's saving's account grew over the past six month.

_____ 19. Bring you're car key.

_____ 20. Each of his brothers has their own golf clubs.

PARAGRAPH PRACTICE

***Directions:* Make corrections where necessary in the following paragraph.**

Many of todays jobs didn't exist twenty-five year ago. All of the job connected with the Internet—from Website designer's to warehouse worker's filling order for Amazon.com— are new. It is difficult to think of a single career that hasn't been effected by the popularity of the computor. Young people today have job opportunity they're parents never dreamed of; this is a hole new world.

45

MASTERY TESTS

On the following pages you will find pull-out Mastery Tests specifically covering the types of problems we've discussed in this book.

FRAGMENTS

Directions: Label the following "F" for fragment or "S" for sentence.

_____ 1. Beneath the orange moon I often see in October.

_____ 2. Flying from one end of the country to the other is tiring.

_____ 3. Because cancer research has led to better treatment.

_____ 4. As if they knew everything about me.

_____ 5. Really serious problems facing older Americans.

_____ 6. When all she wanted to do was give her father a hug.

_____ 7. Getting angry usually doesn't help.

_____ 8. Those games everyone loved as a kid.

_____ 9. After Coco read all of her E-mail.

_____ 10. Two characteristics that all successful doctors seem to share.

FRAGMENTS

Directions: **Label the following "F" for fragment or "S" for sentence.**

_____ 1. Watching the river flow and hoping it would rain.

_____ 2. Written by F. Scott Fitzgerald, the great American novelist.

_____ 3. Before a series of events changed the way I think about college.

_____ 4. A recently discovered letter signed by Thomas Jefferson.

_____ 5. To master the sport of archery and compete in the Olympics was her dream.

_____ 6. Wondering if Juanita will ever get to Paris.

_____ 7. The latest research in genetics.

_____ 8. Entering the construction industry at an early age.

_____ 9. To study constellations in the night sky in preparation for taking Astronomy 101.

_____ 10. That sad looking cat with the gray paws I brought home from the pound watches me wherever I go.

FRAGMENTS

Directions: **Label the following "F" for fragment or "S" for sentence.**

_____   1. To start your own business.

_____   2. The new book I wanted.

_____   3. Belonging to an athletic club offers many advantages.

_____   4. Mowing the lawn wearing shorts, sunglasses, and a bandanna.

_____   5. Watch out!

_____   6. Revising your essay with your dictionary open.

_____   7. Today's children watch too much television.

_____   8. In the decades before the Industrial Revolution began.

_____   9. Because Juanita loved the beach, she convinced Aunt Darlene to rent a condo in Biloxi.

_____   10. After watching six subtitled French movies.

FRAGMENTS

MASTERY TEST 4

Directions: **Underline any fragments you find in the following paragraph.**

For some students, high school is not a fair indicator of college success. After struggling with some subjects in high school. Some students come to college determined to start over again. They develop positive attitudes. About subjects they once thought they didn't like. Subjects they found difficult. This new attitude often gives them the spark they need to achieve success.

RUN-ONS AND COMMA SPLICES MASTERY TEST 5

Directions: Label the following "S" for sentence, "CS" for comma splice, or "RO" for run-on. If it is a CS or RO, correct it.

_____ 1. My favorite show is on let's watch it.

_____ 2. Coco loves to paint, her favorite subject is her dog, Grover.

_____ 3. Many people fear flying they have to take trains or buses if they aren't willing to drive.

_____ 4. There are several reasons for the president's recent trip to Spain, one is the need to discuss trade issues.

_____ 5. Juanita is involved in six activities this semester, the badminton team gets most of her attention.

_____ 6. Thomas Edison invented the lightbulb it was just one of the many inventions that have changed the way we live.

_____ 7. The director of the movie is responsible for many things if the movie is good you can give credit to the director.

_____ 8. After hitting the ball, Cedric ran as fast as he could, he was rewarded with a home run.

_____ 9. Mothers and daughters have a special relationship my wife and daughter finish each other's sentences.

_____ 10. Uncle Waylon got in the car he was going to Timmy's Restaurant for red beans and rice.

RUN-ONS AND COMMA SPLICES   MASTERY TEST 6

Directions: **Label the following "S" for sentence, "CS" for comma splice, or "RO" for run-on. If it is a CS or RO, correct it.**

_____ 1. Discussing the defense budget, the two candidates began to argue.

_____ 2. Right after her twentieth high school reunion. Aunt Darlene decided to return to college she says it's the best thing she ever did.

_____ 3. Some trails are steeper than others that one is the steepest.

_____ 4. Watch the sunset it's beautiful.

_____ 5. Thomas Jefferson designed his home, which is known as Monticello, as well as the campus of the University of Virginia in Charlottesville.

_____ 6. Steven Spielberg has directed many great movies, *Empire of the Sun* is his best.

_____ 7. In the nineteenth century, landscape painters helped to popularize the American West soon everyone wanted to get on a train to California.

_____ 8. Don't go away mad just go away.

_____ 9. Cedric forgave Coco for losing the CD she borrowed, even though she didn't apologize.

_____ 10. Life is just a bowl of cherries, so live and laugh at it all.

RUN-ONS AND COMMA SPLICES   MASTERY TEST 7

Directions: **Label the following "S" for sentence, "CS" for comma splice, or "RO" for run on. If it is a CS or RO, correct it.**

_____   1. Finding good music on the radio isn't easy.

_____   2. Having her own apartment has taught Juanita many things it has helped her grow up.

_____   3. That new medicine is having great results everyone with a cold will want to try it.

_____   4. Getting a bad reputation is easy, living it down is hard.

_____   5. Cities are great places to meet new people if you are outgoing you can make new friends every day.

_____   6. The American farmer has trouble making a profit some feel that federal subsidies are the best way to handle this problem.

_____   7. Cedric has learned to organize his time carefully returning from school, he immediately gets started on his homework.

_____   8. Many advertisers exaggerate, have you ever noticed how gigantic fast food hamburgers look in their TV ads?

_____   9. It is so frustrating to lose things if you want to find something look within a three-foot radius of where you think you left it.

_____   10. It's not so bad to be average, but you should always strive to be better.

RUN-ONS AND COMMA SPLICES MASTERY TEST 8

Directions: Underline and then correct any run-ons and comma splices you find in the following paragraph.

Moving isn't easy it takes careful planning. First of all you need to inventory all of your furniture and belongings to determine how large a truck you need to rent. While you are renting your truck, consider buying boxes and renting furniture pads, both of these things will be essential for your move. If you have friends or relatives lined up to help you move, be sure you notify them of the date of your move as soon as you know it. Having your truck, your boxes and pads, and your helpers ready well in advance will make things go smoothly you might not even mind all of the hard work.

SUBJECT/VERB AGREEMENT   MASTERY TEST 9

Directions: **Underline the correct form of the verbs in the following sentences.**

1. Children who eat dinner with their families grows/grow up with better manners than those who don't.

2. Coco and Juanita has/have invited Cedric to join their sociology study group.

3. People who listens/listen carefully are more successful in life.

4. My uncle was/were important to my development when I was in high school.

5. Hitting golf balls is/are Juanita's favorite way to relax.

6. Astronomy and history is/are my favorite subjects.

7. Sometimes it seems/seem like heroes is/are hard to find.

8. My sister and I has/have the same sense of humor.

9. Having friends helps/help you get through rough times.

10. A wise person invests/invest in a college education.

SUBJECT/VERB AGREEMENT   MASTERY TEST 10

Directions: **Underline the correct form of the verbs in the following sentences.**

1. Planning for the future just makes/make sense.

2. My girlfriend and I is/are going out for tacos.

3. Cedric and Uncle Waylon still collects/collect baseball cards.

4. The Chicago Cubs plays/play at Wrigley Field.

5. At garage sales, I tries/try to find furniture for my new apartment.

6. Late afternoon traffic causes/cause many delays.

7. Those doughnuts is/are deliciously different.

8. The new washer and dryer works/work beautifully.

9. My hands shakes/shake whenever I have to speak before a large audience.

10. Every Sunday Aunt Darlene and Uncle Waylon eats/eat at Timmy's Restaurant.

SUBJECT/VERB AGREEMENT   MASTERY TEST 11

Directions: Underline the correct form of the verb in each of the following sentences.

1. There was/were many people waiting for the box office to open.

2. Those movies was/were exciting and made you think.

3. Juanita and Cedric plans/plan to get together this weekend.

4. Going to parades cheers/cheer me up.

5. That line of cruise ships has/have been very successful.

6. After art class, Cedric always walks/walk over to the coffee house at the mall.

7. All that glitters is/are not gold.

8. It was/were no surprise that the carpenters was/were late again.

9. Here is/are the credit card statement and the refund check.

10. The mandatory retirement age at my company has/have been raised to 70.

SUBJECT/VERB AGREEMENT

MASTERY TEST 12

Directions: Read over the following paragraph and make corrections where necessary.

Family heirlooms is my most prized possessions. I has two chairs that once belonged to my grandmother. One of these chairs were given to her by her grandmother, so you can just imagine how old it is. These chairs make me think of my grandmother and all of the good times we had. They means more to me than anything money could buy.

VERB TENSE

Directions: **Circle any verb tense problems you find in the following sentences and make corrections. Put a "C" beside any sentence that is correct.**

_____ 1. Last night, I seen fireworks over the river.

_____ 2. When Juanita was a child, she search for spare change wherever she went.

_____ 3. I come to this country seven years ago.

_____ 4. Cedric replace the team's usual quarterback right before the game end last Sunday.

_____ 5. Christopher Columbus hoped to find a quick route to the Orient.

_____ 6. Coco had forgot to bring her library card, but they let her check books out anyway.

_____ 7. During World War II, women work in munitions factories.

_____ 8. Before television, family life consist of playing games, talking, and reading books.

_____ 9. At the bowling tournament last Thursday, Aunt Darlene place third in her division.

_____ 10. The first time Richard Nixon run for president, John F. Kennedy was elected.

VERB TENSE

Directions: **Circle any verb tense problems you find in the following sentences and make corrections. Put a "C" beside any sentence that is correct.**

_____ 1. F. Scott Fitzgerald had wrote The Great Gatsby before he turned 30.

_____ 2. Cable has change the way we think about television.

_____ 3. In the 1950s, many people talk about the way Elvis Presley swing his hips.

_____ 4. The architect, Frank Lloyd Wright, design many important buildings during his career.

_____ 5. Back in high school, I enjoy my French class.

_____ 6. Uncle Waylon begun keeping a diary when he turn 14.

_____ 7. For years, I believe that leprechauns exist.

_____ 8. When school was over, the teacher erase the board.

_____ 9. The delegates didn't know that they were suppose to check in before entering the convention hall.

_____ 10. We use to go to the amusement park every summer.

VERB TENSE

Directions: **Rewrite the following sentences in the past tense.**

1. The newly elected president selects his cabinet.

   _____

2. I am performing in my first piano recital this Sunday afternoon.

   _____

3. After adding the eggs, Timmy stirs in two cups of flour.

   _____

4. The stock market is very volatile.

   _____

5. These workers save money by bringing their own lunches.

   _____

6. I do yard work more efficiently when I listen to music.

   _____

7. That artist paints a masterpiece every time he picks up a brush.

   _____

8. Mr. Waylon runs a write-in campaign for mayor.

   _____

9. The department opens early for the holiday sale.

   _____

10. I am concerned about the money problems I've gotten into.

   _____

VERB TENSE

Directions: **Rewrite the following paragraph in the past tense.**

I make New Year's resolutions every year. I don't keep them, but I make them. I usually make the same ones. I swear I will give up chocolate. I promise myself to exercise daily. I say I will read a book every week. I insist I will save money. I usually keep my resolutions for about three weeks.

SPELLING SOUND-ALIKES

MASTERY TEST 17

Directions: **Underline the correctly spelled choices in the following sentences.**

1. (They're, There, Their) are (too, two, to) many people on this (plain, plane).

2. He didn't know (whether, weather) to send more troops to the battlefront.

3. (They're, There, Their) trip has had (its, it's) ups and downs.

4. A (principle, principal) must help teachers do (they're, there, their) jobs.

5. I wanted (to, two, too) take my brother's shirt, but my (concious, conscience) wouldn't let me.

6. (They're, There, Their) going (to, two, too) vote in the next election.

7. Bring those books over (hear, here).

8. After being lost in the (dessert, desert), it's great to (hear, here) a familiar voice.

9. Coco and Juanita told (there, they're, their) new friends to meet them at (to, two, too) o'clock.

10. Come tomorrow (to, two, too) see if you like (there, they're, their) new carpeting.

SPELLING SOUND-ALIKES   MASTERY TEST 18

Directions: Underline the correctly spelled choices in the following sentences.

1. (They're, There, Their) are (too, two, to) many cookies on this plate.

2. (It's, its) time for a change at city hall.

3. (They're, There, Their) friends ordered (to, two, too) many pizzas.

4. (Hear, Here) are the election results.

5. (They're, There, Their) going (to, two, too) move to Seattle.

6. Teachers want (they're, there, their) students to do well.

7. (To, Two, Too) many things in this world are overpriced.

8. The mayor is wondering (whether, weather) to change the parking laws in the business district.

9. Upon being seated in the theater, (it's, its) nice to (hear, here) the orchestra warm up.

10. Ask the (principle, principal) to (write, right) you a letter of recommendation.

Directions: **Underline the correctly spelled choices in the following sentences.**

1. I was tempted (to, two, too) copy the term paper, but my (conscious, conscience) kept me honest.

2. Come on (Wednesday, Wensday) (to, two, too) see if you like the new carpet.

3. He didn't know (weather, whether) to send more troops to the battlefront.

4. Being fair is one of the (principles, principals) I live by.

5. The ambassador (recieved, received) a message from the Chinese delegation.

6. A large rock crashed (through, threw) the window.

7. The children are walking (passed, past) the crossing guard.

8. A security guard (probally, probably) didn't show up for work that (night, nite).

9. The man was (anksious, anxious) about his (anual, annual) check-up.

10. The (restrant's, restaurant's) (buisness, business) address is on (their, there) (calender, calendar).

SPELLING   MASTERY TEST 20

Directions: **Underline the correctly spelled choices in the following sentences.**

1. That new kung-fu movie is (boreing, boring).

2. The prince is (sleeping, sleepping) at the White House.

3. The old (library, liberry) was (beutiful, beautiful).

4. (There, Their, They're) was a (chandeleir, chandelier) hanging from the center of the (ceiling, cieling).

5. The orange stripes on that shirt (compliment, complement) the brown ones.

6. Children have a natural capacity for (mischeif, mischief).

7. (Its, It's) the hospital's (responsibility, responsability) to keep the patient informed.

8. (Neither, Niether) of those patients is running a (temperature, temperture) at the moment.

9. "I'm having a (weird, wierd) (Wensday, Wednesday)," said Coco.

10. That's an (intresting, interesting) word though you have (misspelled, mispelled) it.

PRONOUNS   MASTERY TEST 21

Directions: **Underline the correct pronoun in each of the following sentences.**

1. One of those cowboys left (his/their) money on the bus.

2. Many professors have (his or her/their) own offices.

3. The book club will read (its/their) first biography this winter.

4. Each of the children brought (his or her/their) own lunch.

5. Those drivers need to get (his or her/their) cars inspected.

6. People all over the world want (his or her/their) own cars.

7. Every one of those girls has (her/their) own career plans.

8. The dance company will give (its/their) annual performance this weekend.

9. All of the governors meeting in Chicago have (his or her/their) own agendas.

10. Coco and Juanita brought (her/their) best dishes to the potluck supper.

PRONOUNS

Directions: Underline the correct pronoun in each of the following sentences.

1. Aunt Darlene and Juanita really need (her/their) Disney World vacation this year.

2. The National Park Service has established (its/their) own rules.

3. The Democratic Party will have (its/their) convention in Los Angeles this year.

4. Only one of my brothers will have (his/their) birthday party at the Pizza Place this year.

5. Tell those girls to bring (her/their) books with them to the biology exam.

6. The Vinyl Records Appreciation Society will have (its/their) fund-raiser this month.

7. Six out of ten doctors hang (his or her/their) diplomas in (his or her/their) office waiting rooms.

8. Every one of the soccer players bought (his or her/their) own souvenir T-shirt.

9. Stagecoach drivers in the old west took care of (his or her/their) own horses.

10. Those are the boys who forgot to bring (his or her/their) gym clothes.

Directions: **Add or remove apostrophes where necessary in the following sentences. If the sentence is correct, write "C" beside it.**

_____ 1. The kitchens wallpaper is green and gold.

_____ 2. Many American's live in small towns.

_____ 3. The homeowner's installed new window's and door's.

_____ 4. What would the world's floors be like if we had no vacuum cleaners?

_____ 5. That bands lead singer sings off-key.

_____ 6. The pianists fingers flew across the keys.

_____ 7. The trains whistle sound's so mournful.

_____ 8. Juanita has celebrated her last six birthdays at one of our towns bowling alley's.

_____ 9. There are over 3,000 varieties of mushroom's in America.

_____ 10. The cat sat in the building's shadow.

APOSTROPHES

Directions: **Add or remove apostrophes where necessary in the following sentences. If the sentence is correct, write "C" beside it.**

_____ 1. Cedric doesn't know whether he's going to Juanitas for dinner.

_____ 2. I just got a job at Rosenbergs Fine Furniture.

_____ 3. That trees branches' need to be trimmed.

_____ 4. The shed's lock has been broken.

_____ 5. Automakers have high hope's for the success of this years model's.

_____ 6. The musicians guitar crashed to the stage.

_____ 7. The library's reserve collection is much larger than it used to be.

_____ 8. When I read the journalists account of what happened, I couldn't believe it.

_____ 9. A childrens' museum is a great place to spend a Sunday afternoon.

_____ 10. The girls soccer team will play in this years tournament.

ENDINGS

Directions: **Add "s" or "ed" endings where necessary in the following sentences.**

1. Smoking can irritate your eye.

2. By 9 P.M., the stores will be close.

3. Aunt Darlene loves her newly remodel kitchen.

4. She's proud of the gleaming white appliance.

5. Those scientist are working on a cure for Alzheimer disease.

6. I have ask the manager for a new lock.

7. The blue bowl full of Florida orange is beautiful.

8. This car was design for speed.

9. Let's not talk about problem; let's talk about solution.

10. The dog slid across the freshly wax floor.

Directions: **Add "s" or "ed" endings where necessary in the following sentences.**

1. We have three new car in our driveway.

2. My mother has raise three successful children.

3. There are library in every neighborhood of this city.

4. Dieters usually choose grill chicken.

5. In the country, Cedric saw dozen of insect.

6. I sometime wish I had time to put puzzle together.

7. After years of burning coal, the buildings of London were blacken with soot.

8. Coco has two part-time job at the mall.

9. Uncle Waylon likes a well-starch collar on his shirt.

10. This chair is well design; it's so comfortable.

COMMAS   MASTERY TEST 27

Directions: **Insert commas wherever necessary in the following sentences.**

1. Franklin Roosevelt the U.S. president during the Depression is famous for many things.

2. Cedric brought bread ham mustard and pickles.

3. Come here Uncle Waylon.

4. After flying down to Rio we searched for a hotel room.

5. "You can't change anyone but yourself" said the doctor.

6. Washing clothes cleaning the kitchen and vacuuming the living room are great ways to
   ruin a Saturday.

7. That young man the one wearing the blue top hat sure knows how to attract attention.

8. Because we couldn't wait any longer we left without saying goodbye.

9. For her birthday Juanita received two paperbacks a CD a vanilla candle a gift certificate
   good for two movie tickets and a pair of rhinestone sunglasses.

10. He was born on October 24 1982 in New Orleans Louisiana.

COMMAS   MASTERY TEST 28

Directions: Insert commas as needed in the following sentences.

1. The alarm rang and it was time to get up.

2. To avoid getting sick take vitamins eat right and get enough sleep.

3. We will meet again on September 22 2002.

4. After the summit meeting the two political parties made a joint announcement.

5. My uncle one of the first graduates of this university was honored at graduation.

6. Shopping from a catalog is fun easy and convenient.

7. "It's time for bed" said my mother.

8. A blue whale one of the largest sea creatures was sighted off the coast.

9. Before the war women rarely worked in factories.

10. I went to school in Amherst Massachusetts.

CAPITAL LETTERS

Directions: **Add capital letters where necessary in the following sentences.**

1. On my vacation I visited chicago, washington, d.c. and new orleans.

2. Toni Morrison, the author of *the bluest eye*, won the nobel prize.

3. Uncle Waylon traded in his chevrolet blazer.

4. My best subjects are english and math.

5. We visited the national gallery and the smithsonian institution.

6. Those trees are full of robins and sparrows.

7. Juanita hopes to arrive home from the south by july first.

8. The best florida grapefruit are available in the winter.

9. computer bargain town is having a sale this weekend.

10. That pekinese dog's name is shantalia zarac.

CAPITAL LETTERS   MASTERY TEST 30

Directions: Add capital letters where necessary in the following sentences.

1. My dream is to climb mount Everest with a descendant of sir Edmund Hillary.

2. The national park system maintains shenandoah national park in the blue ridge mountains.

3. While in chicago, aunt Darlene visited the sears tower.

4. I've never been to moscow, but I hear the kremlin is beautiful.

5. Juanita always looks for the big dipper in the night sky.

6. After the civil war, many northerners moved to the south.

7. The band consists of two gibson guitars, a hammond organ and a ludwig drum set.

8. Aunt Darlene's favorite groups are the temptations, the supremes, and the miracles.

9. Can you name the capitals of england and france?

10. The houston astros play at the astrodome.

MISPLACED MODIFIERS   MASTERY TEST 31

Directions: Rewrite the following sentences to eliminate all misplaced modifiers.

1. Made of salsa and cheese, Aunt Darlene couldn't resist the spicy dip.

   _____

   _____

2. He walked out wearing a gray suit with a glass of lemonade.

   _____

   _____

3. By climbing to the top of the mountain, the lights of the city could be seen in the distance.

   _____

   _____

4. After plowing the fields, few words were spoken.

   _____

   _____

5. Being very angry, the president tried to calm the senator down.

   _____

   _____

6. Riding at the front of the parade, hundreds of sports fans could see the winning team.

   _____

   _____

7. When a young driver, my father always told me to be careful.

   _____

   _____

8. While running to the store, a dog jumped in front of my truck.

   _____

   _____

9. Playing loud music at 3 A.M., Aunt Darlene called her neighbors and told them to stop.

   _____

   _____

10. Having no more money, the king gave his subjects the food they needed for free.

   _____

   _____

***Directions:* Rewrite the following sentences to eliminate all misplaced modifiers.**

1. Cleaned and polished to a high sheen, the young woman entered her Chevrolet in the custom car competition.

   _____

   _____

2. While eating fish scraps from a bowl, I petted the cat.

   _____

   _____

3. Having stolen four hubcaps, the policeman chased the thief.

   _____

   _____

4. Burned black and tasting like charcoal, I threw the toast away.

   _____

   _____

5. Not taking proper care of himself, the doctor gave his patient a lecture.

   _____

   _____

6. Although unknown in this country, Hollywood became the destination of the English actor.

   _____

   _____

7. Faded and stretched out, Cedric decided he needed a new sweater.

   _____

   _____

8. To watch television comfortably, the sofa needs to be moved.

   _____

   _____

9. While taking a bath, the phone rang.

   _____

   _____

10. Sold at a profit, I was glad I'd saved my baseball cards.

   _____

   _____

PARALLELISM

Directions: **Rewrite all of the sentences below to make them parallel.**

1. The new computer games entertain, educate, and are amazing.

   _____

   _____

2. Playing the stock market can make you rich, drain your bank account, or leaving you just about the same.

   _____

   _____

3. Aunt Darlene's hobbies include reading cookbooks devoted to spicy food, learning folk dances from other countries, and to paint cat faces on medium sized rocks.

   _____

   _____

4. We watched as the pony jumped the fence, ran up the hill, and then sliding back down.

   _____

   _____

5. The new cars are shinier, roomier, and easy to drive.

   _____

   _____

6. My father thought all car dealers were pushy, deceitful, and full of greed.

   _____

   _____

7. Good writers know how to plan their time, make corrections, and are always looking for ways to increase their vocabularies.

   _____

   _____

8. Her stories are entertaining, thrilling, and they frighten me.

   _____

   _____

9. The judge told the divorcing couple that they were being selfish, unfair, and that they were hurtful to their children.

   _____

   _____

10. Many visitors to the memorial are moved, educated, and changing because of the experience.

   _____

   _____

PARALLELISM

Directions: Rewrite all of the sentences below to make them parallel.

1. Aunt Darlene's nighttime ritual consists of playing the piano, eating saltine crackers, and to go to bed.

_____

_____

2. Cleaning your car means to vacuum the interior, wash the windshield, and polishing the hubcaps.

_____

_____

3. We got lost going to the mall, broke Dad's radio, and running out of gas all in the same afternoon.

_____

_____

4. Mr. Waylon hired someone to paint his living room, sand the floor, and for hanging new drapes.

_____

_____

5. The FBI agent likes to barbecue and horseback riding in his spare time.

_____

_____

6. A summer job on the road crew is exhausting, boring, and something that will irritate you every day.

_____

_____

7. In this city, too many drivers drive too fast, ignore stop signs, and are making illegal turns.

_____

_____

8. Most cats like lounging, sleeping, and to chase mice.

_____

_____

9. Travel opens you to new ways of looking at things, makes you think, and helping you escape your everyday grind.

_____

_____

10. The panel of judges narrowed the field, picked a winner, and awarding the prize.

_____

_____

QUOTATION MARKS   MASTERY TEST 35

Directions: **Add quotation marks wherever necessary in the following sentences.**

1. Raymond Carver's The Car is one of my favorite poems.

2. Don't take any wooden nickels, said Uncle Waylon.

3. In the Cemetery Where Al Jolson Is Buried by Amy Hempel is a good short story.

4. My father always told us, Life's too short to be miserable.

5. The last line of *The Great Gatsby,* and so we beat on, boats against the current, has always touched me.

6. When I was in college, I memorized the poem Degrees of Gray in Phillipsburg by Richard Hugo.

7. The new tax law, declared the senator, should be repealed.

8. That painting is called West of the Sun, East of the Moon.

9. My favorite episode of that TV show, Petunia's Problem Pooch, was nominated for an Emmy.

10. Come over here, said my mother, right this instant!

QUOTATION MARKS

Directions: **Add quotation marks wherever necessary in the following sentences.**

1. Aretha Franklin's most popular hits include Respect and Natural Woman.

2. Have you ever read the poem Trees by Joyce Kilmer?

3. My short story class will be studying The Pit and the Pendulum by Edgar Allan Poe next week.

4. My father always said Don't count your chickens before they're hatched, and now I know why.

5. I've never forgotten the Tom and Jerry cartoon, Tom's Night Out.

6. Ben Franklin is famous for saying, A penny saved is a penny earned.

7. My mother used to recite Little Orphan Annie by James Whitcomb Riley.

8. Kurt Vonnegut's story, Harrison Bergeron, is included in this textbook.

9. One of the strangest songs of the 1960s was MacArthur Park written by Jimmy Webb.

10. Do you like the painting Sunflowers by Van Gogh?

OTHER SENTENCE END PUNCTUATION   MASTERY TEST 37

Directions: **Place the correct mark (period, question mark, exclamation point) at the end of each of the following sentences.**

1. Get down off that ledge

2. Are we almost home

3. If the television breaks, will those children be able to entertain themselves

4. Forget about it

5. Why are these things happening at the beginning of a new century

6. The ruling of the Supreme Court will be read on Tuesday

7. Does that insurance company offer lower rates to college students

8. Don't lose your key

9. Being a chimney sweep has unexpected benefits

10. Am I supposed to go with them or with you

OTHER SENTENCE END PUNCTUATION   MASTERY TEST 38

Directions: Place the correct mark (period, question mark, exclamation point) at the end of each of the following sentences.

1. The house is on fire   Help

2. Let's find a solution before the end of the semester

3. Is there any reason not to support the school tax initiative

4. The boat sank while out on its maiden voyage

5. If we're late, can we still buy tickets at the box office

6. Find those books immediately

7. Run for your life

8. What sort of personality does the average Siamese cat have

9. Many boats come up the river every day

10. When we walk in the woods at night, are we foolish not to carry flashlights

PART 9

FOR SECOND LANGUAGE
LEARNERS

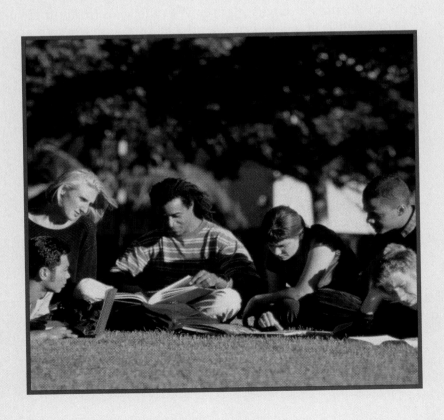

46

ADDITIONAL GUIDELINES FOR ESL STUDENTS

If you are taking a class where this textbook is used, you already know quite a lot about the English language. Learning another language is an ongoing process, and as most native speakers of English will tell you, the process of learning English never ends. There are always new words to discover and new ways to put them together.

One of the reasons why English is such a rich and fascinating language is the fact that it owes so much to other languages. Every day we encounter and/or use words in English that have come to us from other cultures.

The English language is also enriched by the new words and expressions that quickly become incorporated into daily speech. When you are new to a language, it is hard to keep up with all the changes, but when you get the basics down, the rest will come more easily. One of the things you want to be sure to do is to take advantage of every opportunity you can to practice your listening, speaking, reading, and writing skills. All of these skills build on each other and will strengthen your knowledge of English. Since the focus of this section is on improving your reading and writing skills, we'd like to share some suggestions and rules with you.

Reading

Every bit of reading you do helps to improve your understanding of the way English works. Reading allows you to see how English sentences are constructed—from the proper placement of the subject to the form the verb takes. It shows you how punctuation is used effectively to communicate what the author is trying to say. The wonderful thing about reading is that you pick up a lot of information without really trying. As long as you're reading along and understanding the information you're taking in, you're picking up valuable information on writing and reading. Therefore, it's a good idea to make reading a top priority whenever you have free time. Reading material is everywhere—from road signs and billboards on the highway to recipes on a cereal box and the countless forms of print advertising. There are magazines on just about every subject, and books and newspapers are available everywhere. The Internet, of course, also offers endless reading opportunities. The important thing is to take advantage of the words around you—to read them all. Keep your dictionary handy, and take the time to make sense out of all of the words you see.

Writing

With increased exposure to all that there is to read, you will become more secure as you write in English. In this section, we review key concepts in building sentences.

Every sentence must have a subject *and* a verb. The <u>subject</u> is a word that indicates *who or what* is performing or performed the action of the sentence. It tells *who* or *what is* or *who* or *what does*. The <u>verb</u> is a word that indicates the actions in a sentence. It tells what someone or something *does* in the present, *did* in the past, or *will* do in the future. The verb can also tell what someone or something *is* in the present, *was* in the past, or *will be* in the future. Let's look at some examples:

My boss hires new workers every summer.

Who hires? Boss = SUBJECT
What does someone do? Hires = VERB

The mayor talked about neighborhood pride.

Who talked? Mayor = SUBJECT
What did someone do? Talked = VERB

The bus needed to be washed.

What needed? Bus = SUBJECT
What did something do? Needed = VERB

MAKING THE RULES WORK

Here are some examples when the rules about subjects and verbs weren't followed. Following these, we show a few in which the rules were followed.

Doesn't Work!

Is a good father. (No SUBJECT)

The president at the White House. (No VERB)

The president living at the White House. (No VERB)

Without subjects or verbs, these are <u>fragments</u>, not sentences.

Works!

Hector is a good father.

The president lives at the White House.

The president is living at the White House.

Want to know more about subjects and verbs? Refer to Part 7, page 244.

ACTIVITY 46-1

Directions: Decide if the following groups of words are sentences. Write an "S" for sentences and an "F" for fragments in the space provided. Correct all fragments by adding a subject or a verb.

_____ 1. Today's children not studying enough.

_____ 2. My mother needed me to help her at home.

_____ 3. Was not enough money to attend college.

_____ 4. Brought sandwiches to eat at work.

_____ 5. Tam's sister dialing the number of the library.

You must also keep in mind that the subject usually comes before the verb in a sentence. In most English sentences, the subject comes first and the verb follows later. Sometimes the verb will follow directly after the subject.

The soccer <u>team</u> played two games on Sunday.
         S   V

The <u>doctor</u> wrote out a prescription.
    S   V

Sometimes the verb will follow the subject, but other words will separate them.

The soccer <u>team</u> in the red shirts played two games on Sunday.
       S   V

The <u>doctor</u>, after checking the patient's file, wrote out a prescription.
    S   V

MAKING THE RULES WORK

Doesn't Work!

Bought a new car, my brother.

Was appointed to the Supreme Court, Sandra Day O'Connor.

Works!

My brother bought a new car.

Sandra Day O'Connor was appointed to the Supreme Court.

ACTIVITY 46-2

Directions: Check the word order in the following sentences. Use the space below to make any changes that are needed to correct the problems you find.

1. Placed second in the swimming competition, Cedric.

2. Wanting to clean up the environment in general, they decided to clean up their own neighborhood.

3. Is controlled by people who don't know anything about what is good, the music industry.

4. Celebrates his eighty-eighth birthday this year, my grandfather.

5. Beginning to worry that he would miss the bus, the plumber called a cab.

EXCEPTIONS TO THE RULE

Word order changes when you ask a question. Look at the following sentences and notice what happens to the wording when a statement turns into a question. Sometimes you have to use helpers—*did, do, does, has, have,* or *had*—to ask a question.

Statement: The <u>mechanic</u> is fixing my car.

Question: Is the <u>mechanic</u> fixing my car?

Statement: The <u>drugstore</u> was looking for cashiers.

Question: Was the <u>drugstore</u> looking for cashiers?

Statement: <u>Tam</u> had to study hard for her math test.

Question: Did <u>Tam</u> have to study hard for her math test?

Statement: The <u>cost</u> of living went up.

Question: Has the <u>cost</u> of living gone up?

MAKING THE RULES WORK

Doesn't Work!

The winters are long here?

The Mississippi River runs into the Gulf of Mexico?

The Career Placement Center has a new bulletin board?

Works!

Are the winters long here?

Does the Mississippi River run into the Gulf of Mexico?

Does the Career Placement Center have a new bulletin board?

ACTIVITY 46-3

Directions: Reword any of the following questions in the space below that aren't in the correct subject/verb order.

1. The fall semester begins on Monday?

2. He wants to join the athletic club?

3. The newspaper is published every day?

4. The ancient Egyptians worshiped cats?

5. Aunt Darlene went fishing with Timmy?

SENTENCES STARTING WITH "HERE" OR "THERE"

The usual subject/verb order also changes when you start a sentence with "here" or "there." Under these circumstances, the verb comes before the subject. Here are some examples:

There are several <u>reasons</u> to own a home computer.
     V   S

Here is your <u>wallet</u>.
  V   S

MAKING THE RULES WORK

Doesn't Work!

Here the questions you need to answer are.

There the new librarian's cat is.

Works!

Here are the questions you need to answer.

There is the new librarian's cat.

ACTIVITY 46-4

Directions: Check the word order in the following sentences. Use the space below to make any changes that are needed to correct the problems you find.

1. There fresh tomatoes and apples are at the farmer's market.

2. There are many ways to fix potatoes.

3. Here the kind of melon I love is.

4. Here the bushels of sweet corn are.

5. There the manager of the farmer's market is.

In addition to knowing the proper subject/verb order, you must use the right punctuation at the end of every sentence.

MAKING THE RULES WORK

Doesn't Work!

Listening to music is my favorite leisure activity, it relaxes me.

Listening to music is my favorite leisure activity it relaxes me.

Works!

Listening to music is my favorite leisure activity. It relaxes me.

Listening to music is my favorite leisure activity because it relaxes me.

Listening to music is my favorite leisure activity; it relaxes me.

ACTIVITY 46-5

Directions: Determine whether the following sentences have correct end punctuation. Correct any sentence end punctuation problems you find.

If it's a comma splice (Sentence, Sentence mistake), put "S,S" in the blank.
If it's a run-on (SentenceSentence mistake), put "SS" in the blank.
If the end punctuation is correct, put a "C" in the blank.

_____ 1. The new chair is made of solid wood, Aunt Darlene likes oak and maple furniture.

_____ 2. Summer is my favorite season I can go swimming every day.

_____ 3. This is an excellent production of <u>The Tempest</u> all of the performers practiced for weeks.

_____ 4. Aunt Darlene has never been to South America, but she hopes to go soon.

_____ 5. I am sorry I sold my literature book it contained many interesting stories.

MAKING WORDS PLURAL

When you want to show that there is more than one of something in English, you usually add the letter "s." This is what you do with words that are *countable*; that is, words that can be counted.

1 bicycle... 2 bicycles

1 cat... 14 cats

1 cookie... 6 cookies

1 television... 3 televisions

Some words are things that are *uncountable*. This means that they *can't* be counted.

faith	charity	gossip
grease	intelligence	music
bravery	wealth	corruption
furniture	news	

To review, if you can count something, then you can make it plural by adding an "s." If you can't count it, then you can't make it plural.

MAKING THE RULES WORK

Doesn't Work!

I have a lot of faiths.

Juanita bought new furnitures for her apartment.

Works!

I have a lot of faith.

Juanita bought new furniture for her apartment.

ACTIVITY 46-6

Directions: Correct any problems with countable and uncountable words that you find in the following sentences.

1. My suitcases were packed with many clothing.

2. The store delivered the new furnitures last Saturday.

3. His father told him he had faiths in him.

4. I advise you to put the monies he gave you in the bank.

5. The soldiers were rewarded for their braveries.

Some words become plural without adding "s." These words change their spelling to indicate more than one of something.

1 woman... 2 women

1 man... 6 men

1 person... 4 people

MAKING THE RULES WORK

Doesn't Work!

Tell those persons to turn down the music.

Many womens are running for political office in this country.

Works!

Tell those people to turn down the music.

Many women are running for political office in this country.

ACTIVITY 46-7

Directions: Correct any problems you find in the formation of plurals in the following sentences.

1. Would you please put some ices in my Coke?

2. My daughter invited six childs to her birthday party.

3. Gooses from the North fly south for the winter.

4. The seafood plate comes with six shrimps.

5. Those mans haven't registered to vote yet.

USING THE VERB "DO"

The verb "do" (PRESENT: *do* or *does*, PAST: *did*) used with another verb can mean only three things:

❶ *A question:*

Do you want to read this book?

❷ *A negative when used with not:*

Tam does not want to read this book.

❸ *Emphasis:*

This book does have beautiful illustrations.

Be sure you do not confuse the verbs "do" and "make." They do not mean the same thing. "Do" usually means to finish or to perform a particular job or procedure.

Do the laundry.

Do the best you can.

Do the first three steps.

"Make" usually means to build or create:

Make a grocery list.

Make an effort.

Make a cake.

MAKING THE RULES WORK

Doesn't Work!

Did you make your homework last night?

Did you make a good job on your project?

Works!

Did you do your homework last night?

Did you do a good job on your project?

ACTIVITY 46-8

Directions: Correct any problems you find with "do" and "make" in the following sentences. If the sentence is correct, leave it alone.

1. Let's do a grocery list before we go to the store.

2. Aunt Juanita does a chocolate cake every Sunday.

3. I did my apology and left early.

4. She did a last attempt to capture the gold ring.

5. Cedric makes well in his history class.

PRONOUNS

As we told you on page 281, pronouns are words that substitute, or replace nouns. Here are some pronoun rules to keep in mind:

❶ You don't need a pronoun to repeat the subject.

MAKING THE RULES WORK

Doesn't Work!

The teacher she is very helpful.

The new CD player it is fantastic.

Works!

The teacher is very helpful.

The new CD player is fantastic.

ACTIVITY 46-9

Directions: Eliminate any unnecessary pronouns in the following sentences.

1. The forest ranger she is very concerned about a fire that is out of control down by the river.

2. The sculptors of the nineteenth century they mainly worked with bronze.

3. The trees surrounding the lake they have just begun to turn orange.

4. Coco, who was just elected president of the student government, she wants to give students a refund.

5. The marketing executive he announced his plan for the new products.

❷ You don't need a pronoun to replace a word that *who, whom, whose, which,* or *that* already refers to.

Doesn't Work!

Those are the cashiers who they ignored me.

Works!

Those are the cashiers who ignored me.

ACTIVITY 46-10

Directions: Eliminate any unnecessary pronouns in the following sentences.

1. This is the kind of situation that it really makes me mad.

2. I met the woman who she wants to buy your car.

3. I lost the keys which he left them in my kitchen.

4. Did you find the dog that it got lost in the park?

5. These are the people who they won the prize.

MODIFIERS

Modifiers are words used to describe a noun (person, place, or thing).

❶ If you are going to use *a, an,* and *the* correctly, you need to understand the difference between "countable" and "uncountable" nouns (see explanation on p. 380).

> ◆ With singular countable nouns whose identity is not specified, use *a* or *an*.
>
> My sister read *a* book over the weekend.

> ◆ With a singular countable noun whose identity is specified, use *the*.
>
> My sister read *the* book that is number one on the bestseller list.

> ◆ With plural nouns or uncountable nouns never use *a* or *an*.
>
> We bought a new furniture for our living room.
>
> We bought new furniture for our living room.

MAKING THE RULES WORK

Doesn't Work!

It took me the hour to do my homework last night.

She couldn't buy the coat because she didn't have a cash with her.

Works!

It took me an hour to do my homework last night.

She couldn't buy the coat because she didn't have the cash with her.

ACTIVITY 46-11

Directions: Underline the correct choice in the following sentences using the rules presented on the previous page.

1. I am going to (a, the) Christmas Party my grandmother gives every year on December 7.

2. She was watching the movie that won (an, the) Academy Award for Best Picture.

3. The coach gave the team (a, the) break.

4. This is (a, the) dream house my parents just built for our family.

5. Most of the students have already passed (a, the) driver's license test.

◆ If the reader already knows the identity of your noun, use *the*.

Here is the pen that I borrowed. (The reader knows which pen you're talking about.)

◆ If an uncountable noun names one member of a larger group, use *the*.

This is the president of our science club.

MAKING THE RULES WORK

Doesn't Work!

She is a most talented member of the theater group.

Works!

She is the most talented member of the theater group.

ACTIVITY 46-12

Directions: Underline the correct word in each of the following sentences.

1. They are restoring (a, the) painting of President Washington that hangs in (a, the) National Gallery.

2. Al Gore was (a, the) Democratic candidate who ran against George W. Bush.

3. You are (a, the) best friend I've ever known.

4. Please bring me (a, the) bag of potato chips from the snack machine.

5. She threw away (a, the) most recent letter her boyfriend sent to her.

❷ Adverbs that show frequency (like *always, often, never,* and *usually*) come after forms of *be* and before other verbs.

After a form of *be*: Tam's car is always breaking down.

Before other *verbs*: Tam's car never breaks down.

MAKING THE RULES WORK

Doesn't Work!

The scientists always are making discoveries.

Works!

The scientists are always making discoveries.

ACTIVITY 46-13

Directions: Decide if the following sentences are correct. Place a "W" for "works" if the sentence is correct or a "DW" for "doesn't work" if it's not. Use the space below to correct any errors you find.

_____ 1. My loan check usually is late.

_____ 2. Juanita listens never to Elvis records.

_____ 3. I often wonder what my life would be like if I won the lottery.

_____ 4. The circus is coming never to our town.

_____ 5. I am always having to make decisions I'm not ready to make.

PREPOSITIONS

Prepositions are words used to show the relation of a noun or pronoun to another word in the sentence. A prepositional phrase is a group of words that begins with a preposition. For further discussion of prepositions and prepositional phrases see page 221.

❶ In English the subject of a sentence never appears in a prepositional phrase.

One of the baseball players is my roommate.

"One" is the subject; "players" is the object of the preposition *of*.

❷ *In*, *on*, and *at* are used in different ways.

◆ Use *in* when you're talking about seasons, months, and years with no specific date.

They are getting married in June.

◆ Use *on* when you're going to give a specific date.

They are getting married on June 5, 2004.

MAKING THE RULES WORK

Doesn't Work!

I'm going on a bus trip to see the autumn leaves on October.

Works!

I'm going on a bus trip to see the autumn leaves in October.

◆ Use *in* for a period of the day (morning, afternoon, night, etc.)

   Juanita and Cedric play cards in the afternoon.

◆ Use *on* for a specific day (Monday, Tuesday, June 12, etc.)

   The semester began on Monday.

◆ Use *at* for a specific time or period of the day (3 P.M., dawn, midnight, etc.)

   The horn sounds at midnight.

MAKING THE RULES WORK

Doesn't Work!

The party was in Saturday.

Coco eats breakfast on the morning.

I left for my afternoon job on noon.

Works!

The party was on Saturday.

Coco eats breakfast in the morning.

I left for my afternoon job at noon.

ACTIVITY 46-14

Directions: Underline the correct choices in the following sentences.

1. People usually take their vacations (in, on, at) July or August.

2. (In, On, At) sunset, we are planning to have a cook-out on the levee.

3. St. Valentine's Day is (in, on, at) February 14.

4. Many stores are open (in, on, at) the afternoon (in, on, at) Sunday.

5. We will leave for the haunted house (in, on, at) midnight (in, on, at) October 31st.

◆ Use *in* for a place surrounded by something else.

The mall is in the center of a large housing development.

◆ Use *at* for a specific place.

She got the books she needed at the public library.

MAKING THE RULES WORK

Doesn't Work!

I will see you in the corner of State and Lake.

Mr. Waylon's dart landed at the middle of the dart board.

Works!

I will see you at the corner of State and Lake.

Mr. Waylon's dart landed in the middle of the dart board.

ACTIVITY 46-15

Directions: Underline the correct choice in each of the following sentences.

1. The postman was (in, at) the middle of his route when he decided to take a break.

2. Aunt Darlene bought a table and two chairs (in, at) the antiques fair.

3. The professor placed his desk (in, at) the center of the classroom.

4. The old man lives (in, at) 1776 Washington Avenue.

5. Cedric got a summer job drying off cars (in, at) the car wash.

❸ You cannot use "to + verb" as objects of prepositions.

MAKING THE RULES WORK

Doesn't Work!

He is asking for to help.

Works!

He is asking for help.

ACTIVITY 46-16

Directions: Revise the following sentences as necessary.

1. She bought that book for to give him.

2. There is a good reason for to give money to charities.

3. His mother made him go to the school of to dance.

4. The lifeguard was hired to teach the finer points of to swim.

5. This truck is used for to transport mail from one post office to another.

❹ Keep in mind that some prepositions are made up of two or more words. Here are some examples:

absent from	according to	accustomed to
on account of	in addition to	as well as
aside from	on behalf of	capable of
familiar with	in front of	guilty of
next to	out of	

This won't be a hard test *according to* my teacher.

They will serve hot dogs and hamburgers *in addition to* the pizza.

When she's in a good mood, my sister is *capable of* being nice.

If Kiki wants to get her driver's license, she will have to be *familiar with* all the driving regulations in this state.

This pen is *out of* ink.

IDIOMS

Idioms are groups of words that cannot be defined by analyzing the meaning of each word. You can look up all of the words in an idiom individually and still not be able to figure out what the idiom means. Sometimes looking up a key word in a dictionary will help, but the best way to deal with idioms is to memorize them.

We are including a list of some of the more common idioms below, but you may want to purchase a dictionary of American idioms.

a bit   a small amount

I need *a bit* more money so I can afford the large French fries.

a lost cause   a hopeless case

My broken down bicycle is *a lost cause.*

above all   mainly

Her parents, *above all,* want her to try hard.

all wet   entirely wrong, mistaken

If you think your ex-girlfriend will help you, you're *all wet.*

be in someone's shoes to experience the same thing as another person

If you were *in my shoes,* you wouldn't be happy either.

can of worms   complicated situation

The argument over whether to build a grocery store in our neighborhood is a *can of worms.*

cross one's heart to promise you've told the truth

I *cross my heart;* I've never said a bad word about you.

down in the dumps discouraged and/or sad

When Coco's car broke down and she couldn't get in touch with Cedric, she was *down in the dumps.*

few and far between infrequent, unusual

Motels that allow you to have pets in your room are *few and far between.*

fly off the handle become very angry

When Mr. Waylon lost all his change in the candy machine, he *flew off the handle.*

get in touch with   contact

If you need a loan, you should *get in touch with* a bank.

goof off   waste time

After the exam, Juanita and Coco went to *goof off* at the bowling alley.

hard-nosed   tough, strict

That policeman is *hard-nosed* about litter.

let up   lessen intensity

After two days, the rains still hadn't *let up*.

on hand   available

We need to know how many people will be *on hand* to help us move.

out to lunch   unaware; distracted and confused.

He made so many mistakes he must have been completely *out to lunch*.

over the hill   old or past the peak of effectiveness

After her car broke down seven times, Coco realized that it was *over the hill*.

play by ear   act spontaneously, without a plan

We may or may not be going out for dinner. After the movie we plan to *play it by ear*.

pick up the tab   pay the bill

Juanita was delighted when Aunt Darlene *picked up the tab* for her birthday party at the bowling alley.

see the light   to understand or agree

After talking to the salesperson for three hours, Coco finally *saw the light* and decided to buy a new car.

show up   arrive or appear

It's a good idea to *show up* for class before the bell rings.

sooner or later   eventually

If I save my money, I'm sure I will make it to London *sooner or later*.

under the weather   not feeling well

Cedric didn't attend the party because he was *under the weather*.

up-to-date   current

Computer technicians need to be *up-to-date* on the latest changes.

write off   cancel (as in a debt), accept as a loss

The library said it would *write off* my late book fines if I brought a can of food for the food bank.

Remember that this is not a complete list of idioms. It's not even close! We encourage you to become a collector of idioms and have fun with them.

Helpful Sections of the Book for "ESL" Learners

You may want to review the sections that cover the following topics in this book:

◆ Sentence fragments
(page 218)

◆ Run-on sentences and comma splices
(page 233)

◆ Subject/verb agreement problems
(page 244)

◆ Verb tense problems
(page 257)

◆ Pronoun agreement
(page 281)

◆ Commonly confused words
(page 272)

PART
10

SEVENTEEN READINGS

"'Goodnight room. Goodnight moon.'"

Before you start any of the readings in this section, take a moment to think about your life as reader and how you feel about it.

The Reader's Inventory

Did your parents or anyone else read to you while you were growing up? Who? Write a little about the experience of being read to:

◆ What is the first book you remember being read to you? If you can't remember the title, tell what it was about, what happened.

◆ What do you remember about learning to read? Did you learn to read at home or at school?

◆ Was learning to read exciting? Why or why not?

◆ What is the first book you read completely on your own? If you can't remember exactly, don't worry. What sort of book was it?

◆ Did you go to the library as a child? How often?

◆ Did you have any books at home?

◆ How did you feel about the reading you had to do in grade school? In junior high or middle school? In high school?

◆ How do you feel about reading today?

◆ Do you ever read just for fun?

◆ What do you like to read best?

◆ What kind of reading bores you?

Writing Idea

Take your answers to the questions above and write an essay called "My Autobiography as a Reader." Tell the story of your whole experience as a reader from being read to as a young child to how you feel about reading today.

Something to Think About

Good readers make good writers. If you're working to become a better writer, and we certainly hope you are, it's a good idea to put more effort and energy into your reading. If in the past you haven't been much of a reader, it's time to give reading a second chance. Take the time to do it right and have fun!

In this section of the book you will find a wide variety of reading selections: informative articles, essays, short stories, and poems. No matter what you are reading, there are steps you can follow to make the experience more enjoyable and more profitable. Here are some ideas:

◆ **Get comfortable and get ready** Whenever you've got reading to do, take some time to get as comfortable as you can. Find a chair with a good light next to it. Turn off the music and the television, and cut out any other distractions. Make sure you have a pencil or highlighter nearby.

◆ **Sneak preview** You are no doubt familiar with the "previews" they show at movie theaters before the feature begins. In the space of a couple of minutes or less, you see scenes from a movie that give you a general idea of what the movie is about and are designed to convince you to see it. When you read, it helps if you give yourself a "sneak preview" before you get started. The more you know about something you're reading before you start, the better. Check and see how long the piece is. If there is information about the author (his or her background and experience), read it. Look for visual clues like boldface type, bullets, or checkmarks to see what is being emphasized. You might want to skim the essay, paying particular attention to the introductory and concluding paragraphs as well as the topic sentences of each paragraph in between.

◆ **Read awake** Reading requires your full attention. Unlike going to the movies with a friend, there's no one to nudge and say, "What happened?" if your attention slips. One way to stay focused is to keep a pencil or highlighter in your hand and actively look for points to underline. If you just let the words wash over you, you'll find yourself finishing your reading with no idea what you've read. Stay active, jotting down questions in the margin, and putting stars beside the points that mean the most to you.

◆ **Instant replay** When you've finished your reading, go back over it, reviewing the points you've underlined or highlighted in some way. Try to summarize what you've read in a sentence or two. Remember

what it's like after you've seen a movie with friends? Everyone talks about the movie, describing his or her favorite scenes. When you run into someone who hasn't seen the movie, you try to summarize it. Put these same skills to use with your reading. When you read something, tell others about it. The more you talk about it, the better you'll remember it and be able to make use of what it said.

SUCCESS TAKES TIME, SACRIFICE, AND HARD WORK

by Tim O'Brien

☆ **SNEAK PREVIEW** ☆ Tim O'Brien writes continuing-education courses and presents seminars in stress management.

Everyone hopes to be a success in life. In this essay, Tim O'Brien makes the case that success at anything is liable to take a long time. Though it's difficult in our fast-paced lives to be patient, we have to stay focused on our goals.

☆ ☆ ☆

1   Ours is an instant society of 30-second sound bit communication and MTV-like rapid imagery advertisements. Many of us want everything now. We don't want to put forth time, effort, or money. We want the government to take care of our health needs even when we don't take care of ourselves. We overeat, we don't exercise, 25 percent of us smoke, many drink alcohol excessively. These can lead to heart disease, cancer, diabetes, and premature death. As a result of hectic lifestyles, many people do not enjoy the success they hoped to achieve.

2   The road to success is easy to define. Achieving that success will probably involve considerable time, personal sacrifice, and much hard work.

The observations I make are not scientific. However, patterns become obvious in the letters that people write, in the comments they make, and in the questions they ask at seminars.

3   The most recent trend disturbs me. For many people life itself is stressful. In this mental and physical state of exhaustion, they long for an easier life. They want success, but hope that success and security will somehow just fall into their life. Many people have difficulty developing a strong work ethic or delaying gratification. Look no further than the number of personal bankruptcies filed each year and the level of credit card debt carried by the average person.

4   What does it take to succeed? What is a reasonable time to become successful? Can everyone become successful? The quick answer to these questions is yes and many years.

5   Each person must define what success is for them. Do you want financial independence? Do you want life-long relationships, a family, and a career? Write your definition of success until it is clear in your mind. Don't change your definition as soon as you hit an obstacle, but recognize that it may change when you or your

circumstances change. You will also need to redefine what success is for you when you reach your present definition of it.

6   How long will it take to be successful? Earl Nightingale defined success as "the progressive realization of a worthy goal." And Cervantes said: "The road is more important than the inn." These quotes remind us that success is a process, not a destination. Another good reminder is: "If you can't find happiness along the way, you won't find it at the end of the road."

7   The willingness to take calculated risks is another quality of the successful. This characteristic causes many people to decide to settle for less than what they could have or be. And, if they do take risk and lose, they often want someone else to bail them out. The "victim mentality" is compatible with being successful in the business world. Successful persons take 100 percent responsibility for their lives.

8   Outer evidence of material success might take years to get. What does it take to succeed?

9   Self-discipline, perseverance and a clear vision of what you want to accomplish.

10   Brian Tracy, the internationally known success trainer, says research shows that fewer than 4 percent of the population has written goals. They have no map to guide them. We can use self-discipline to focus our time, energy, and resources to achieve what we want to the exclusion of anything that would keep us from it. Success is not usually easy, or you'd see more successful people. And when shown what those successful few endured to reach their level of accomplishment, most people respond, "No thank you." However, they continue to envy and covet what the successful have. Those attitudes nearly ensure their continued failure.

11   Choose success. Plan a significant future. You have to live your life somehow. Why not live as successfully as possible? Roll up your sleeves. Sharpen your pencil. Use your brain and stay focused. That should lead you to the life of your dreams.

What Was It About?

1. Does the title of this essay adequately prepare you for what the author has to say?

2. What does the author rely on to draw his conclusions?

3. According to Brian Tracy, do most people write down their goals?

What Did You Think?

1. Was the author successful in motivating you to change your behavior? Why or why not?

2. The article suggests that most people resent the success of those few who have "made it." Do you agree?

3. Do you think your own success rests 100 percent in your own hands?

Get It Down On Paper!

1. Discuss a different goal you set for yourself and succeeded in reaching. (Process, Cause/Effect)

2. What does being a success mean? (Definition, Example, Classification)

3. Can you identify behavior (in yourself or others) that can sabotage success? (Example, Cause/Effect)

MERICANS

by Sandra Cisneros

☆ **SNEAK PREVIEW** ☆ Sandra Cisneros grew up traveling between three worlds: the Mexican world of her father's family in Mexico City, the Latino world of the neighborhood in Chicago where she grew up, and the Anglo world of the Midwest. She graduated from the M.F.A. program at Iowa State University and has published a number of books of poetry and fiction, including *The House on Mango Street* (1983) and *Woman Hollering Creek* (1991).

☆ ☆ ☆

1   We're waiting for the awful grandmother who is inside dropping pesos into la ofrenda box before the altar to La Divina Providencia. Lighting votive candle and genuflecting. Blessing herself and kissing her thumb. Running a crystal rosary between her fingers. Mumbling, mumbling, mumbling.

2   There are so many prayers and promises and thanks-be-to-God to be given in the name of the husband and the sons and the only daughter who never attend mass. It doesn't matter. Like La Virgen de Guadalupe, the awful grandmother intercedes on their behalf. For the grandfather who hasn't believed in anything since the first PRI elections. For my father, El Periquin, so skinny he needs his sleep. For Auntie Light-skin, who only a few hours before was breakfasting on brain and goat tacos after dancing all night in the pink zone. For Uncle Fat-face, the blackest of the black sheep—Always remember your Uncle Fat-face in your prayers. And Uncle Baby—You go for me, Mama—God listens to you.

3   The awful grandmother has been gone a long time. She disappeared behind the heavy leather outer curtain and the dusty velvet inner. We must stay near the church entrance. We must not wander over to the balloon and punch-ball vendors. We cannot spend our allowance on fried cookies or Familia Burron comic books or those clear cone-shaped suckers that make everything look like a rainbow when you look through them. We cannot run off and have our picture taken on the wooden ponies. We must not climb the steps up the hill behind the church and chase each other through the cemetery. We have promised to stay right where the awful grandmother left us until she returns.

4   There are those walking to church on their knees. Some with fat rags tied around their legs and others with pillows, one to kneel on and one to flop ahead. There are women with black shawls, crossing and uncrossing themselves. There are armies of penitents carrying banners and flowered arches while musicians play tinny trumpets and tinny drums.

5   La Virgen de Guadalupe is waiting inside behind a plate of thick glass. There's also a gold crucifix bent crooked as a mesquite tree when someone once threw a bomb. La Virgen de Guadalupe on the main altar because she's a big miracle, the crooked crucifix on a side altar because that's a little miracle.

6   But we're outside in the sun. My big brother Junior hunkered against the wall with his eyes shut. My little brother Keeks running around in circles.

7   Maybe and most probably my little brother is imagining he's a flying feather dancer, like the ones we saw swinging high up from a pole on the Virgin's birthday. I want to be a flying feather dancer too, but when he circles past me he shouts, "I'm a B-Fifty-two bomber, you're a German," and shoots me with an invisible machine gun. I'd rather play flying feather dancers, but if I tell my brother this, he might not play with me at all.

8   "Girl, we can't play with a girl." Girl. It's my brothers' favorite insult now instead of "sissy." "You girl," they yell at each other. "You throw that ball like a girl."

9   I've already made up my mind to be a German when Keeks swoops past again, this time yelling, "I'm Flash Gordon. You're Ming the Merciless and the Mud People." Something wants to come out of the corners of my eyes, but I don't let it. Crying is what girls do.

10   I leave Keeks running around in circles—"I'm the Lone Ranger, you're Tonto." I leave Junior squatting on his ankles and go look for the awful grandmother.

11   Why do churches smell like the inside of an ear? Like incense and the dark and candles in blue glass? And why does holy water smell of tears? The awful grandmother makes me kneel and fold my hands. The ceiling is high and everyone's prayers are bumping up there like balloons.

12   If I stare at the eyes of the saints long enough, they move and wink at me, which makes me a sort of saint too. When I get tired of winking saints, I count the awful grandmother's mustache hairs while she prays for Uncle Old, sick from the worm, and Auntie Cuca, suffering from a life of troubles that left half her face crooked and the other half sad.

13   There must be a long, long list of relatives who haven't gone to church. The awful grandmother knits the names of the dead and the living into one long prayer fringed with the grandchildren born in that barbaric country with its barbarian ways.

14   I put my weight on one knee, then the other, and when they both grow fat as a mattress of pins, I slap them awake. Micaela, you may wait outside with Alfredito and Enrique. The awful grandmother says it all in Spanish, which I understand when I'm paying attention.

15   "What?" I say, though it's neither proper nor polite. "What?" which the awful grandmother hears as "Guat?" But she only gives me a look and shoves me toward the door.

16   After all that dust and dark, the light from the plaza makes me squinch my eyes like if I just came out of the movies. My brother Keeks is drawing squiggly lines on

the concrete with a wedge of glass and the heel of his shoe. My brother Junior squatting against the entrance, talking to a lady and man.

17   They're not from here. Ladies don't come to church dressed in pants. And everybody knows men aren't supposed to wear shorts.

18   "Quierres chicle?" the lady asks in a Spanish too big for her mouth. "Gracias." The Lady gives him a whole handful of gum for free, little cellophane cubes of chicklets, cinnamon, and aqua and the white ones that don't taste like anything but are good for pretend buckteeth.

19   "Por favor," says the lady. "Un foto?" pointing to her camera.

20   "Si."

21   She's so busy taking Junior's picture, she doesn't notice me and Keeks.

22   "Hey, Michele, Keeks. You guys want gum?"

23   "But you speak English!"

24   "Yeah," my brother says, "we're Mericans."

25   We're Mericans, we're Mericans, and inside the awful grandmother prays.

What Was It About?

1. Why is the grandmother referred to as "awful"?

2. Why does the grandmother have so many prayers to say?

3. Why are all the men and women surprised to hear Junior speak English?

What Did You Think?

1. How does the author feel about her brothers?

2. What might tempt the children to stray from their post at the church entrance?

3. How does the author feel about being a girl? Why?

Get It Down On Paper!

1. What in your community or family might seem strange to a visiting tourist? (Description, Example, Comparison/Contrast)

2. What does it mean to be an American? (Definition, Classification, Example)

3. Who in your family might be described as an "oddball" or a "real character?" (Description, Example, Definition)

HOW TO ENJOY POETRY

by James Dickey

⭐ **SNEAK PREVIEW** ⭐ James Dickey was a poet (author of *Buckdancer's Choice*) and novelist (*Deliverance*). Here he shares his love of poetry through an essay designed to increase the reader's enjoyment of it.

What is poetry? And why has it been around so long? Many have suspected that it was invented as a school subject, because you have to take exams on it. But that is not what poetry is or why it is still around. That's not what it feels like, either. When you really feel it, a new part of you happens, or an old part is renewed, with surprise and delight at being what it is.

From the beginning, men have known that words and things, words and actions, words and feelings go together, and that they can go together in thousands of different ways, according to who is using them. Some ways go shallow, and some go deep.

⭐ ⭐ ⭐

1   The first thing to understand about poetry is that it comes to you from outside you, in books or in words, but that for it to live, something from within you must come to it and meet it and complete it. Your response with your own mind and body and memory and emotions gives the poem its ability to work its magic; if you give to it, it will give to you and give plenty.

2   When you read, don't let the poet write down to you; read up to him. Reach for him from your gut out, and the heart and muscles will come into it, too.

3   The sun is new every day, the ancient philosopher Heraclitus said. The sun of poetry is new every day, too, because it is seen in different ways by different people who have lived under it, lived with it, responded to it. Their lives are different from yours, but by means of the special spell that poetry brings to the fact of the sun—everybody's sun; yours, too—you can come into possession of many suns as many as men and women have ever been able to imagine. Poetry makes possible the deepest kind of personal possession of the world.

4   The most beautiful constellation in the winter sky is Orion, which ancient poets thought looked like a hunter, up there, moving across heaven with his dog Sirius. What is this hunter made out of stars hunting for? What does he mean? Who owns him, if anybody? The poet Aldous Huxley felt that he did, and so, in Aldous Huxley's universe of personal emotion, he did.

5   Up from among the emblems of the
              wind into its heart of power.

6   The Huntsman climbs, and all his
          living stars
      Are bright, and all are mine.

7   The beginning of your true encounter with poetry should be simple. It should bypass all classrooms, all textbooks, courses, examinations, and libraries and go straight to the things that make your own existence exist: to your body and nerves and blood and muscles. Find your own way—a secret way that just maybe you don't know yet—to open yourself as wide as you can and as deep as you can to the moment, the now of your existence and the endless mystery of it, and perhaps at the same time to one other thing that is not you, but is out there: a handful of gravel is a good place to start. So is an ice cube—what more mysterious and beautiful interior of something has there ever been?

8   As for me, I like the sun, the source of all living things, and on certain days very good feeling, too. "Start with the sun," D. H. Lawrence said, "and everything will slowly, slowly happen." Good advice. And a lot will happen.

9   What is more fascinating than a rock, if you really feel it and look at it, or more interesting than a leaf?

10   Horses, I mean; butterflies, whales;
      Mosses and stars; and gravelly
      Rivers, and fruit.

11   Oceans, I mean; black valleys; corn;
      Brambles, and cliffs; rock, dirt, dust, ice...

12   Go back and read this list—it is quite a list, Mark Van Doren's list!—item by item. Slowly. Let each of these things call up an image out of your own life.

13   Think and feel. What moss do you see? Which horse? What field of corn? What brambles are your brambles? Which river is yours?

14   Part of the spell of poetry is the rhythm of language, used by poets who understand how powerful a factor rhythm can be, how compelling and unforgettable. Almost anything put into rhythm and rhyme is more memorable than the same thing said in prose. Why this is, no one knows completely, though the answer is surely rooted far down in the biology by means of which we exist; in the circulation of the blood that goes forth from the heart and comes back, and in the repetition of breathing. Croesus was a rich Greek king, back in the sixth century before Christ, but this tombstone was not his:

15   No Croesus lies in the grave you see;
      I was a poor laborer, and this suits me.

16   That is plain-spoken and definitive. You believe it, and the rhyme helps you believe it and keep it.

17   Writing poetry is a lot like a contest with yourself and if you like sports and games and competitions of all kinds, you might like to try writing some. Why not?

18   The possibilities of rhyme are great. Some of the best fun is making up your own limericks. There's no reason you can't invent limericks about anything that comes to your mind. No reason. Try it.

19   The problem is to find three words that rhyme and fit into a meaning. "There was a young man from..." Where was he from? What situation was he in? How can these things fit into the limerick form—a form everybody knows—so that the rhymes "pay off," and give that sense of completion and inevitability that is so deliciously memorable that nothing else is like it?

20   The more your encounter with poetry deepens, the more your experience of your own life will deepen, and you will begin to see things by means of words, and words by means of things.

21   You will come to understand the world as it interacts with words, as it can be re-created by rhythms and by images.

22   You'll understand that this condition is one charged with vital possibilities. You will pick up meanings more quickly—and you will create meaning, too, for yourself and for others.

23   Connections between things will exist for you in ways they never did before. They will shine with unexpectedness, wide-openness, and you will go toward them, on your own path. "Then..." as Dante says, "...Then will your feet be filled with good desire." You will know this is happening the first time you say of something you never would have noticed before, "Well, would you look at that! Who'd a thunk it?" (Pause, full of new light)

24   "I thunk it!"

What Was It About?

1. What is the author's purpose in writing this essay?

2. How does the essay suggest that poetry is like the sun?

3. How does the author suggest enabling yourself to understand what a poem is trying to say?

What Did You Think?

1. Has the essay changed the way you feel about poetry? Why or why not?

2. Which lines of poetry quoted in the essay were most meaningful to you?

3. Do you think the analogy between writing poetry and competing in athletics is valid? Why or why not?

Get It Down On Paper!

1. Explain why you do or do not read poetry. (Example, Cause/Effect, Comparison/Contrast)

2. What is poetry? (Definition/Example)

3. How has reading poetry (or literature) changed your life? (Cause/Effect, Example)

LIFE LESSONS FOR STUDENTS

by Jeff Herring

☆ **SNEAK PREVIEW** ☆ Jeff Herring is a nationally syndicated columnist who hopes to inspire his readers to change their lives. In this piece, he takes on the problems that students face and offers some advice.

☆ ☆ ☆

1   It's time for the start of a new school year. So, for all the students out there, from preschool to graduate school, here are a few tips just for you.

2   The Law of a Good Start. Many people with whom I work say that they can start off a school year very well, but then seem to fade as the year goes on. While it's important to have a good start, it's equally important to have a good middle and end.

3   The Law of Keeping Up. This may be one of the most important laws for students. Do what you need to do to keep up. It's tough to play catch-up, and all too easy to give up when you get behind.

4   The Law of Forever. School is not forever. It will pass, and hopefully so will you. Learning, however, can and should be forever—a lifetime kind of thing.

5   The Law of Importance. If you are going to succeed in school, at some point school has to become more important to you than to your parents or anyone else. Doing it primarily for someone else will eventually drain your energy. Bottom line: Do it for you and your future.

6   The Law of the Clock. What is the slowest moving invention in the world? A clock that you constantly check and watch. The more you watch the clock the slower it goes.

7   The Law of Personalities. Sometimes in your school career, you may encounter what is called a "personality conflict" with a teacher. You may not like them, they may not like you, or both. As tempting as it may be, do not choose to get bad grades and otherwise sabotage yourself. This is simply practice for the real world, where you will not like everyone and everyone will not like you. You may have to work with them, however.

8   The Law of Once. The best way to handle a class and/or teacher you don't like is to take the class only once.

9   The Law of Your Ticket. When you find yourself stuck in a boring class that you know you will never use no matter how much they try to convince you otherwise, here's a tip: This class is merely a very small piece of the ticket to the rest of your life.

10   Here's what I mean—back when Disney World opened, you didn't pay one huge admission fee and then ride whatever you wanted. You purchased "ticket coupons" marked A-E. An "A" ticket got you something simple like the carousel or Dumbo's ride. An "E" ticket got you on the good stuff like the Haunted Mansion.

11   Your education is much the same: Don't finish high school and you've got an "A" ticket for life. Finish and you've got at least a "B" ticket.

12   In other words, the more education you get, the better your ticket can be.

What Was It About?

1. What is the author's attitude toward education?

2. What does the author mean by using the word "law"?

3. What is the meaning of "The Law of Once"?

What Did You Think?

1. Which law did you think was most helpful? Least helpful? Why?

2. Do you agree with the author's opinion about the importance of education? Why?

3. If you use "The Law of Your Ticket," what ticket would you get?

Get It Down On Paper!

1. Explain your strategy for starting a new school year. (Process, Cause/Effect)

2. Has your attitude about education changed from high school to college? (Compare/Contrast, Cause/Effect, Definition, Example)

3. Pick one of the laws from the article and apply it to your situation. (Cause/Effect, Process, Example)

THE STORY OF AN HOUR

by Kate Chopin

☆ **SNEAK PREVIEW** ☆ Kate Chopin was an important American writer who lived in Louisiana in the late nineteenth century. Her most famous novel is The Awakening, a work that reflected her interest in the issues facing the women of her time.

☆ ☆ ☆

1   Knowing that Mrs. Mallard was afflicted with heart trouble, great care was taken to break to her as gently as possible the news of her husband's death.

2   It was her sister Josephine who told her, in broken sentences; veiled hints that revealed in half concealing. Her husband's friend Richards was there, too, near her. It was he who had been in the newspaper office when intelligence of the railroad disaster was received, with Brently Mallard's name leading the list of "killed." He had only taken the time to assure himself of its truth by a second telegram, and had hastened to forestall any less careful, less tender friend in bearing the sad message.

3   She did not hear the story as many women have heard the same, with a paralyzed inability to accept its significance. She wept at once, with sudden, wild abandonment, in her sister's arms. When the storm of grief had spent itself she went away to her room alone. She would have no one follow her.

4   There stood, facing the open window, a comfortable, roomy armchair. Into this she sank, pressed down by a physical exhaustion that haunted her body and seemed to reach into her soul.

5   She could see in the open square before her house the tops of trees that were all aquiver with the new spring life. The delicious breath of rain was in the air. In the street below a peddler was crying his wares. The notes of a distant song which someone was singing reached her faintly, and countless sparrows were twittering in the eaves.

6   There were patches of blue sky showing here and there through the clouds that had met and piled one above the other in the west facing her window.

7   She sat with her head thrown back upon the cushion of the chair, quite motionless, except when a sob came up into her throat and shook her, as a child who has cried itself to sleep continues to sob in its dreams.

8   She was young, with a fair, calm face, whose lines bespoke repression and even a certain strength. But now there was a dull stare in her eyes, whose gaze was fixed away off yonder on one of those patches of blue sky. It was not a glance of reflection, but rather indicated a suspension of intelligent thought.

9   There was something coming to her and she was waiting for it, fearfully. What was it? She did not know; it was too subtle and elusive to name. But she felt it, creeping out of the sky, reaching toward her through the sounds, the scents, the color that filled the air.

10   Now her bosom rose and fell tumultuously. She was beginning to recognize this thing that was approaching to possess her, and she was striving to beat it back with her will—as powerless as her two white slender hands would have been.

11   When she abandoned herself a little whispered word escaped her slightly parted lips. She said it over and over under her breath: "free, free, free!" The vacant stare and the look of terror that had followed it went from her eyes. They stayed keen and bright. Her pulses beat fast, and the coursing blood warmed and relaxed every inch of her body.

12   She did not stop to ask if it were or were not a monstrous joy that held her. A clear and exalted perception enabled her to dismiss the suggestion as trivial.

13   She knew that she would weep again when she saw the kind, tender hands folded in death; the face that had never looked save with love upon her, fixed and gray and dead. But she saw beyond that bitter moment a long procession of years to come that would belong to her absolutely. And she opened and spread her arms out to them in welcome.

14   There would be no one to live for her during those coming years; she would live for herself. There would be no powerful will bending hers in that blind persistence with which men and women believe they have a right to impose a private will upon a fellow-creature. A kind of intention or a cruel intention made the act seem no less a crime as she looked upon it in that brief moment of illumination.

15   And yet she had loved him—sometimes. Often she had not. What did it matter! What could love, the unsolved mystery, count for in the face of this possession of self-assertion which she suddenly recognized as the strongest impulse of her being!

16   "Free! Body and soul free!" she kept whispering.

17   Josephine was kneeling before the closed door with her lips to the keyhole, imploring for admission. "Louise, open the door! I beg; open the door—you will make yourself ill. What are you doing, Louise? For heaven's sake open the door."

18   "Go away. I'm not making myself ill." No; she was drinking in a very elixir of life through that open window.

19   Her fancy was running riot along those days ahead of her. Spring days, and summer days, and all sorts of days that would be her own. She breathed a quick prayer that life might be long. It was only yesterday she had thought with a shudder that life might be long.

20   She arose at length and opened the door to her sister's importunities. There was a feverish triumph in her eyes, and she carried herself unwittingly like a goddess of Victory. She clasped her sister's waist, and together they descended the stairs. Richards stood waiting for them at the bottom.

21   Someone was opening the front door with a latchkey. It was Brently Mallard who entered, a little travel-stained, composedly carrying his gripsack and umbrella. He had been far from the scene of the accident and did not even know there had been one. He stood amazed at Josephine's piercing cry; at Richards' quick motion to screen him from the view of his wife.

22   But Richards was too late.

23   When the doctors came they said she had died of heart disease—of joy that kills.

What Was It About?

1. How does the beginning of the story foreshadow the end?

2. What was Mrs. Mallard's initial reaction to the news of her husband's death? How did it change?

3. How did the doctors explain Mrs. Mallard's death?

What Did You Think?

1. What kind of marriage did the Mallards likely have?

2. Did Brently Mallard consider himself a good husband? Do you think he was?

3. Do you think Mrs. Mallard's grief at first hearing of her husband's death was genuine? Why?

Get It Down On Paper!

1. What makes a good marriage? (Definition, Cause/Effect, Example)

2. How important is "self-assertion" in a relationship? (Cause/Effect, Definition, Example)

3. Discuss an emotion of yours that was misinterpreted by someone else. (Comparison/Contrast, Definition, Example)

THE GREAT AMERICAN COOLING MACHINE
by Frank Trippett

☆ **SNEAK PREVIEW** ☆ Frank Trippett wrote his essay that discusses the effects of air conditioning on modern life for *Time* magazine.

☆ ☆ ☆

1   "The greatest contribution to civilization in this century may well be air-conditioning—and America leads the way." So wrote British Scholar-Politician S. F. Markham 32 years ago when a modern cooling system was still an exotic luxury. In a century that has yielded such treasures as the electric knife, spray-on deodorant and disposable diapers, anybody might question whether air-conditioning is the supreme gift. There is not a whiff of doubt, however, that America is far out front in its use. As a matter of lopsided fact, the U.S. today, with a mere 5% of the population, consumes as much man-made coolness as the whole rest of the world put together.

2   Just as amazing is the speed with which this situation came to be. Air-conditioning began to spread in industries as a production aid during World War II. Yet only a generation ago a chilled sanctuary during summer's stewing heat was a happy frill that ordinary people sampled only in movie houses. Today most Americans tend to take air-conditioning for granted in homes, offices, factories, stores, theaters, shops, studios, schools, hotels, and restaurants. They travel in chilled buses, trains, planes, and private cars. Sporting events once associated with open sky and fresh air are increasingly boxed in and air cooled. Skiing still takes place outdoors, but such attractions as tennis, rodeos, football and, alas, even baseball are now often staged in synthetic climates like those of Houston's Astrodome and New Orleans' Superdome. A great many of the country's farming tractors are now, yup, air-conditioned.

3   It is thus no exaggeration to say that Americans have taken to mechanical cooling avidly and greedily. Many have become all but addicted, refusing to go places that are not air-conditioned. In Atlanta, shoppers in Lenox Square so resented having to endure natural heat while walking outdoors from chilled store to chilled store that the mall management enclosed and air-conditioned the whole sprawling she-bang. The widespread whining about Washington's raising of thermostats to a mandatory 78 degrees, defied and denounced the Government's energy saving order to cut back on cooling. Significantly, there was no popular outrage at this judicial insolence; many citizens probably wished that they could be so highhanded.

4   Everybody by now is aware that the costs of the American way is enormous, that air-conditioning is an energy glutton. It uses some 9% of all electricity pro-

duced. Such an extravagance merely to provide comfort is peculiarly American and strikingly at odds with all the recent rhetoric about national sacrifice in a time of menacing energy shortages. Other modern industrial nations such as Japan, Germany and France have managed all along to thrive with mere fractions of the man-made coolness used in the U.S. and precious little of that in private dwellings. Here, so profligate has its use become that the air conditioner is almost as glaring a symptom as the automobile of the national tendency to overindulge in every technical possibility, to use every convenience to such excess that the country looks downright coddled.

5   But not everybody is aware that high cost and easy comfort are merely two of the effects of the vast cooling of America. In fact, air-conditioning has substantially altered the country's character and folkways. With the dog days at hand and the thermostats ostensibly up, it is a good time to begin taking stock of what air-conditioning has done besides lower the indoor temperature.

6   Many of the byproducts are so conspicuous that they are scarcely noticed. To begin with, air conditioning transformed the face of urban American by making possible those glassy, boxy, sealed-in-skyscrapers on which the once humane geometries of places like San Francisco, Boston and Manhattan have been impaled. It has been indispensable, no less, to the functioning of sensitive advanced computers, those high operating temperatures require that they be constantly cooled. Thus, in a very real way, air-conditioning has made possible the ascendancy of computerized civilization. Its cooling protection has given rise not only to moon landings, space shuttles and Sky labs but to the depersonalized punch-cardification of society that regularly gets people hot under the collar even in swelter-proof environments. It has also reshaped the national economy and redistributed political power simply by encouraging the burgeoning of the sultry southerly swatch of the country, profoundly influencing major migration trends of people and industry. Sunbelt cities like Phoenix, Atlanta, Dallas and Houston (where shivering indoor frigidity became a mark of status) could never have mushroomed so prosperously without air conditioning; some communities—Las Vegas in the Nevada desert and Lake Havasu City on the Arizona-California border—would shrivel and die overnight if it were turned off.

7   It has, as well, seduced families into retreating into houses with closed doors and shut windows, reducing the commonalty of neighborhood life and all but obsoleting the front porch society whose open casual folkways were an appealing hallmark of a sweatier America. Is it really surprising that the public's often noted withdrawal into self-pursuit and privatism has coincided with the epic spread of air-conditioning? Though science has little studied how habitual air-conditioning affects mind or body, some medical experts suggest that, like other technical avoidance of natural swings in climate, air-conditioning may take a toll on the human capacity to adapt to stress. If so, air-conditioning is only like many other greatly

useful technical developments that liberate man from nature by increasing his productivity and power in some ways—while subtly weakening him in others.

8   Neither scholars nor pop sociologists have really got around to charting and diagnosing all the changes brought about by air-conditioning. Professional observers have for years been preoccupied with the social implications of the automobile and television. Mere glancing analysis suggests that the car and TV, in their most decisive influences on American habits, have been powerfully aided and abetted by air-conditioning. The car may have created all those shopping centers in the boondocks, but only air conditioning has made them attractive to mass clienteles. Similarly, the artificial cooling of the living room undoubtedly helped turn the typical American into a year-round TV addict. Without air-conditioning, how many viewers would endure reruns on one of those pestilential summer nights that used to send people to collapse on the lawn or to sleep on the roof.

9   Many of the side effects of air-conditioning are far from being fully pinned down. It is a reasonable suspicion, though, that controlled climate, by inducing Congress to stay in Washington longer than it used to during the swelter season, thus presumably passing more laws, has contributed to bloated government. One can only speculate that the advent of the super cooled bedroom may be linked to the carnal adventurism associated with the mid-century sexual revolution. Surely it is a fact—if restaurant complaints about raised thermostats are to be believed—that air conditioning induces at least expense-account diners to eat and drink more; if so, it must be credited with adding to the national fat problem.

10   Perhaps only a sophist might be tempted to tie the spread of air-conditioning to the coincidentally rising divorce rate, but every attentive realist must have noticed that even a little window unit can instigate domestic tension and chronic bickering between couples composed of one who likes it on all the time and another who does not. In fact, perhaps surprisingly, not everybody likes air-conditioning. The necessarily sealed rooms or buildings make some feel claustrophobic, cut off from the real world. The rush, whir and clatter of cooling units annoys others. There are even a few eccentrics who object to man-made cool simply because they like hot weather. Still, the overwhelming majority of Americans have taken to air-conditioning like hogs to a wet wallow.

11   It might be tempting, and even fair, to chastise that vast majority for being spoiled rotten in their cool ascendancy. It would be more just, however, to observe that their great cooling machine carries with it a perpetual price tag that is going to provide continued and increasing chastisement during the energy crisis. Ultimately, the air conditioner, and the hermetic buildings it requires, may turn out to be a more pertinent technical symbol of the American personality than the car. While the car has been a fine sign of the American impulse to dart hither and yon about the world, the mechanical cooler more neatly suggests the maturing national compulsion to flee the natural world in favor of a technological cocoon.

12   Already architectural designers are toiling to find ways out of the technical trap represented by sealed buildings with immovable glass, ways that might let in some of the naturally cool air outside. Some have lately come up with a remarkable discovery: the openable window. Presumably, that represents progress.

What Was It About?

1. In what way is America's use of air-conditioning different from that of Europe's and Asia's?

2. How does the article connect air conditioning to the rise in computer technology?

3. What does the last line of the essay suggest?

What Did You Think?

1. Do you rely on air-conditioning? Why or why not?

2. Which of the effects that air-conditioning has had on society do you think has the greatest impact?

3. How does the article compare the car to air-conditioning?

Get It Down On Paper!

1. Which invention do you think has had the greatest impact on society? Why? (Cause/Effect, Example)

2. Which invention could you least stand to live without? Why? (Cause/Effect, Example)

3. What is progress? (Definition, Cause/Effect, Example)

A BLUE PLATE SPECIAL TOWN
by Sue Pace

☆ **SNEAK PREVIEW** ☆ Sue Pace is a writer who lives in Arlington, Washington.

Do you live in a small town or a big city? If you live in a small town, the world Sue Pace describes may sound very familiar to you. If you don't, you will begin to understand what it might be like to live in a small town and what makes it unique.

☆ ☆ ☆

1   I live in a small town 50 miles north of Seattle, and we're getting our first fast-food restaurant this year. No need to drive elsewhere to get a hamburger, chicken nuggets or fishwich in two minutes or less. This lumber and dairy town of 5,000 will have its very own McDonald's.

2   It isn't that we don't have restaurants, delis or pizza joints. We do, along with a 7-Eleven for microwave burritos and a grocery store with a deli. There is a drive-in called Rotten Ralph's which serves fish and chips and locally made mountain-black-berry ice cream. Townsfolk brag that Ralph's cones are the largest in the state. There's also The Blue Bird Cafe, which specializes in Swiss steak and mashed pota-toes. These businesses don't have a huge advertising budget. They hire locals, offer decent food and expect adults as well as children to clean their plates.

3   But the modern world is starting to push in at us now. We've got malls and housing developments. We've got Costco and Eagle and clothing outlets within a half hour's drive. When Arlington's only clothing store went out of business last month, after more than 40 years, I started thinking about what it means to live in a small town. Sometimes, I feel there's an entire economy dedicated to wiping out my town.

4   I grew up in a hamlet of 250 in eastern Washington. I knew everybody and they knew me. I actually lived in that mythical village it takes to raise a child. There weren't many jobs, so when the siren song of a more exciting future beckoned, I left for college, marriage and employment in what could be called a real city. But when I had my first child, it became clear to me that I didn't want to raise a family in a place where I'd have to entrust my kids to strangers.

5   That's when my husband and I set out to find a new home. On an afternoon's drive, I saw a white house with a garden and fruit trees, an elementary school just a block away, and I knew I was there. Arlington is a town where the mill owner's children go to school with the logger's kids. Everyone has an opinion, and a letter to the editor of the local paper has real consequences.

6   We settled in a place where young and old live on the same street and have to make some kind of peace with that. We have an informal block watch because it isn't just some woman getting beat up by her boyfriend—it's the grocery-store checker's daughter. The one who graduated with your son. Neighbors look out for each other and when renters at the end of the block turned out to be drug dealers, the landlord heard about it. From us.

7   In Arlington, we go to soccer matches, baseball and fast-pitch games, dance recitals and concerts because we know the kids who are involved. They go to our church and buy stuff from our stores. The youngsters may be classmates of our grandkids or best friends or worst enemies with the neighbor's kid.

8   This is a town that smells like cow manure when the wind blows the wrong way. But that happens only a couple of days a month. It's balanced by the fact that I can walk one block to the Stillaguamish River and pick blackberries along its banks. I can wade in it. I can catch fish in it. On a hot day—or a cold one—I can listen to its rushing water, raise my eyes to the mountains and be drop-to-my-knees grateful I live here.

9   I can walk the five-block stretch that is Main Street and know the blessings and tragedies of each shopkeeper. I know more about my city-council members than they might like. I talk easily to the emergency-room physician because his daughter and mine played in the same piano recital. I'm part of a community.

10   I've always been more distrustful of big business than of government—maybe that comes from growing up in the '60s—and I guess that's how you separate the conservatives from the liberals. It's no secret that I'm the latter. Lately I've been thinking that we need to worry less about saving our nation and the world and worry more about saving our cities and towns. That's where people congregate in sickness and in health and where children learn about life and death. It's where kids learn about fair play, trade-offs and tolerance—and where the buck really stops.

11   That's why I want my town to survive. It bothers me when the citizens of Arlington go elsewhere to shop. They say there's a wider selection in the big stores. That may be true for some things but certainly not for all. Not even, to be truthful, for most things. I've heard that it's more expensive to buy in town, but our hardware store has sales that can match most warehouse prices from paint to flashlights. Doesn't spending $4 on gas, $3 on beverages and $10 on lunch cancel out much of what is "saved" driving to the mall? Is it all that economical living in a community that's had its heart torn out because citizens don't support local businesses, activities and schools? It isn't just loyalty we're talking here. It's property values and hard-nosed common sense.

12   These so-called bargain hunters forget that the city budget relies on local taxes. They don't buy cars at the car dealership or lumber at the lumber store and then wonder why local government is having budget problems. They complain that the streets aren't clean and the police aren't plentiful. They forget the basic math that

says nothing is free. If you want something you have to pay for it. With votes. With energy and time. With money.

13   Maybe this new McDonald's is going to help people stick around with their money. Perhaps it will put new life back into the empty storefronts I see up and down Main Street. If folks start staying in town to eat, perhaps they'll also stay in town to shop. For lumber and sporting goods. For sewing needles and tires, tables and shoes, stationery and books, bicycles and gardening supplies, haircuts and bouquets and watches and linoleum. Maybe this fast-food restaurant is the start of something good.

What Was It About?

1. How does the author feel about living in a small town?

2. Why does the author suggest it's just as economical to shop in Arlington, even if the merchandise costs more?

3. In what ways might the new McDonald's help Arlington?

What Did You Think?

1. Do you shop mostly at Mom 'n' Pop stores or at big chain stores? Why?

2. Would you be willing to do without some of the convenience and excitement of city living to feel safer and more connected to your neighbors? Why?

3. Do you agree with the author that it's the responsibility of small town residents to support local merchants? Why?

Get It Down On Paper!

1. Would you prefer to live in a small town or a big city? Why? (Comparison/Contrast, Cause/Effect)

2. How has your neighborhood changed in the past five to ten years? (Comparison/Contrast, Cause/Effect, Description)

3. What is the ideal hometown? (Definition, Description, Classification)

WHAT'S WRONG WITH PLAYING "LIKE A GIRL?"

by Dorothea Stillman

☆ **SNEAK PREVIEW** ☆ Dorothea Stillman is a freelance writer who lives in New York.

What do you think of boys and girls playing on the same sports teams? How would you feel about having a woman coach? Stillman explores the role of women in children's sports in this essay.

☆ ☆ ☆

1 I started out watching my sons' games and practices just to cheer the boys on, but I quickly learned another important reason to be there. I found that, as often as not, while the coaches showed the kids how to shoot a basket, throw a strike or head a soccer ball, they were also teaching them to regard girls as inferior to boys.

2 The coed basketball program was the worst offender. For three weeks I watched as the coaches belittled the girls and humiliated the boys by saying they were "playing like girls." The seven-year-old's division was about 30 percent girls. In the ten-year-old's division there were no girls. Clearly, they were so discouraged by that age that they gave up.

3 One typical Saturday morning the gym rang with shouts as four groups of seven-year-olds excitedly waved their arms and urged their teammates to hurry. It was a relay dribbling race in my younger son's practice.

4 An all-girl team won against three other teams, all of which were made up exclusively or mostly of boys. As the last girl came to the finish, her teammates jumped up and exploded into cheers. A smirk came over the coach's face. He stood in the middle of the gym with a hand on one hip. "Are you going to let a bunch of girls beat you?" he roared at the boys.

5 The message was clear: if the girls won, it was because the boys hadn't been trying hard enough. The girls should feel no pride in their victory because it was a fluke. The natural order of things was that the boys should be superior to the girls— and be ashamed if they weren't.

6 The girls giggled uncertainly. The boys looked at each other sheepishly and shrugged. The fathers, helping out on the floor, smiled. The mothers, sitting on the sidelines, showed no reaction.

7 But I was riled, and I wasn't going to take it. For three weeks the director of the program had been asking for a volunteer to coach the ten-year-olds, and no one had come forward. When he made the appeal again at the end of practice, I said I'd do

it. He looked shocked, but he could hardly say no. The alternative was to cut ten kids from the program, and he knew it.

8   But it wasn't going to be that simple. No sooner had I picked up the assignment than men swooped in to take it away from me. A big man standing nearby pushed his way between me and the program director. "Ron can run the practices," he said. "He just can't be there for the games on Saturdays because he has to work." Ron joined in: "You could be there for the games, and sometimes I'll be able to coach them, too, if I rearrange my lunch hour."

9   I went home and seethed. Ron would have been a fine coach if he had seen fit to volunteer on his own. But he hadn't. Ron never would have tried to use a man the way he was proposing to use me, and I was not willing to be used. I pulled myself together, called Ron and told him thanks but no thanks. If I was going to be the coach, I wanted to run the practices myself.

10   Then I got busy. I knew next to nothing about basketball (neither did most of the fathers who were coaching), but I gave myself a crash course. I read books. I attended every game the local high-school team played. I watched the game on TV every day.

11   At first I could only recognize the obvious: the fast break, the slam-dunk. But before long I noticed the finer points—the fake, the curl, the pick-and-roll. At home my kids and I talked basketball day and night. I researched and watched and learned and developed drills and plays. I was so enthusiastic I even allowed my sons to dribble basketballs to the living room.

12   Before each of our games, the referees would ask the coaches for a roster of the players. My assistant was a man, and they approached him first every time.

13   "That's the coach over there," he would say, pointing to me. The refs would turn and scan the gym for another man. When they realized I was the one they were looking for, their eyebrows would shoot up. Or they'd break into a grin. Or their faces would freeze.

14   Out on the court the boys would be warming up. "Watch this, Coach," they'd call to me, eager to show off their fanciest moves, taking three-point shots or dribbling between their legs. "You guys are looking good," I'd say, and they would beam with pride. To them I was no different from any other coach.

15   When I watched my younger son's practices, I chatted with the other mothers. My coaching had sent a ripple through them. One woman asked, "Is there someone helping you? How can you do it?" She seemed to think women were incapable of understanding basketball. Another was more supportive: "It's about time we had a woman coach," she said. Best of all, a third woman joined the men on the floor and helped run the last practice.

16   The season was ending but something big was starting.

What Was It About?

1. How long did you read before you discovered the author's attitude about the way society treats girls and boys?

2. Why does the author think there were no girls in the ten-year-old's division?

3. What did the author's younger son's coach, Ron, and the referees have in common?

What Did You Think?

1. Does the author have any biases of her own? If so, what are they?

2. Do you admire the author for deciding "not to take it"? How is she different from the other mothers in the article?

3. How do you think the boys reacted to having their mom be their coach?

Get It Down On Paper!

1. Do you think boys and girls receive equal treatment? Why or why not? (Example, Comparison/Contrast, Classification)

2. Discuss a time you were treated unfairly because of a societal stereotype. (Narration, Cause/Effect)

3. The author states that by the end of the season "something big was starting." Can one person make a difference in another's attitude? (Narration, Example, Cause/Effect)

TROUBLEMAKERS IN THE OFFICE

by Staff Writers at *Time* magazine

⋆ **SNEAK PREVIEW** ⋆ This article, written by staff writers at *Time*, classifies the different kinds of workers who end up causing problems in modern offices. If you've ever had a job, you've probably encountered some of the "types" described here.

☆ ☆ ☆

1   In Shepherd Mead's satire *How to Succeed in Business Without Really Trying,* office workers are so committed to devious little games and personality conflicts that everyone seems to have forgotten what it is that the company produces and sells. In fact, a good deal of fiction has depicted the office as a war zone of neurotic combat. But according to Management Consultant Robert M. Bramson, who studies such matters, that concept is unfair. Only 10% of office workers are relentlessly difficult says Bramson, and anyone can learn how to cope with a troublesome minority.

2   Over the past few years, Bramson has studied the behavior of some 400 managers and other workers at dozens of companies and public agencies. He has concluded that they, like Gaul, are divided into three parts: 10% troublemakers, 70% unable to cope with troublemakers and 20% not bothered by troublemakers. By paying particular attention to the manner and techniques of the resilient 20%, he has constructed a strategy for achieving office harmony and teaches it (for $1,000 a session) to employers and employees alike at daylong seminars throughout California.

3   Bramson's "method-oriented" program is designed around a basic premise: "People who are difficult have learned that behavior precisely because in the short run it has worked for them. The reason the bad behavior works is that it elicits predictable, typical reactions from other people."

4   Bramson has identified several categories of troublemakers—hostile-aggressives, complainers, indecisives, unresponsives and know-it-alls—and in his seminars suggests how to cope with each. The Bramson way:

5   Hostile-aggressives: There are three subspecies in this category—"Sherman tanks," "snipers" and "exploders"—and the basic strategy for dealing with all of them is not to rise to the bait. The Shermans are straight-ahead pushy folk known for their jabbing fingers, loud talk and complete knowledge of what is good for their fellow workers. "You have to stand up to him, but don't fight," says Bramson. His advice: look Sherman straight in the eye, call him by name, and state your disagreement with defusing phrases such as "in my opinion," and "it's my judgment

that..." Then let the tank blow off some steam. Says Bramson: "Sherman tanks are experts at escalating. If you fight you lose."

6   Snipers shoot at people through the camouflage of sarcasm or irony and should be asked to explain and expand their remarks. "Smoke them out," says Bramson. "Make them be overt in their attack, or backtrack. Don't push. It's hard for hostile people to lose face. Let them get out from under their attack." The behavior of exploders—sudden yelling, cursing or crying—requires no action at all. Simply let the tirade or crying jag spin itself out and end in a guilty apology. If that fails, Bramson recommends a distancing line: "This is a very serious matter, but we can't handle it this way." The final line of defense is to leave the room, saying you will return in five minutes.

7   Complainers lace their speech with "always" and "never," and usually insist on sitting down before detailing their gripes—the fellow who complains standing up wants action, but the sitter wants to whine in comfort. It is a serious mistake to either agree or disagree with complainers. Instead, says Bramson, paraphrase the whiner's complaints back to them with "limiting concrete statements that let them know you understand." Noncommittal but encouraging "ums" and "ahs" are helpful too.

8   Indecisives come in two varieties: "analysts," who are afraid of making a mistake, and "be-nicers" who are afraid of making enemies. Bramson says analysts should be given plenty of documentation: if a memo has complicated figures, attach the adding machine slip or note saying, "I've checked these numbers." Despite their indecision, he says, analysts respond well to deadlines, if the lead time is stretched a bit. In dealing with be-nice people, the point is to keep the employee talking long enough to find out what is really going on. Don't push, or an impulsive decision will result, and never show enthusiasm, which indecisives find alarming. Instead, appeal to the employee's sense of what is best for the company, which usually works. If this fails, says Bramson, keep the initiative by saying something like, "I'll be back Thursday to see where we are."

9   Unresponsives are too frightened, confused or hostile to discuss matters. Bramson suggests trying to outwait them: by saying nothing. As the growing silence produces anxiety, throw your eyebrows up expectantly. Chances are the unresponsive will break first, particularly if you have practiced coping with awkward silences yourself.

10   Know-it-alls come in two types: "real experts," who are right about 75% of the time, and "phony experts," who are inept and usually wrong. The real experts are highly valuable, but dogmatic, stubborn and often "so superior in tone that they make others feel useless." Coworkers who must face a know-it-all should do their homework carefully, and instead of arguing, ask "extensional" questions, such as "How will this approach work with our five kinds of customers?" The questions may lead know-it-alls to see their errors because they are among the few troublemakers

"who can be influenced by clear logic, especially if their logic is off." If the know-it-all is too intimidating, says Bramson, an employee might want to knuckle under. "Take a frank, subordinate stance as an alternative to sitting and seething. If nothing else, it will relieve tension."

11   Though Bramson's advice may strike some as manipulative, he prefers to call it "managing your own behavior." His argument: candor and self-assertiveness are valuable tools, but they are not automatically useful in getting along with difficult colleagues. Says he: "People should do something different from what comes naturally. Being candid is always worth trying once, but it won't always solve the problem." Bramson also has a surefire cure for office problems, but it may not be practical for too many employees. "The best way to cope with difficult people," he says, "is to get as far away from them as you can."

What Was It About?

1. On what does Robert M. Bramson base his theories?

2. Why does Bramson suggest that bad behavior in the office works?

3. How many categories of office troublemakers does Bramson identify?

What Did You Think?

1. Have you ever encountered one of Bramson's troublemakers?

2. Do you agree that being candid is not always the best way to deal with difficult colleagues?

3. Do Bramson's categories apply to areas outside the workplace?

Get It Down On Paper!

1. Can you identify categories of troublemakers among your faculty or classmates? (Classification, Description, Definition)

2. "Nice guys finish last." When it comes to business, do you agree or disagree? (Cause/Effect, Example, Comparison/Contrast)

3. Have you ever encountered a troublemaker in the workplace? How did you cope? (Process, Cause/Effect, Example)

HARRIET TUBMAN

by David Ramsey

★ SNEAK PREVIEW ★ David Ramsey is a journalist.

Harriet Tubman played an important role in American history. In this article you'll find out how her courage made a difference on the Underground Railroad.

★ ★ ★

1   In her youth, Harriet Tubman had dreams of liberty. She lived in Maryland as a slave, but in her slumber she could soar to freedom.

2   As she slept, she saw herself flying over fields and towns, over rivers and mountains. She looked down on the sights she later told a friend, "like a bird."

3   She always arrived at a massive fence that halted her flight, but help arrived in the form of women, in Tubman's words, "all dressed in white." The women held out their arms to Harriet and pulled her past the barrier to liberty.

4   After 30 years of living as a slave, Tubman realized her dream in 1849, when she sneaked away to freedom in Philadelphia.

5   She wasn't through. She vowed to become one of those women dressed in white who helped those seeking to break through the barriers to freedom.

6   Details of Tubman's life (1819–1913) are sketchy, and she did little to promote her many acts of bravery.

7   What we do know comes from oral histories.

8   We know she despised slavery and dedicated her energies to aiding those who wanted to flee north to freedom. She was one of the great conductors of the Underground Railroad, a group of women and men who assisted fugitive slaves. Frederick Douglass, an escaped slave who became an abolitionist and a journalist, and Jermain Loguen, a Syracuse, N.Y., minister, were key figures, too, but they performed their work in the relative safety of free states.

9   Tubman performed a more dangerous role. She returned 19 times across the line of freedom. Defying U.S. laws, defying slave owners who wanted to capture her, she boldly traveled into Southern states and led approximately 300 slaves to freedom. She walked thousands of miles during these journeys, mostly at night.

10   A humble woman who usually declined to talk about herself, Tubman was heard to say that she never lost any of the slaves she sought to save.

11   After the outbreak of the Civil War, she served as a nurse and spy for the Union army.

12   She earned the admiration in the 19th century from those who understood her work and her devotion.

13   In 1868, Douglass wrote Tubman a letter to thank her for her work.

14   "I have had the applause of the crowd and the satisfaction that comes of being approved by the multitude," Douglass wrote, "while the most that you have done has been witnessed by a few trembling, scarred and foot-sore bondmen and women, who you have led out of the house of bondage, and whose heartfelt 'God bless you' has been your only reward.

15   "The midnight sky and the silent stars have been the witness of your devotion to freedom and of your heroism. It is to me a great pleasure and a great privilege to bear testimony to your character and your works."

16   John Brown, the fiery abolitionist who was hanged by the state of Virginia after his failed raid on Harpers Ferry, Va. (now W. Va.) called Tubman "General" and once introduced her as "one of the best and bravest persons on this continent." She helped him plan the raid but did not participate.

17   She spent her final years in relative obscurity, settling in Auburn, N.Y., where she lived quietly with her second husband, Nelson Davis.

18   Her ability to inspire remains strong. She still stands as a symbol of sacrifice, a symbol of a determined woman's ability to overcome any obstacle.

19   An experimental rock band currently playing clubs in New York city calls itself Harriet Tubman, because the group is all about the "journey to musical freedom."

20   A shelter for abused women and children in Minneapolis is called Harriet Tubman Center. In its mission statement, the center declares its goal to be "to provide safe passage from abuse."

21   And those who admire Tubman and her work make the pilgrimage to her final home in Auburn. Hillary Rodham Clinton, actress Cicely Tyson and painter Jacob Lawrence are among the thousands who have traveled to Auburn to honor Tubman.

22   When Clinton visited Auburn in 1998, she told a large crowd to remember Tubman's "terrific courage and personal triumph" and posed a question to those who might take the privilege of freedom for granted: "Do we fritter it away or do we attach ourselves to a greater mission such as the education of our children? Do we keep going as Harriet Tubman urged, to greater things?"

23   Most of the visitors to the Tubman home are not famous. They come to consider the life of a woman who, in many ways, was utterly ordinary but who managed to perform extraordinary feats. Visitors have traveled from South Africa, India, Great Britain and across the United States to pay tribute to Tubman.

24   The Rev. Paul G. Carter, the resident manager of the Tubman house, says Tubman's story retains its power because she "was willing to put her life on the line to free those who had been enslaved because of injustice. She was willing to fight for a cause. She was willing to keep pushing no matter what the cost.

25   "She offers light and hope now to a darkened world that is desperately looking for someone to look up to."

What Was It About?

1. How does the author convince us that Harriet Tubman remains an inspiration today?

2. How have we learned about Harriet Tubman's life and accomplishments?

3. How was Tubman's work on the Underground Railroad different from the work of Frederick Douglass and Jermain Loguen?

What Did You Think?

1. How was Tubman's dream prophetic?

2. Do you think Tubman's accomplishments are sufficiently recognized?

3. When Tubman achieved freedom for herself, why did she risk it by going back into slave states?

Get It Down On Paper!

1. Discuss what lessons Tubman's life can teach us. (Definition, Cause/Effect)

2. Is there someone you know that deserves to be recognized for inspirational work? (Narrative, Cause/Effect)

3. What is a hero? (Definition)

THE FREEDOM OF LIVING ALONE
by Patricia Leigh Brown

 SNEAK PREVIEW Patricia Leigh Brown is a respected journalist who writes on many subjects.

Do you currently live alone? Have you ever lived alone? How did you feel about it? In this piece, Patricia Leigh Brown takes a look at the lives of a number of people who live alone and how it affects their lives.

☆ ☆ ☆

1   They have nothing in common and everything in common. "We eat over the sink and in bed, and sometimes at a table," said the photographer Adrienne Salinger of people like herself who live alone. "We find things where we left them. We always know where the good scissors are."

2   In her recent book, "Living Solo" (Andrews McMeel Publishing, $18.95), Salinger—no relation to J. D.—investigates the inner lives, dwelling places and somewhat eccentric indulgences of people who, either by choice or circumstance, find themselves living alone.

3   They are an expanding tribe. The motley array of questers that Salinger befriended at laundromats, in department stores, in bookstores, even at the side of the road, represent possibly the first generations for which, in her words, "Living alone is presumed to be a legitimate choice rather than a declaration of defeat."

4   No longer perceived as simply a transient state with no respect, solo living— sometimes elegant, sometimes scraggly and unkempt—is a statistical reality: the number of women living alone doubled between 1970 and 1996, to 15 million, while the number of solitary men tripled, to 10.3 million, the Census Bureau says.

5   Among their ranks is Salinger, 42, an associate professor at the University of New Mexico, who lives alone in a one-story adobe house in Albuquerque with interiors she calls "fairly neutral."

6   "I'm fascinated with how people define themselves in their spaces," she said. "People who live alone are marginalized in our culture. But when you live alone, you're not compromised in your space. Living with others, you develop a shorthand for communicating. You don't consider your own life as clearly, because you don't have to." Opening the shutters on 50 lives, Salinger finds that they defy conventional expectations.

7   Among her subjects are Judd Hostetler, who was dismissed from his job as a bookkeeper after 22 years for doing a somersault, and Anne Meredith, a Hollywood screenwriter, who is shown in Salinger's photograph in front of an altar assembled from her home's earthquake debris. She recalls the summer weekdays of her youth

on Cape Cod—the "unspoken conspiracy" of women living a "totally free and joyous life" when their husbands were away.

8   Salinger portrays divorcees, widowers, recovering heroin addicts and alcoholics, a personal chef, a woman battling multiple sclerosis alone in her bathroom. They are shown in rooms that are at times at odds with their stories. Gordon Harrington, who served two tours in Vietnam, stands in his living room surrounded by rose-brocade balloon shades and lace curtains, holding his rifle amid scented candles and a carved bunny on the coffee table.

9   Reflecting on an unhappy marriage of 27 years, Abby Bayouth observes that interiors don't always reveal inner truths. "People thought it was a very happy home," she says, "because we had a very beautiful house."

10 The author's decision to explore the lives of people she saw grocery shopping—people that "you always assume don't have complex inner lives, which is completely untrue"—evolved gradually from her own solo life, though she acknowledged the down side: "When you're sick and want someone to take care of you."

11 The daughter of an artist and a furniture manufacturer who now live in Sedona, Arizona, and "have the perfect relationship," she said, Salinger grew up in Los Angeles and San Francisco and worked briefly as a pastry chef before getting a master of fine arts degree at the Chicago Art Institute. She taught at Syracuse University and moved to Albuquerque a year and a half ago. "I wanted to change my life, so I just kind of did it," she said. "I didn't want to be one of those people who stayed in the same place forever. Those people just become bitter."

12 The project is her second book. The first was *In My Room: Teen Agers in Their Bedrooms* (Chronicle Books, 1995).

13 "I became interested in whether or not we are in fact a group," she said. "It's not that simple, because there are 25 million of us living alone. Yet, we're invisible." She began her odyssey, in which she trekked across the country with a 4-by-5 view camera, by photographing herself in her own home, surrounded by hundreds of books whose spines remained obsessively unbroken. "I was appalled," she said of how she looked. "Which anyone would be unless they're Gwyneth Paltrow."

14 Salinger, who relishes the "terrifying invasion" of photographing people at home, has lived alone on and off since college. She is not committed to the solitary life and is involved with someone, but finds lone souls to be more open and articulate about themselves.

15 In her view, eccentricity has gotten a bad rap, and even the loopiest characters have profundities to reveal. "The reason my marriages didn't work is because I was very much involved in cocktails," says Vivian Grace, a former alcoholic turned substance abuse counselor.

16 Such solo fliers have been largely unheralded until now. "It takes an enormous amount of courage to live alone," Salinger said. "You have no escape from looking at yourself."

What Was It About?

1. Why does the author think now is a good time to study those living alone?

2. What aspect of living alone fascinates Salinger?

3. How do you think Salinger feels about the people she photographs?

What Did You Think?

1. Have you ever lived alone? Would you like to? Why or why not?

2. Salinger says those living alone may be seen as a group. Do you agree? Why or why not?

3. Does Salinger see "solo fliers" as superior to those who live with others? Do you?

Get It Down On Paper!

1. Is it better to live alone or with others? (Compare/Contrast, Cause/Effect)

2. How would your life change if you suddenly found yourself living alone/living with someone else? (Comparison/Contrast, Cause/Effect)

3. What does it mean to be lonely? To be alone? (Definition, Comparison/Contrast, Classification)

THE RICH DON'T NEED IT ALL

by Leonard Pitts, Jr.

☆ **SNEAK PREVIEW** ☆ Leonard Pitts, Jr. is a syndicated columnist for the *Miami Herald* who often covers issues of particular interest to African Americans.

In this essay, he takes a look at greed in America and talks about what the very rich should be doing with their money.

☆ ☆ ☆

The Man who dies … rich, dies disgraced.
—Andrew Carnegie

1   It's not that I have anything against money. Hey, I'd love to have enough of the green stuff to ensure that my heirs and I never want for anything again. It might be fun to have that much.

2   But here's the question: What if I had more?

3   That's what I find myself wondering each time *Forbes* magazine releases its annual ranking of the world's richest people, as it did just a few days ago. To the surprise of no one, Microsoft founder Bill Gates tops the list. Indeed, his estimated $90 billion in net worth exceeds that of the next three billionaires combined.

4   Let's pause to put that figure into context. If Gates were to spend his fortune at the rate of a million dollars a day, it would take him 246 years to exhaust it all. If he spent a hundred thousand an hour, he'd still last 102 years. He could take the PLANET to lunch and keep $30 billion socked aside for a rainy day.

5   Not to pick on the uber nerd. The wondering that the *Forbes* ranking inspires in me applies as much to the lowliest billionaire on the list as it does to him.

6   I mean, I just can't picture sitting on a $90 billion fortune. Not just because the number is beyond my understanding, but also because there are too many hospitals that need building, too much pain that needs healing. There is ignorance that needs learning, hunger that needs feeding, wrong that needs righting.

7   I just can't figure it out: After you have enough to cover everything you could possibly want or need, why have more? What's the point? Why not give it away?

8   I'll admit that in asking the question, I feel not unlike an ant trying to understand the thinking of a human. Or a human trying to comprehend the mind of God.

9   Fiscally, at least, the distance between me and your average billionaire is about that dramatic. So I keep figuring there must be things here I'm not wealthy enough to understand, motivations and machinations that fly over my head like a private jet.

10   But I'll tell you what it looks like from down here. Like acquisition for its own sake, like obtainment as its own reward. Like greed.

11   Of course the rich, as F. Scott Fitzgerald once famously observed "are different from you and me."

12   And the *Forbes* list, I assume, is meant as celebration of the difference, an opportunity for the rest of us to indulge our daydreams. Why not? It's only human to wonder what wealth must feel like.

13   And yet...you look at these folks sitting atop their fortunes and you wonder whether they ever reach sufficiency, a point where another dollar is irrelevant.

14   For most, I suspect, the answer is no. Which is sad. Because acquisition without purpose is empty. And in a world where want is at the root of so much suffering, it also seems vaguely...obscene.

15   Yes, you're right. I overstep my bounds here. It's not my place to tell another man how to spend his money. I don't know what's in Bill Gates' heart. And indeed, published reports say he has already given as much as $800 million to charity.

16   Of course, that's rather like you or me giving a few hundred to Goodwill, but it's the thought that counts.

17   Besides, Bill Gates isn't the point. Rather, the point is that we have an unfortunate tendency to judge success—our own and someone else's—by what is gained rather than by what is given.

18   Hard to blame us, I admit. Money greases the wheels of American culture. So most of us who aren't wealthy spend our time praying for riches. And *Forbes'* ranking only offers that prayer a little vicarious gratification.

19   Ultimately, though, I'm glad it'll never be more than that for me. It would be an embarrassment to find my name on that list.

20   I'd take it as a sign that I had sought sufficiency in all the wrong places. That I was rich in money, but dead broke in every other way that matters.

What Was It About?

1. What is the author's attitude toward wealth?

2. What is the *Forbes* list?

3. Why would the author be embarrassed to find his name on the list?

What Did You Think?

1. Would you like to be as rich as Bill Gates? Why or why not?

2. Is money a valid measure of success? Why or why not?

3. Can money solve society's problems? How?

Get It Down On Paper!

1. If you could pick the level of wealth that would make you happiest, what would it be? (Classification, Definition, Example)

2. Fitzgerald said, "The rich are different from you and me." Do you agree? Why or why not? (Definition, Classification, Comparison/Contrast)

3. "Money is the root of all evil." Agree or disagree. (Example, Cause/Effect)

LOOKING FOR MY PRINCE CHARMING

by Shamali Pal

⭐ **SNEAK PREVIEW** ⭐ Shamali Pal is an Indian writer who lives in San Francisco.

Every country has its own courtship and marriage customs. Maybe you grew up in a family with very specific ideas about how you were to select a husband or wife. In this essay, Shamali Pal discusses her family's traditions in regard to marriage.

⭐ ⭐ ⭐

1   For some reason, an Indian mother finds it necessary to stretch the truth when it comes to her son's height. "You're very tall. That's good, because my son is six feet," said a potential mother-in-law while perched on my uncle's sofa in Calcutta. When I found myself face to face with the aforementioned son on a street corner in New York City about two months later, I couldn't help noticing that he had perhaps an inch or two on my 5 feet 7 inches. Taking into consideration this man's many appealing characteristics—he's a successful investment banker, well mannered, well traveled—it seems odd that his mother chose to describe him in terms of inches. Welcome to the world of arranged marriages where height is only a few notches below moral rectitude on the desirability scale.

2   Born and raised in America by parents who moved from Calcutta more than 30 years ago, I grew up on the prevailing notion that first comes love, then comes marriage. I watched Prince Charming fall for Cinderella and her slipper, and followed Laurie Partridge, the oldest sister of television's *The Partridge Family*, on countless dates with her beau d'episode.

3   Fast forward 20 years and I'm singing a slightly different tune. While I haven't gone so far as to allow my parents to pick a mate virtually sight unseen and cast my lot with a stranger (as is still the tradition in many Indian families), I have agreed to the occasional discreet introduction.

4   Fortunately, my parents have respected my preferences in a mate. I would prefer someone who also was raised outside of India. I'd like it if he weighed more than I do. I want no mustaches. But most important, I don't want to be featured in any matrimonial advertisements, such as this one I found on the Web: "Renowned Physician's Family seek Bengali surgeons, physicians, others, 32–42, for US citizen, Bengali, Brahmin, bright, pretty, adorable, petite, US raised, educated daughter. Two degrees, Business Administration, Computer Science, 37—looks 20ish, 3 day unconsummated convenient marriage annulled."

5   When people ask why I've agreed to my family's setups, I could say it's about preserving my cultural heritage or maintaining a link to a homeland that my parents have fought to preserve. But in the end, I'm just lazy. Marrying an Indian means a lot less explaining: Why don't my parents call one another by their first names? Why do they eat with their hands? What is that red dot on my mother's forehead?

6   Marriage strikes me as stressful enough, what with having to learn the ins and outs of any "normal" (i.e. slightly dysfunctional) family. Fitting into a family with ties that are several time zones away could be too much to ask.

7   In the last two years I've phoned, e-mailed and dined with three potential "ideal husbands." (This is according to the aunts or cousins who talk up the suitors to my parents. Marriage brokering is a favorite pastime for my extended family.) The investment banker was my first blind date. The timing couldn't have been worse. He'd made his mark and was searching for a full-fledged adult companion, not a recent journalism-school graduate who spent most of lunch whining about being unemployed.

8   After that came drinks with the San Francisco-based attorney. He rattled on about himself for an hour and then we said polite goodbyes. It was a superficial meeting, as initial conversations usually are. Two days later he sent me a long-winded e-mail explaining that he wasn't ready for a serious commitment—which was a shame because I'd already mailed the invitations, set up the bridal registry and commissioned the cake.

9   Finally, there was the multimedia artist raised in London. We had been e-mailing each other for a few months and for the most part, it was a pleasant exchange. When we met in person, he complimented my apartment, but said he would like it better if I weren't in it (I think he was joking). He made me see *Deep Impact.* Enough said.

10   Obviously, none of these gentlemen wound up being "the one." And compared with the agony that can follow a breakup after just a few months of dating, I came up relatively unscathed. However, just because there wasn't an emotional investment, the rejection didn't smart any less.

11   In my most dire moments, I consider surrendering my marital future to the scientists at the University of Hawaii who successfully cloned a couple of mice. If I could take elements of my three suitors and fuse them together, maybe I would have the perfect man. I could just relax while genetic engineering caught up with my needs. Of course, I don't see the anxious aunts and cousins waiting it out with me. In fact, my father seems keen on sending me on an extended holiday to India. I can just picture myself rolling out of Calcutta customs, bleary-eyed and jet-lagged, to be greeted by a line of eligible young men, holding up little cards with their respective heights printed on them, well-intentioned mothers hovering close at hand.

What Was It About?

1. What is the author's attitude toward the would-be suitors her family arranged for her to meet?

2. How would you describe the tone of this essay?

3. Why does the author allow her family to fix her up with dates?

What Did You Think?

1. Have you ever been on a blind date?

2. Do you believe in love (or hate) at first sight?

3. Do you think the author would have better luck finding someone on her own?

Get It Down On Paper

1. How important is a similar cultural background in making a relationship work? (Example, Cause/Effect)

2. Discuss the best or worst date you've ever had. (Narration, Example, Definition)

3. Should family traditions be followed or should young people find their own ways of dating and marrying? (Comparison/Contrast, Cause/Effect, Example)

CHANGING THE RULES OF THE GAME

by Dennis Williams

★ **SNEAK PREVIEW** ★ Dennis Williams directs the Center for Minority Educational Affairs and teaches English at Georgetown University. He is also the author of two novels.

Does your college have athletic teams? What academic standards do athletes have to maintain at your school?

★ ★ ★

1   To a lot of people, it seemed like a good idea at the time: minimum academic standards for college athletes. The set of rules first known as Proposition 48, handed down by the NCAA in the mid-1980s, promised to cure the plague of all-but-illiterate athletes' appearing in collegiate stadiums and arenas.

2   However, there were a few loud voices insisting that the new rules would merely limit opportunities for young people to learn as well as play—and that African-Americans, whatever the rule makers' intentions, would end up losers. Earlier this month a federal judge in Philadelphia sided with the naysayers, striking down the NCAA's initial-eligibility standards for college athletes. And when the same judge refused to grant a stay, it was clear that coaches, recruits and admissions officers would have to begin playing a much different game—immediately—with no rules to guide them.

3   The court ruled that the NCAA's minimum SAT score of 820 has an "unjustified" discriminatory effect on African-American students and therefore violates federal law. The judge did not rule out the possibility of a minimum score altogether, and so some speculate that an even lower cutoff might do the trick. But using SAT scores is an inherently discriminatory approach (in general admissions, too, I contend, but that's another issue). African-American students consistently score lower on the test than white students, although the gap has narrowed. The original Proposition 48 SAT line was drawn close to what was then the median score for all black students. Furthermore, as opponents have consistently argued, using the SAT to determine athletic eligibility is a blatantly inappropriate use of a test designed, simply, to set a point spread for the first semester academic success in college.

4   Still, the discriminatory effect, predicted and predictable as it was, might have been minimized had so many colleges not abdicated their own responsibility. As an educator I would not have been saddened to see any student barred from competition for a year in order to complete the first year of college satisfactorily. What happened in practice, however, was far different: most students found ineligible to receive athletic scholarships and compete as freshmen were simply not admitted to

division I and Division II schools. Why "waste" a classroom seat on some large young person who could not benefit the school until the following year—especially when there is no danger of the competitions suiting him up?

5   The primary stated purpose of the NCAA regulations was to increase graduation rates of recruited athletes. The implication was that prospective college athletes would have an incentive to arrive better prepared and therefore be better able to accomplish four years of collegiate course work. Graduation rates have risen slightly since 1984 for Division I athletes. But so have the rates for all students at those schools, with no externally legislated SAT cutoffs. Raising SAT entrance requirements is a lazy and inefficient way to boost graduation rates. A better way to help any student succeed is to improve teaching, tutorial support, instruction in time management and note-taking skills. And for athletes, it is to schedule fewer games, reduce travel and end freshman eligibility so that everyone gets a chance to be a student for a full year before competing.

6   These, however are educational concerns, and NCAA regulations have nothing to do with either education or the well-being of the young people involved. They have everything to do with competitive balance and with public relations. The fundamental issue with initial-eligibility requirements is that they inevitably become entrance requirements, and the NCAA simply has no business deciding whom a college can admit. Even eligibility to compete should be determined by individual colleges as long as the students are at least in good standing and making satisfactory progress toward a degree.

7   If this solution sounds hopelessly naive, that indicates only the bankruptcy of the NCAA's cherished notion of "student-athlete" as it applies to high-profile, revenue-generating sports. This is not to say that many athletes don't see and gain an education, and that many colleges are not conscientious in providing that opportunity. But they do so in spite of a system engineered for maximum exploitation and minimum embarrassment. Yet we cannot afford to admit that we no longer regard these young men and women as actual students. Without the thin veil of "scholarships" and the pretense of compensation by education (no degree required), some judge would no doubt someday force us to consider these young folks employees of our institutions, paid entertainers. The most talented of them would command far more than the $30,000 or so they cost now for a year's classes and keep at places like Stanford and Duke—not to mention the in-state tuition rate at Tennessee or Connecticut. It is madness, but it does not end in March.

What Was It About?

1. What does the author state as the primary purpose of the NCAA regulations?

2. What does the author think is an appropriate role for the NCAA? What is an inappropriate role?

3. What does the essay suggest would be a better way to raise graduation rates for student athletes?

What Did You Think?

1. Do you think student athletes are treated fairly on your campus? Why or why not?

2. Should student athletes be subject to the same set of admission standards as all other students applying to college?

3. Have you had any experience with college sports or college athletes?

Get It Down On Paper!

1. Are athletics a valid part of college life? (Cause/Effect, Example, Comparison/Contrast)

2. How are student athletes different from other students (or from each other)? (Comparison/Contrast, Classification)

3. Does collegiate athletic competition take advantage of college athletes? (Cause/Effect, Narration)

UFOs—A SECOND LOOK

by Randy Fitzgerald

☆ **SNEAK PREVIEW** ☆ Randy Fitzgerald is a journalist.

What do you think about UFOs? Do you know anyone who has seen one? Do you think it's possible that they exist?

☆ ☆ ☆

1 To James and Fawn Clemens of Kingman, Arizona, the bright but fuzzy amber light hanging above the northwestern horizon seemed odd. It was 8 P.M., March 13, 1997, and the couple, both 42, were in their yard.

2 Looking through binoculars, the Clemenses seemed to see five intense orange lights, in a "V" formation, heading southeast. Then reports began streaming into local law enforcement agencies, media outlets and civilian UFO groups.

3 Retired Northwest Airlines Captain Trig Johnston says an object the size of 25 airliners floated slowly and soundlessly past his home in north Scottsdale. "It was the most incredible thing I've ever seen," he told *Reader's Digest*. A 43-second videotape, recorded at 8:28 P.M. by a man in north Phoenix, shows five white lights in a "V" formation. At 8:30 P.M. the cockpit crew of an American West 757 airliner at 17,000 feet near Lake Pleasant, Arizona, noticed the lights off to the right and just above them.

4 "There's a UFO!" co-pilot John Middleton said kiddingly to pilot Larry Campbell. They queried the regional air-traffic-control center in Albuquerque, N.M. A controller radioed back that it was a formation of CT-144s flying at 19,000 feet.

5 Overhearing this exchange, someone claiming to be a pilot in the formation radioed Middleton. "We're Canadian Snowbirds flying Tutors," a man said.

6 The Canadian Snowbirds are the elite air-show performance team of the Canadian air force. Snowbird pilots fly CT 144s, a two-seat training jet nicknamed the Tutor, which has a single landing light in its nose.

7 But Captain Michael Perry, squadron logistics officer for the Snowbirds, denied that any of his planes were in Arizona that month. "We don't travel in a V-shaped formation, and we don't cruise with landing lights on," he told *Reader's Digest*.

8 Officials at Luke AFB in Phoenix, Nellis AFB in Las Vegas and Edwards AFB in Rosamund, California, all denied that any of their planes were responsible for the sightings. FAA officials profess to be baffled. "We don't have any knowledge of the incident," says Martin Hardy, the Phoenix air-traffic-control manager.

9 Was it a secret military exercise, an elaborate hoax—or something else? The mass sightings of whatever flew over northern Arizona that night have added new fuel to the UFO controversy.

An Old Mystery

10   Unexplained aerial phenomena have been observed for centuries, but the modern UFO era began in 1947, when there was an unprecedented number of reported sightings. Observers have offered a wide range of reasons for the surge—from Cold War hysteria to visitors from outer space investigating nuclear explosions.

11   The U.S. Air Force investigated some 12,618 sightings over the next 22 years. Most were explained as misidentifications of natural atmospheric phenomena, such as meteors or planets, or as weather balloons and other man-made flying craft. Still, 701 remained unexplained and Northwestern University astronomer J. Allen Hynek, the Air Force's scientific consultant on UFOs, concluded that some of these could be extraterrestrial in origin.

12   That view was challenged by a 1969 University of Colorado study funded by the Air Force, which examined 59 of the more celebrated cases. Some were also revealed as misidentifications or hoaxes. Although 23 still remained unexplained, project director Dr. Edward Condon concluded that no evidence of extraterrestrial visitation existed and "further extensive study of UFOs probably cannot be justified."

13   Nevertheless, UFO reports continue, and interest in the subject remains widespread. In 1997 a panel of nine scientists from France, Germany and the United States, all affiliated with universities, laboratories and observatories, examined the reports of eight UFO investigators. The panel, funded by Laurance S. Rockefeller, a wealthy philanthropist long interested in the subject, took up cases where physical evidence of some sort existed—such as radar trackings, damage to vegetation or documentable injuries to witnesses.

14   The panel concluded that some of the incidents may have been due to rare atmospheric phenomena. They found no proof that any UFOs were extraterrestrial. But they didn't rule out the possibility either.

15   The panel's report was met with skepticism from the committee for the Scientific Investigation of Claims of the Paranormal, a group that specializes in debunking fringe science. CSICOP fellow Philip J. Klass, a contributing editor at *Aviation Week & Space Technology,* dismisses the idea that UFOs are extraterrestrial: "In 50 years there hasn't been a single piece of credible physical evidence."

16   Perhaps not. At any rate, I've taken a second look at a pair of cases examined by the Rockefeller panel, interviewing eyewitnesses and reviewing official documents. Like the lights over Arizona, these episodes remain fascinating—and mysterious.

Molten Metal

17   At 7:45 P.M.. on December 17, 1977, Mike and Criss Moore, both 24, were driving to visit Mike's mother in Council Bluffs, Iowa, when they say they saw a bright red ball glowing above the treetops about a half-mile away. Three other individuals

report watching an object fall in Big Lake Park. Motorists who converged on the site found a pond levee glowing red-orange from a mass of molten metal that was boiling over the frozen ground.

18   Council Bluffs assistant fire chief Jack Moore, Mike's father, arrived within 15 minutes to discover "a big puddle of metal about four inches thick, bubbling and red in spots." Local astronomer Robert Allen forwarded samples of the debris to metallurgists at Iowa State University and the U.S. Air Force's Foreign Technology Division at Wright-Patterson AFB in Ohio.

19   The sample was composed chiefly of iron with small amounts of nickel and chromium, making it carbon steel. "Analytic results make it highly unlikely that the material is of meteoric origin," reported Robert S. Hansen, director of the Amers Laboratory at Iowa State.

20   Government scientists offered no explanation for the object's origin, but were certain the material was unrelated to military or space projects. "Re-entering spacecraft debris does not impact the earth's surface in a molten state," Col. Charles Senn wrote to Allen in 1978.

21   Was this an elaborate hoax? Allen could find only one local foundry with the equipment to produce molten metals. It had not been operating the night of the incident. "Even then," adds Allen, "no one can explain how a thousand pounds of molten metal could have been dropped from such a height."

Fire in the Sky

22   Shortly after 9 P.M. on December 29, 1980, Betty Cash, 52, was driving through a pine forest on a deserted rural road toward her home in Dayton, Texas. In the car with her was her friend Vickie Landrum, 57, and Landrum's grandson, six-year-old Colby.

23   The two women say a brilliant object descended directly ahead of them, spitting flames from its underside. Cash jammed on her brakes and brought the car to a halt about 150 feet from the object. Immediately they felt intense heat inside the car and heard a loud roaring sound.

24   They got out of the car and stared at a blinding light and a metallic structure, big as the 200-foot-tall water tower in Dayton, and shaped like a diamond with a blunt top. The object seemed to be struggling to ascend above the treetops, emitting blasts of fire and a continuous roar that reminded the women of a shrill welding torch, only much louder.

25   After ten minutes the object rose above the trees, tilted itself onto one side, and began moving slowly south. Then by their account, up to 23 helicopters eventually appeared, apparently following the object.

26   On the drive home, Landrum, Cash and Colby said they suffered headaches and later nausea, and over the next few days experienced bouts of vomiting, diarrhea and skin burns. Cash also lost large clumps of hair, and on January 2, 1981 was

admitted to Houston's Parkway General Hospital as a burn patient. She spent four of the next five weeks under supervised care.

27   Cash and Landrum contacted the state's police agencies and military bases, but no one could provide an explanation. Cash was advised to contact John F. Schuessler, a NASA contractor, project manager for the Space Shuttle Flight Operations, and an authority on UFOs. Schuessler and NASA physicist Alan Holt also interviewed Landrum and Colby, who led them to the encounter site.

28   "Where the object came down, the highway's yellow line wiggled from the melting of a heat blast," Schuessler told *Reader's Digest*. "A roughly twenty-foot circle of the road surface appeared to have melted and then resolidified. On the trees about twenty feet up there were blackened areas facing the road."

29   Schuessler found five witnesses who had observed a similar UFO the same night; another eight witnesses, including Dayton police officer, claimed to have seen the swarm of helicopters but not the UFO. Over the next five years Schuessler tried without success to identify the helicopters and where they came from.

30   The incident was examined by an Inspector General from the Department of the Army. He found no answer, but did conclude that there "was no perception that anyone was trying to exaggerate the truth."

31   Meanwhile, health problems continued to plague Cash, Landrum and Colby. Cash moved to Birmingham, Alabama, where, as Dr. Bryan McClelland said in an interview, "The illness that she suffered after her exposure was an absolute classic radiation injury in which she lost skin and hair, then had diarrhea and vomiting. She could not have made it up."

A New Dimension

32   Von R. Eshleman, a retired Stanford University electrical engineer who co-chaired the Rockefeller panel, says the panel acknowledges that a few recent UFO cases may "have their origins in secret military activities." Still the explanation for others may live elsewhere. Computer scientist Jacques Vallee, an advisor to the panel, notes that "the UFO debate has always been locked into two points of view—that it's either all nonsense or it's extraterrestrial." Maybe the real answer will be stranger than we can now imagine.

What Was It About?

1. How does the author attempt to convince us of the existence of UFOs?

2. How do the section headings direct our attention?

3. What evidence offered is factual? What is anecdotal?

What Did You Think?

1. Was the article convincing? Why or why not?

2. Which of the cases presented was most compelling to you? Which was the least? Why?

3. Do you think the author is impartial in his approach?

Get It Down On Paper!

1. Have you ever experienced something that couldn't be explained by ordinary expectations? (Narration, Cause/Effect)

2. Is the idea of UFOs exciting or threatening? (Cause/Effect, Example)

3. What conclusions might first-time UFO visitors draw about Earth if they landed at your house, school, or city? (Narration, Classification, Cause/Effect)

WITCHDOCTORS AND THE UNIVERSALITY OF HEALING

by E. Fuller Torrey

☆ SNEAK PREVIEW ☆ E. Fuller Torrey is a psychiatrist. In this selection from his book *The Mind Game: Witchdoctors and Psychiatrists,* Dr. Torrey compares the activities and societal positions of witchdoctors and psychiatrists and comes to some conclusions that may be surprising.

☆ ☆ ☆

1   Witchdoctors and psychiatrists perform essentially the same function in their respective cultures. They are both therapists; both treat patients, using similar techniques; and both get similar results. Recognition of this should not downgrade psychiatrists—rather it should upgrade witchdoctors.

2   The term "witchdoctor" is Western in origin, imposed on healers of the Third World by eighteenth and nineteenth century explorers. The world was simpler then, and the newly discovered cultures were quickly assigned their proper status in the Order of Things. We were white, they were black. We were civilized, they were primitive. We were Christian, they were pagan. We used science, they used magic. We had doctors, they had witchdoctors.

3   American psychiatrists have much to learn from the therapists in other cultures. My own experience observing and working with them includes two years in Ethiopia and briefer periods in Sarawak, Bali, Hong Kong, Colombia, and with Alaskan Indians, Puerto Ricans, and Mexican-Americans in this country. What I learned from these doctor-healers was that I, as a psychiatrist, was using the same mechanisms for curing my patients as they were—and not surprisingly, I was getting about the same results. The mechanisms can be classified under four categories.

4   The first is the naming process. A psychiatrist or witchdoctor can work magic by telling a patient what is wrong with him. It conveys to the patient that someone— usually a man of considerable status—understands. And since his problem can be understood, then, implicitly, it can be cured. A psychiatrist who tells an illiterate African that his phobia is related to a fear of failure, or a witchdoctor who tells an American tourist that his phobia is related to possession by an ancestral spirit, will be met by equally blank stares. And as therapists they will be equally ineffective. This is a major reason for the failure of most attempts at cross-cultural psychotherapy. Since a shared world-view is necessary for the naming process to be effective, then it is reasonable to expect that the best therapist-patient relationships will be

those where both come from the same culture or subculture. The implications for our mental health programs are obvious.

5 The second healing component used by therapists everywhere is their personality characteristics. An increasing amount of research shows that certain personal qualities of the therapist—accurate empathy, nonpossessive warmth, genuineness—are of crucial importance in producing effective psychotherapy. Clearly, more studies are needed in this area, but if they substantiate the emerging trend, then radical changes in the selection of therapists will be in order. Rather than selecting therapists because they can memorize facts and achieve high grades, we should be selecting them on the basis of their personality. Therapists in other cultures are selected more often for their personality characteristics; the fact that they have not studied biochemistry is not considered important.

6 The third component of the healing process that appears to be universal is the patients' expectations. Healers all over the world use many ways to raise the expectations of their patients. The first way is the trip itself to the healer. It is a common observation that the farther a person goes to be healed, the greater are the chances that he will be healed. This is called the pilgrimage. Thus, sick people in Topeka go to the Lahey Clinic in Boston. The resulting therapeutic efforts of the trip are exactly the same as have been operating for centuries in Delphi or Lourdes. The next way to raise patients' expectations is the building used for the healing. The more impressive it is, the greater will be the patients' expectations. This has been called the edifice complex. Therapists in different cultures use certain paraphernalia to increase patient expectations. In Western cultures nonpsychiatric healers have their stethoscope and psychotherapists are supposed to have their couch. Therapists in other cultures have their counterpart trademark, often a special drum, mask or amulet. Another aspect of patients' expectations rests upon the therapists' training. Some sort of training program is found for healers in almost all cultures. Blackfoot Indians, for instance, had to complete a seven-year period of training in order to qualify as medicine men.

7 Finally, the same techniques of therapy are used by healers all over the world. Let me provide a few examples: drugs are one of the techniques of Western therapy of which we are most proud. However, drugs are used by healers in other cultures as well. Rauwulfia root, for example, which was introduced into Western psychiatry in the 1950s as reserpine, a major tranquilizer, had been used in India for centuries as a tranquilizer, and has also been in wide use in West Africa for many years. Another example is shock therapy. When electric shock therapy was introduced by Cerletti in the 1930s, he was not aware that it had been used in some cultures for up to 4000 years. The technique of applying electric eels to the head of the patient is referred to in the writings of Aristotle, Pliny, and Plutarch.

8 What kind of results do therapists in other cultures—witchdoctors—achieve? A Canadian psychiatrist, Dr. Raymond Prince, spent 17 months studying 46 Nigerian

witchdoctors, and judged that the therapeutic results were about equal to those obtained in North American clinics and hospitals.

9   It would appear, then, that psychiatrists have much to learn from witchdoctors. We can see the components of our own therapy system in relief. We can learn why we are effective—or not effective. And we can learn to be less ethnocentric and arrogant about our own therapy and more tolerant of others. If we can learn all this from witchdoctors, then we will have learned much.

What Was It About?

1. What is being compared in Torrey's piece?

2. What is Torrey's main point?

3. How does Dr. Price support Torrey's views?

What Did You Think?

1. Was Torrey's viewpoint persuasive?

2. Did Torrey's writing change your mind about psychiatrists? How about witchdoctors?

3. Why do you think Torrey begins by explaining the origins of the term "witchdoctor"?

Get It Down On Paper!

1. Would you seek treatment from a psychiatrist? Why or why not?

2. Is all progress really bringing positive changes in our society?

3. Do you trust scientific knowledge?

IT'S TIME TO OPEN THE DOORS
OF OUR PRISONS

by Rufus King

☆ **SNEAK PREVIEW** ☆ Rufus King is a Washington lawyer with a lifelong interest in criminal justice.

In this essay, he questions the methods America uses to punish law-breakers.

☆ ☆ ☆

1   Americans, once so kind-hearted, have become lusty punishers. Since President Nixon's "war" on crime, the public has become increasingly intolerant of wrongdoers, a group with no lobbyists or spin doctors to look out for them. In the late 1960s, America, like most of the rest of the world, forsook capital punishment. Since reviving it almost a decade later, we have executed more than 500 people. Now governors brag about the number of death warrants they sign.

2   The U.S. prison population, 1.2 million not counting short-term jail inmates, is the largest in the Western world. A number of states are spending more on prisons than on schools, and along with the federal government are turning some of their prisoners over to private custody—so that skimping on accommodations directly boosts stockholders' dividends. Lawmakers trample one another to pose as tough crime fighters and mandatory minimums force judges to hand out long sentences, sometimes life, automatically upon conviction. Parole programs have atrophied.

3   The situation is aggravated by America's hysteria over drugs. Self-administered opiates (heroin and morphine) and cocaine together cause fewer than 8,500 deaths per year—compared with tobacco, 430,000, and alcohol, 100,000 dead, plus millions drunk in the gutter or otherwise incapacitated. I don't think marijuana has ever killed anyone.

4   Yet the White House campaign to be "drug free" not only costs billions, but concentrates on prohibition and punishment at the expense of notably cheaper and more effective treatment. The elaborate U.S. campaign to compel drug crop-growers abroad to give up their livelihoods is one of the most fatuous national efforts ever undertaken. Imagine Turks and Andeans trying to keep Yankee farmers from growing their truly deadly tobacco!

5   Nearly all the nation's prison systems are overcrowded, many critically. In state and federal prisons, more than half of all inmates are serving their time for nonviolent offenses. Some percent are first offenders. African-Americans are a grossly disproportionate 49 percent. Drug-law convictions account for almost one-fourth, and nearly one-third of these are for simple possession. Genuine hardship cases

abound, with stunning sentences for minor wrongs, the separation of parents and young children and a wide disproportion among convictions for identical offenses.

6   After working for many years in the development of criminal law, I've become increasingly concerned about our clogged prison system. My proposal to relieve the problem is simple systematic use of pardon and commutation powers to clear out worthy first-offense long-termers to make room for serious felons. It should stir compassion and appeal to common sense. But there is another consideration that Americans may understand even better: costs. At an estimated $20,000 per year to hold each prisoner, we are spending more than $25 billion annually for simple, non-productive warehousing of convicted offenders.

7   Altogether, our annual layout for corrections is more than $35 billion, curving steadily upward even as crime rates drop. We are developing a powerful "prison industrial complex," a national growth industry exploiting today's hostility toward wrongdoers. There is scant evidence that long prison terms alone are causing the drop. Most observers credit other factors such as progress in reducing poverty, the improved economy, tighter gun laws and the increasing average age of the population. Criminologists agree that about-to-be lawbreakers don't look up penalties in the law books; they plan, if at all, on how to avoid being caught.

8   Every system for administering justice has, since ancient times, included some provision for tempering punishment, usually a power to pardon and commute sentences, vested in the executive. Royal pardons were well known to most of our European forebears. American presidents draw the power directly from the constitution, and every state governor enjoys some such prerogative. Historically, the power has been freely, often liberally used, sometimes to grant amnesty to entire classes of offenders.

9   So I urge an immediate review of all sentences now being served in order to identify nonviolent first offenders held for disproportionately long terms, to release those who have paid their debts to society and are good risks, and to make room for menacing recidivists and other serious offenders.

10 There would inevitably be a few Willie Hortons, but the process might be designed to include further screening in each case. Release should be strictly conditioned on good behavior and other factors where appropriate.

11 The president could initiate such a program simply by directive or Congress could set up a new authority for it. And any governor or state legislature could give it a try. I only need to convince enough economy minded people that some of the nation's prison-budget billions could be better spent elsewhere. Perhaps I've convinced you.

What Was It About?

1. How does the author characterize the present prison system?

2. What does the essay say about the "war on drugs"?

3. What solution does the author propose?

What Did You Think?

1. Do you agree with the author's distinction between first-time, nonviolent offenders and the rest of the inmate population?

2. The essay ends with a statement directed at the reader. How effective was this approach?

3. Which appeal do you think Americans would respond to: compassion or cost cutting?

Get It Down On Paper!

1. Should drug use be legalized? (Cause/Effect, Example)

2. Does the court system treat all citizens equally? (Example, Narration, Comparison/Contrast, Classification)

3. If you were a judge, which offenders would you consider for parole? (Classification, Example, Comparison/Contrast)

CREDITS

Photo Credits

Page 2: R.J. Erwin/Photo Researchers, Inc.; **6:** Tim Davios/Stone Images; **7:** Chip Simons/FPG International LLC; **11:** © The New Yorker Collection 1987 Warren Miller from cartoonbank.com. All Rights Reserved; **18:** Jim Cummins/FPG International LLC; **19:** © The New Yorker Collection 1992 Michael Crawford from cartoonbank.com. All Rights Reserved; **29:** © The New Yorker Collection 2001 Mike Twohy from cartoonbank.com. All Rights Reserved; **43:** Stephen Simpson/FPG International LLC; **44:** Michael Newman/PhotoEdit; **47:** Jeff Greenberg/PhotoEdit; **53:** © The New Yorker Collection 2000 Donald Reilly from cartoonbank.com. All Rights Reserved; **66:** © The New Yorker Collection 2001 Mick Stevens from cartoonbank.com. All Rights Reserved; **69:** © The New Yorker Collection 1988 Ed Fisher from cartoonbank.com. All Rights Reserved; **72:** Carolyn A. McKeone/Photo Researchers, Inc.; **75:** Petrified Collection/Imagebank; **76:** Bill Aron/PhotoEdit; **84:** The Kobal Collection; **91:** Tom Brakefield/The Image Works; **92:** © The New Yorker Collection 2000 J.C. Duffy from cartoonbank.com. All Rights Reserved; **93 (left):** Ron Edmonds/AP/Wide World Photos; **93 (right):** M. Spencer Green/AP/Wide World Photos; **94:** © The New Yorker Collection 2001 Victoria Roberts from cartoonbank.com. All Rights Reserved; **99 (left):** Richard Lord/PhotoEdit; **99 (right):** John Dominis/TimePix; **103:** Tom & Pat Leeson/Photo Researchers, Inc.; **105:** Reprinted with special permission of King Feature Syndicate; **114:** Imagebank; **120:** © VCG 2000/FPG International LLC; **121:** Deborah Davis/PhotoEdit; **123:** The Kobal Collection; **127:** Photofest; **131:** © The New Yorker Collection 1973 Warren Miller from cartoonbank.com. All Rights Reserved; **139:** © The New Yorker Collection 2000 Liza Donnelly from cartoonbank.com. All Rights Reserved; **147:** Sachs/PhotoEdit; **157:** © The New Yorker Collection 1990 Al Ross from cartoonbank.com. All Rights Reserved; **159 (top):** Syracuse Newspapers/The Image Works; **159 (center):** Martin Barraud/Stone Images; **159 (bottom):** Sarraute/Imagebank; **162:** Reprinted with special permission of King Feature Syndicate; **164:** David Young-Wolff/PhotoEdit; **167:** © The New Yorker Collection 2001 Jack Ziegler from cartoonbank.com. All Rights Reserved; **168:** Renee Lynn/Stone Images; **170:** John Giustina/FPG International LLC;

Text Credits

INDEX